Family Circle
CHRISTMAS TREASURY

Family Circle
CHRISTMAS
TREASURY

WINGS BOOKS
New York • Avenel, New Jersey

This 1994 edition is published by Wings Books,
distributed by Random House Value Publishing, Inc.,
40 Engelhard Avenue, Avenel, New Jersey 07001,
by arrangement with The New York Times Company Women's Magazines.
Family Circle is a registered trademark of
The New York Times Company Women's Magazines.

Random House
New York • Toronto • London • Sydney • Auckland

Printed and bound in the United States of America

A CIP catalog record for this book is available from the Library of Congress

ISBN 0-517-11956-0

8   7   6   5   4   3   2   1

CONTENTS

	INTRODUCTION	1
Chapter I:	*COME HOME TO THE HARVEST*	2
	Set A Harvest Table	4
	Harvest Touches	8
	Harvest Home Accents	10
	Cold Weather Crafts	19
	Giving Thanks	28
	Cozy Meals for Chilly Days	38
	Soup and Salad Italian-Style	39
	Microwave Mexican Fiesta	42
Chapter II:	*COUNTRY CELEBRATIONS*	46
	A Heartland Holiday	48
	Country Gifts from the Heart	62
	Just for Kids	74
	Darling Dolls	82
	Country Touches	86
	A Country Christmas Breakfast	89
Chapter III:	*VICTORIAN SPLENDOR*	98
	Splendid Christmas Decorations	100
	O' Christmas Tree	106
	Visions of Victoriana	108
	Victorian Touches	118
	Grand Gifts	120
	Just For Kids	130
	A Victorian Christmas Dinner	141

Chapter IV: *OLD-FASHIONED FESTIVITIES* 150
               Turning Back the Clock 152
               Old-Fashioned Touches 164
               Timeless Treasures 166
               Just For Kids: Wonderful Wooden Toys 176
               Cuddly Critters 182
               Sweet Serendipity 192

Chapter V: *WINTERFEST* 202
               Throw a Theme Party! 204
               Happy Healthy New Year 208
               Just For Kids: Fun Stuff to Do Indoors 210
               Winterfest Touches 212
               A Hero's Welcome 214
               Ring In The New Year! An Open House Cocktail Party 220

               CRAFTS BASICS AND ABBREVIATIONS 230
               INDEX 242
               PHOTO, CRAFT AND FOOD CREDITS 250

INTRODUCTION

T is the season . . . . .

. . . of shared smiles, the sweet, clear sound of children caroling, a shy kiss stolen under the mistletoe. On the busiest street corner you can hear the ringing of Salvation Army bells, and even strangers greet each other warmly with "Merry Christmas!" It is a time for the gathering together of good friends and family . . . a time of reflection, a time for peace. This is the season that makes the rest of the year worthwhile.

For over fifty years, our Family has been helping you to create the Christmas of your dreams. And this year, as always, we hope that all your Christmas wishes come true.

$\mathcal{S}$ing a song of
seasons!
Something bright in all!
Flowers in the summer,
Fires in the fall.

— ROBERT LOUIS STEVENSON

A Touch of Spice Table Setting
(directions, page 5)

CHAPTER 1

COME HOME TO THE HARVEST

Autumn is special, any way you look at it. The changing colors of the season, leaves that crackle beneath your step and a crisp bite in the air signal that the harvest has come. This is a time for giving thanks, a time when family and friends gather together and preparations for the coming winter are made.

In this chapter, you'll find a wonderful Thanksgiving menu, featuring scrumptious recipes from appetizers to desserts. And since the temperature is dropping, there are two other chill-chasing meals.

We'll help you bring the rich colors of autumn into your home with harvest accents, such as a grapevine wreath centerpiece, a quilted wall hanging or a trio of pillows that you can use throughout the cold-weather months.

And . . . Christmas is just around the corner! Get a jump on the season by making some of your gifts in advance. Stitch a red flannel quilt, knit a woolly sweater for a loved one, or make your own scented soaps. We know the satisfaction that comes from crafting a gift by hand, so we've included a wide variety of projects.

As all are joined together, toast the season and welcome the coming holidays with joy.

SET A HARVEST TABLE

Let the bounty of the harvest inspire your seasonal decor. Autumn fruits—grapes, apples, pears and citrus—whole spices, pine cones and touches of green are delightful decorative accents.

Grapes & Pine Cones Centerpiece Wreath

GRAPES & PINE CONES CENTERPIECE WREATH

Easy: Achievable by anyone.

Materials: 12-inch-diameter grapevine wreath; real or artificial bunches of green grapes; pine cones of varying sizes; freesia, carnations, roses or other white flowers; floral wire.

Directions:

1. Using the floral wire, attach the grapes and the pine cones to the grapevine wreath in a pleasing arrangement.

2. Intersperse the white flowers among the grapes and pine cones.

3. Use the wreath alone as a centerpiece, or place it around an arrangement of white candles or a bowl of fruit.

Merry Christmas

BOUNTIFUL BASKETS

Fill cornucopias with autumn fruits, vegetables and nuts.

✳

Use baskets at the table, for everything from serving rolls to holding individual soup bowls.

✳

Fill mushroom baskets with Spanish moss and tuck in hostess soaps for a cozy touch in your bathroom.

✳

For a "Midas touch" centerpiece, spray paint a basket gold. Then spray artichokes, Indian corn, gourds, crab apples and nuts with the same paint, or use a bronze color. Let everything dry completely, then create an arrangement of the vegetables and nuts in the basket.

A TOUCH OF SPICE TABLE SETTING

Easy: Achievable by anyone.

Materials: Fabric with small print in blue, white and yellow; matching threads; blue bias tape; rust-colored fabric; 1-inch-wide yellow satin ribbon; 1-inch-wide craft ribbon in blue and yellow; 12-inch-long cinnamon sticks; candles, grapevine wreath and dried flowers *(optional).*

Directions:

1. Measure the length and width of your dining table. Add 3 feet to both these measurements, and cut or piece together the print fabric to equal these measurements. Turn under all the edges ¼ inch, press and turn ¼ inch again to make a hem. Stitch the hem.

2. Cut as many 16-inch squares from the print fabric as needed for napkins. Trim all the corners of the squares in a curve. Open one side of the bias tape and pin it to a napkin, right sides together and edges even. Stitch the bias tape to the napkin, using the first fold of the tape as a stitch guide. Fold the tape up and over the raw edge of the napkin, matching the second fold edge of the tape to the first stitch line, and edgestitch.

3. Cut 6-inch-wide strips from the rust fabric. Measure the diagonals of your dining table and add 3 feet to this measurement. Piece together enough strips to equal the diagonal measurement. Fold under all the edges ¼-inch, press and turn ¼-inch again. Stitch in place.

4. Place the tablecloth on the table. Arrange the rust streamers on the table as shown in the photo on page 2. Cut lengths of the craft ribbon and glue them down on the center of the streamers.

5. Fold the napkins to stand upright. Cut 1-foot lengths of the satin ribbon for each napkin. Tie a ribbon in a bow around three or four cinnamon sticks, and insert a bundle into each napkin.

6. Add the candles, wreath and dried flowers, if you wish.

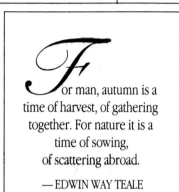

For man, autumn is a time of harvest, of gathering together. For nature it is a time of sowing, of scattering abroad.

— EDWIN WAY TEALE

AUTUMN LEAVES TABLE SETTING

Easy: Achievable by anyone.

Materials: Several yards of plaid fabric in autumn hues; matching threads; darning needle; pumpkins; acorn squash; gourds, Indian corn and nuts; straw cornucopia; large ceramic bowls; artificial autumn leaves; candle lanterns with candles, candles in brass candlesticks or votive candles; scissors; sewing machine *(optional)*.

Directions:

1. Cut as many 12 x 18-inch rectangles from the plaid fabric as needed for the place mats. Fold under the edges of each rectangle ¼ inch all around, and hand sew or machine zigzag stitch the hems.

2. Cut as many 10 x 10-inch squares from the plaid fabric as needed for napkins. Fold under the edges of the napkins ¼ inch all around, and hand sew or machine zigzag stitch the hems.

3. Using the photo as a guide, fill the cornucopia with the gourds, Indian corn and nuts, letting some spill out of the opening onto the table. Place the pumpkins and an acorn squash or two on the table as desired. Fill the ceramic bowls with the remaining acorn squash and the nuts, and place the bowls on the table or on a sideboard, as desired. Spread some of the autumn leaves around the cornucopia, and around each individual place setting.

4. Place one candle lantern, candles in brass candlesticks, or a grouping of votive candles, at each end of the table.

CRANBERRIES AND ORANGES

This colorful garland is too heavy for a tree, so use it to adorn a mantel or on the table for a centerpiece.

✳

Make a loop at one end of a length of sturdy floral wire. String four cranberries and one clementine orange onto the wire. Repeat for the length of the wire, ending with four cranberries. Make a loop at the other end of the wire to secure the fruits.

✳

String about 20 cranberries onto a second, shorter piece of floral wire. Join the wire ends together to form a loop, and gently bend the loop into a heart shape.

✳

Lay the cranberry heart and cranberry and orange garland on a bed of pine boughs and holly leaves.

Autumn Leaves Table Setting

Harvest Touches

A grapevine or cornhusk wreath is the perfect base for a harvest wreath. Use floral wire to attach small gourds, Indian corn, nuts, pine cones and bunches of dried flowers to the wreath. Add a big bow in autumnal hues, and hang your wreath on the front door to herald the season.

✳

Make wonderful, rich soups from the flesh of acorn squash, pumpkins or other winter squash, and serve the soup in the hollowed-out squash shells.

Colorful Indian corn makes a lovely harvest centerpiece. Add marigold yellow or rust brown candles in brass candlesticks to complement the corn.

✳

Put away your summer pastels and bring out the deeper colors of fall in sheets, pillowcases, and towels. Try using cranberry in a pink room, forest green in a yellow or pastel room, ultramarine or charcoal gray with pale earth tones.

Whip up a fun treat by making your own popcorn balls. Melt caramel candies in a saucepan over low heat. Toss the melted caramel with freshly popped corn, and form the mixture into balls with lightly greased hands. Place the balls on wax paper to cool. Let the caramel set for a few hours.

✳

Add a dash of cinnamon to the plain ground coffee in your coffee maker. This will make your regular coffee taste like a more expensive gourmet blend, and the spice is extra nice when there's a chill in the air.

Stitch sumptuous covers for your sofa throw pillows. A simple change of color, fabric or pattern can give your sofa a different look for the fall. Check fabric stores for remnants in wintery hues and fabrics — touchable brocade, jewel-toned raw silk, lush velvet or sturdy wool. A yard of fabric will cover a standard square pillow. Cut two squares from the fabric to size, leaving a ½-inch seam allowance. Place the squares right sides together, and stitch around three sides and four corners. Turn the cover right side out, slip the pillow inside, and slipstitch the opening closed *(see Stitch Guide, page 240)*. To remove the cover, carefully snip the threads along the hand-stitched edge.

✳

Personalize your Thanksgiving grace by letting each family member take a turn offering thanks in his or her own words. You're bound to hear some witty and wacky comments, but the sentiments will be heartfelt and genuine.

Fill a glass bowl with autumn leaves to use as a centerpiece or coffee table accent. For a longer-lasting arrangement, use artifical leaves. Add a little glitz by spray painting nuts gold and interspersing them among the leaves.

✳

Pick up a new tablecloth and napkins. Tapestry prints, paisley and plaid all set the mood for cold-weather dining.

✳

This holiday, if you're using your folding bridge table and chairs for extra seating, dress them up a bit. Fold a square shawl or fabric scrap into a triangle shape. Place the long side of the triangle on the front of a chair, and flop the point of the triangle over the back. Tie the other two corners of the shawl around the back and over the point to secure it. Try this with brightly checked gingham or Christmas prints for the "children's table."

When you no longer have fresh flowers from your garden, fill your favorite vases with a bouquet of autumn leaves, branches of eucalyptus or "silver dollars," or even bare branches, spray-painted or left in their natural state.

✳

Replace a painting over the mantel with a framed mirror. The mirror will reflect light back into the room — a bonus in these days of early sunsets.

Tiny pieces of orange peel added to the fire give your home a wonderful citrus smell. Pine cones can bring the scent of the woods indoors. Cinnamon sticks fill the house with a rich, spicy fragrance.

✳

Make fireplace cleanup easier by sprinkling the ashes with water from a spray bottle before sweeping them out. For even easier cleanup, line the bottom of the fireplace with heavy-duty aluminum foil.

✳

To keep yarn neat and manageable while you work at your cold-weather crafting, punch a hole in the lid of a clean, wide-mouthed jar. Thread the yarn end through the hole, place the ball of yarn in the jar, and replace the lid. Be sure to punch the lid from the inside out, to keep the sharp edges facing away from the yarn.

This fall, make leaf-raking easier. Shred the leaves with your lawnmower before raking and bagging them. You'll find you have fewer bags to fill. You also can use the shredded leaves as mulch to cover flower and vegetable beds, and to fill in areas beneath your shrubbery. The mulch enriches the soil and cuts down on weeds.

✳

Fill glass jars with red, green and white pasta, and tie the jars with ribbons in holiday colors. The jars will look festive on your kitchen counter, or as accents in the dining room or breakfast nook. As a treat for the kids, cook up some holiday-colored pasta for lunch.

Order your Christmas cards from charitable organizations. A portion of the money you pay for the cards goes to support their causes. Write to these organizations for catalogs and further information:

American Cancer Society, P.O. Box C19140, Seattle, WA 98109-1140

The Arthritis Foundation, Rocky Mountain Chapter, 2280 South Albion, Denver, CO 80222

The Association for Retarded Citizens, ARC National Headquarters, P.O. Box 6109, Arlington, TX 76006

The National Committee for the Prevention of Child Abuse, Attn: Holiday Cards, P.O. Box 94283, Chicago, IL 60690

Your local branch of the A.S.P.C.A.

✳

Press flowers and brightly-colored fall leaves and use them to make unique, lovely stationery to send or give as gifts. Flower presses are available in most craft stores. Flowers that press well include geranium, marigold, nasturtium, petunia, Queen Anne's lace, rose, salvia and yarrow.

HARVEST HOME ACCENTS

Dress your home for the cold winter months with these warm and wonderful projects, crafted in the rich hues of autumn.

Carolina Lily Quilted Shade

CAROLINA LILY QUILTED SHADE

(30 x 44 inches, for a 28 x 42-inch window opening)

Challenging: Requires more experience in sewing and quilting.

Materials: 30 x 44 inches of firm, closely woven cotton for shade front; matching quilting thread; 30 x 54 inches of insulated lining fabric for shade back; ½ yard of 45-inch-wide fabric for binding; fabric scraps for appliqués; matching sewing threads; 30 x 44 inches of synthetic batting; firm template material; darner needles; between needles; masking tape; scissors; pencil; iron; five 30-inch-long thin adjustable sash rods with a loop at each end; 10 L-shaped shoulder hooks, 2 of them long enough to hold 2 rods at the same time.

Directions:

1. Shade Front: Fold the shade front in half twice, once in each direction, and press the folds to mark the horizontal and vertical centerlines. Then fold each short end to meet the horizontal center fold, and press to mark the casing positions.

2. Cutting: Using the dimensions in FIG. I, 1 *(page 12)*, draw the appliqué patterns on firm template material, and cut out the templates. Trace them on the right side of the fabric scraps, and cut out the pieces ¼ inch outside the traced lines. For each large flower of the center design, cut one large base and two pairs of large petals; to cut one pair, trace once with the template right side up, and once with the template right side down. For each small flower, cut one small base, two pairs of small petals, and one pair of small leaves. For the center design, also cut two large leaves and one large base. For the large flower stems, cut 1-inch-wide bias strips. For the small flower stems, cut ⅞-inch-wide bias strips.

3. Large Flowers: When sewing the petals, stop stitching ¼ inch from each edge. Stitch together a pair of large petals along one long edge. Repeat. Stitch the two pairs together along a short edge *(see photo)*. Press the seams open. Stitch the four petals to a large base. Make two more large flowers.

4. Small Flowers: Stitch together the small flowers following the directions in Step 3. Make ten small flowers.

5. Appliquéing: Using the photo as a guide, pin the appliqués to the shade front, turning under the edges along the traced lines. Center the large flowers on the vertical centerline. Slide the stem ends under the flowers, with the small flower stems running into the 1-inch seam allowance for the binding. Leave at least ¾ inch between the flowers and the creases that mark the casings placement. Edgestitch the flowers in place.

6. Shade Back: Cut a shade back from the insulated lining the same size as the shade front. Use the excess lining to make three rod casings. To determine the width of the casings, lay a rod flat on a table and smooth the lining fabric over it. Mark the fabric on each side where it touches the table. Measure the distance between the marks. Add ⅜ inch for easing, and a ½-inch seam allowance. Cut three casings of this width x 29 inches long. Turn under ¼ inch at each long edge and press. Turn under ⅝ inch at each short end. Stitch across the short ends. Pin one long edge of a casing along each horizontal quarter fold, with the other edge toward the center. (Pin the remaining casing, centered, on the horizontal center fold.) Keep each end 1⅛ inches away from the shade edge to leave room for the 1-inch-wide binding. Stitch each pinned edge, and remove the pins. Slide a rod under each casing with the shade back flat on the table. Pin each loose edge to the shade back over the rod, to prevent the shade front from bulging. Remove the rods, stitch the pinned edges, and remove the pins.

7. Quilting: Lay the shade back, wrong side up, on the table, and tape down the edges. Place the batting and the shade

The autumn always gets me badly, as it breaks into colours. I want to go south, where there is no autumn, where the cold doesn't crouch over one like a snow-leopard waiting to pounce.

— D.H. LAWRENCE

front, right side up on the shade back, edges even. Using the darner needles, baste from the center of the shade outward diagonally to each corner and straight to each edge. Using the between needles and quilting thread, quilt about ¼ inch outside the appliqués.

8. *Binding:* Cut four 4-inch-wide binding strips, two 44 inches long and two 32 inches long. Fold each strip in half lengthwise (2 x 44″; 2 x 32″), and press. Fold each long edge to meet the center fold on the wrong side and press. Pin a 44-inch strip to one long edge of the shade, right sides together and raw edges even. Stitch the strip to the shade along the first crease. Fold the binding to the back, and slipstitch the last fold to the seam *(see Stitch Guide, page 240).* Repeat at the opposite long edge. Repeat the process using the 32-inch strips at the top and bottom edges of the shade, turning under the strips 1 inch at each short end.

9. Make a top and bottom casing from the binding fabric, and stitch them to the back of the binding following the directions in Step 6.

10. Slide the rods through the casings. Place the shade over the window, centers matching and bottom flush with the sill. Mark the hook positions. Attach the top hooks. Hang the shade. Attach the remaining hooks, with the long hooks holding the second rod from the top. To raise the shade, overlap it so that only the flower borders are showing.

FIG. I, 1 CAROLINA LILY QUILTED SHADE

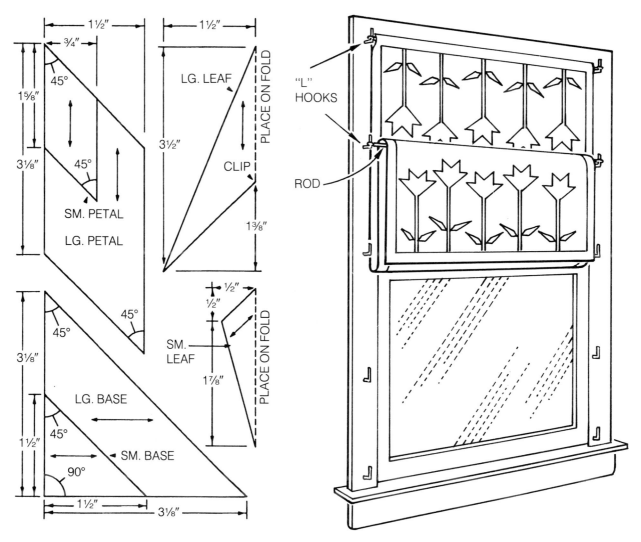

BUFFALO PLAID AFGHAN

Average: For those with some experience in knitting.

Materials: Eight 100-gram skeins each of Reynolds Icelandic Lopi yarn in red and black; one 24-inch size 10½ circular needle; plastic sewing needle.

Gauge: In Garter stitch (knit every row), 3 stitches = 1 inch, 4 rows = 1 inch.

Pattern:
Work in Garter stitch throughout.

Rows 1 through 12: Black.
Rows 13 through 24: Red.
Rows 25 through 30: Black.
Rows 31 through 36: Red.

Directions:

1. With black yarn, cast on 144 sts. Work rows 1 through 36 following the pattern above. Repeat the pattern until the afghan measures 48 inches. Repeat the pattern for more length, if you wish. The multi-striped pattern keeps all the yarn color changes on the wrong side.

2. To convert the striped pattern to a plaid, weave vertical stripes through the first pattern. Spread out the afghan with the stripes on the horizontal. Use a strand of yarn, doubled on the needle, that is 8 inches longer than the afghan when it is held across the stripes. The Garter stitch results in linking rows of loops, one row facing up, the other facing down. Weave through the **up** loops only to the top of the afghan. Start at the bottom right corner, with black yarn in the needle, and weave through the **up** loops of the twelve black rows, then through the **up** loops of the red, and so forth until you reach the top of the afghan. Leave several inches at each end to weave into the back.

3. Following the process in Step 2, weave enough black strands to equal the width of the black stripe (10 strands woven one at a time should create a solid square). Change to red and repeat the process. Change to black and weave a narrow stripe (5 strands). Repeat with red. Alternate wide and narrow stripes of weaving to match the horizontal knit stripes. You will have alternating blocks and stripes of solid color, and a textured red and black combination.

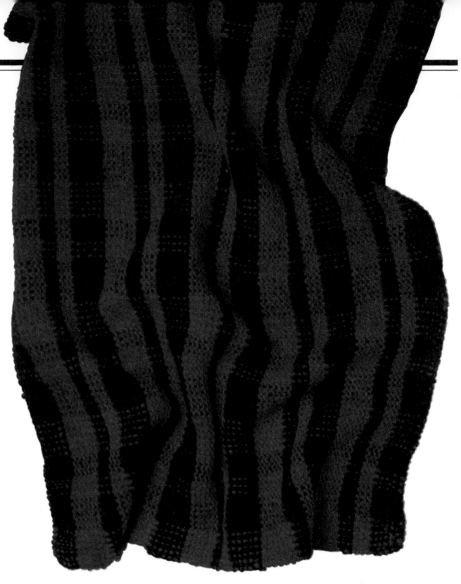

Rainbow Pillow; Sunburst Pillow; Autumn Hues Pillow

SUNBURST PILLOW
(12 inches in diameter)

Average: For those with some experience in crocheting.

Materials: DMC Cebelia No. 10 yarn (50-gram ball): 1 of red; size 1 crochet hook, OR ANY SIZE HOOK TO OBTAIN GAUGE BELOW; 45-inch-wide broadcloth: ½ yard of orange and 1 yard of red; matching threads; needle; scissors; stuffing.
Gauge: 8 dc = 1 inch; 7 rows = 2 inches; each square = 1¾ inches; center circle = 7 inches in diameter.
Directions:
1. Squares (make 11): Starting at the center, ch 5. Join with sl st to form ring. **Rnd 1:** Ch 5 (counts as 1 dc, ch 2), in ring work (4 dc, ch 2) 3 times; 3 dc. Join with sl st to 3rd ch of ch-5. **Do not** turn rnds. **Rnd 2:** Sl st in next ch-2 sp, ch 5, 2 dc in same sp, * 1 dc in each dc to within corner ch-2 sp, in corner work 2 dc, ch 2, 2 dc; rep from * around, end 1 dc in each dc, 1 dc in corner. Join with sl st to 3rd ch of ch-5. **Rnd 3:** Rep Rnd 2. Fasten off.
2. Circle: Starting at the center, ch 5. Join with sl st to form ring. **Rnd 1:** Ch 4 (counts as first tr), work 18 tr in ring. Join with sl st to top of ch-4 — 19 tr. **Do not** turn rnds. **Rnd 2:** Ch 4, 1 tr in same st as joining, 2 tr in each st around — 38 tr. Join with sl st to top of ch-4. **Rnd 3:** Rep Rnd 2 — 76 tr. **Rnd 4:** Ch 4, 1 tr in each st around. Join with sl st to top of ch-4. **Rnd 5:** Ch 4, * 2 tr in next st, 1 tr in next st; rep from * around, end 2 tr in last st — 114 tr. Join with sl st to top of ch-4. **Rnd 6:** Rep Rnd 4. **Rnd 7:** Ch 4, * 1 tr in each of next 2 sts, 2 tr in next st; rep from * around, end 1 tr in each of last 2 sts — 152 tr. Join with sl st to top of ch-4. **Rnd 8:** Sl st in each st around. Join with sl st to first sl st. Fasten off.
3. Cut two 13-inch-diameter circles, one from the orange fabric and one from the red fabric. Cut 7-inch-wide red strips to measure 2 yards when pieced together.
4. Sew together the red strips at the short

ends to make a loop. Fold the loop in half lengthwise and press. Sew a gathering row along the raw edges. Pin the ruffle to the orange circle, right sides together and raw edges even, pulling up the gathers to fit; stitch in place.
5. Pin together the orange and red circles, right sides together, with the ruffle between. Stitch together the circles using a ½-inch seam allowance, leaving an opening for turning. Turn right side out, stuff, turn in the open edges, and slipstitch the opening closed *(see Stitch Guide, page 240).*
6. Center the crocheted circle over the orange front; stitch edges in place. Using the photo as a guide, tack squares around the circle to form a ring of diamonds.

RAINBOW PILLOW
(about 16 inches square)

Average: For those with some experience in needlepoint.

Materials: Persian yarn (10-yard skeins): 9 of pink, 10 of purple, 11 of yellow, 6 of turquoise, 7 of orange and 7 of green; ½ yard of 14-mesh needlepoint canvas; tapestry needle; 18-inch square of yellow fabric for pillow back; 2 yards of yellow piping; stuffing; scissors; masking tape.
Directions:
1. Cut an 18-inch needlepoint canvas square, and bind the edges with masking tape. From the center hole, baste diagonally to each corner.
2. Using full strands of yarn and the tapestry needle, work four 7-mesh squares of pink Scotch stitch *(see Stitch Guide, page 240)* at the center. Using the photo as a color guide, surround the squares with 7-mesh-wide bands of Straight stitch, mitering the bands at the corners. Block the finished needlepoint *(see How To Block Like A Pro, page 239).*
3. Trim the canvas ½ inch beyond the needlepoint. Trim the pillow back to match. Pin the piping to the pillow front,

right sides together and raw edges matching. Using a ½-inch seam allowance, stitch the piping to the pillow front close to the needlepoint, clipping at the corners.
4. Right sides together, stitch the pillow back to the front around three sides and four corners. Turn right side out, stuff, turn in the open edges, and slipstitch the opening closed *(see Stitch Guide).*

AUTUMN HUES PILLOW
(14 inches square)

Average: For those with some experience in sewing.

Materials: 45-inch-wide corduroy: ¼ yard each of blue and beige, and 1 yard of red; matching threads; scissors; 1¾ yards of piping cord; stuffing.
Directions:
1. From the red corduroy, cut one 15-inch square for the pillow back, six 5¼-inch squares, and enough 2-inch-wide bias strips to measure 57 inches when pieced together. From the beige corduroy, cut four 4½-inch squares and two 5¼-inch squares. From the blue corduroy, cut four 5¼-inch squares.
2. Cut all the 5¼-inch squares diagonally in half. Lay out the pillow top, using the photo as a placement guide. With right sides together, stitch the long edges of the triangles together to form squares. Stitch the squares together to make four rows. Stitch the rows together, matching seams, to finish the pillow top.
3. Using a zipper foot, enclose the cord, centered, in the bias strips for piping.
4. With raw edges out and using a ½-inch seam allowance, stitch the piping to the seamline around the pillow front, clipping at the corners. With right sides together, stitch the pillow back to the pillow front around three sides and four corners. Turn the pillow right side out, stuff, turn in the open edges, and slipstitch the opening closed *(see Stitch Guide, page 240).*

The owl hunts in the
evening and it is pretty
The lake water below him
rustles with ice
There is frost coming from
the ground, in the air mist
All this is pretty, it could not
be prettier.

— STEVIE SMITH

STAINED GLASS AFGHAN
(48 x 62 inches)

Challenging: For those with more experience in crocheting.

Materials: Reynolds Reynelle yarn (4-ounce skein): 7 skeins of Black (A), 2 skeins of Clay (B), and 1 skein each of Raspberry (C), Purple (D), Royal (E), Turquoise No.3 (F), Gold (G), Cardinal (H), and Kelly (I); size I afghan hook, OR ANY SIZE HOOK TO OBTAIN GAUGE BELOW; size H crochet hook; No.14 tapestry needle; yarn bobbins.

Gauge: In Afghan Stitch, 4 upright bars = 1 inch; 3 rows = 1 inch.

Note: *Wind each color yarn on a yarn bobbin. Keep the bobbins on the wrong side of the work. To change colors at the beginning of a row, work off the last 2 lps of the previous row with the new color. To change colors in the middle of a row, draw up a lp with the new color in the next upright bar. Twist the old and new color yarns once when changing colors to prevent holes in the work. The black outlines are embroidered later.*

Afghan St: With the afghan hook, ch the required number of sts. **Row 1:** Draw up a lp in 2nd ch from hook and each ch across; work off lps as follows: yo, thru 1 lp on hook, * yo, thru 2 lps on hook; rep from * across—1 lp on hook counts as first lp on next row. **Row 2:** Sk first upright bar at edge, draw up a lp in next upright bar and each upright bar across; work off lps as for Row 1. Rep Row 2 for afghan st. **Note:** *The number of lps drawn up on each row will be the same as the number of sts in starting ch. Each upright bar, formed by a lp, counts as one st.*

Directions:
1. Panel (make 3): Starting at the lower edge with the afghan hook and A, ch 33. **Row 1:** Work afghan st, changing to D at end—33 upright bars. **Row 2:** With D, draw up a lp in next 5 upright bars (6 D lps on hook); join C, with C draw up a lp

in next 21 upright bars; join D, with D draw up a lp in last 6 upright bars; work off lps in colors as established. Follow the chart in Fig. I, 2A *(page 18)* for the afghan st Panel Rows 3 to 43; turn the chart upside down and work Rows 44 through 85. With A, sl st in each upright bar on the last row. Fasten off.

2. Embroidery: With the tapestry needle and A, outline each color section in chain stitch *(see Stitch Guide, page 240)*. Following Fig. I, 2A, work the rows of chain stitch indicated by the broken lines.

3. Panel Edging, Rnd 1: With right side facing, and the crochet hook, join A in a corner of the Panel, ch 1, * 3 sc in corner, work an odd number of sc to opposite corner; rep from * around, working the same number of sc on the corresponding sides and spacing the sts to keep the edge flat; join with sl st to first sc. **Rnd 2:** Sl st to center st at corner, ch 6, dc in same st *(first corner)*; ch 1, sk 1 sc, * dc in next sc, ch 1, sk 1 sc; rep from * to next corner st, (dc, ch 3, dc) in corner st, ch 1, sk 1 sc; rep from * around, end ch 1, sk 1 sc, join in 3rd ch of ch-6. **Rnd 3:** Working 5 sc in each corner ch-3 sp, sc in each dc and ch-1 sp around; join. Fasten off.

4. Long Side Edging, Row 1: Wrong side facing, join C in first sc after center sc at corner on a long edge; in same sc as joining, work sc and dc *(group made)*, * sk 1 sc, sc and dc in next sc; rep from * across long edge, end in sc before corner sc. Fasten off. Turn. **Row 2 (right side):** Join A in corner sc before first group, ch 1, sc in same sc, * ch 1, sc between next 2 groups; rep from * across, end ch 1, sc in corner after last group. **Row 3:** Ch 4; turn, sk first ch-1 sp, dc in next sc, * ch 1, sk next ch-1 sp, dc in next sc; rep from * across. **Row 4:** Ch 1, turn, sc in each dc and ch-1 sp across, sc around ch-4, sc in 3rd ch of ch-4. Fasten off. Turn. **Row 5:** With D, sk first sc, join in next sc, work as for Row 1 to sc before last sc. Fasten off. Turn.

Continued on page 18

Stained Glass Afghan

Row 6: Beg in st before first group and ending in st after last group, work as for Row 2. **Rows 7 and 8:** Rep Rows 3 and 4. **Row 9:** With F, rep Row 5. **Rows 10 to 12:** Rep Rows 6 to 8. Fasten off. Work the opposite long edge to correspond.

5. Short Side Edging: On one short edge of the Panel, work as for the Long Side Edging, working Row 1 with color I, Row 5 with E, Row 9 with H. Work the opposite short edge to correspond.

6. Small Square (make 12): With the afghan hook and B, ch 12. Follow the chart in Fig. I, 2B for the Small Square for 10 rows. Fasten off.

7. Embroidery: With the tapestry needle and A, outline each color and follow the broken lines in Fig. I, 2B in chain stitch.

8. Small Square Edging, Rnd 1: With A, rep Rnd 1 of the Panel Edging. **Rnd 2:** Sc in each sc, working 3 sc in center st at each corner; join. Fasten off. With A, sew or sl st the squares into the corners between the Long and Short Side Edgings on the Panels.

9. Finishing: Block the Panels *(see How To Block Like a Pro, page 239),* being careful to block the corners at right angles. With A, sew or sl st the long edges of the Panels together.

10. Afghan Side Edging, Row 1: With right side facing, and the crochet hook, join A in the right corner on one long edge of the Afghan, ch 4, sk next st, dc in next st, * ch 1, sk next st, dc in next st; rep from * across. **Row 2:** Rep Row 4 of the Long Side Edging. Rep Rows 5 to 8 of the Long Side Edging 3 times, working the first Row 5 with D, the 2nd Row 5 with E, and the 3rd Row 5 with H. Fasten off. Work same edging along opposite edge of Afghan; *do not* fasten off after 3rd rep.

11. Afghan Outer Edging, Rnds 1 to 3: Work the same as Panel Short and Long Side Edgings Rnds 1 to 3 around the entire Afghan. **Rnd 4:** Sl st in each sc around; join. **Rnd 5:** * Sc in next st, ch 2, sk 3 sts, (dc, ch 3, tr, ch 3, dc) in next st, ch 2, sk 3 sts; rep from * around; join. **Rnd 6:** * 3 sc in next ch-2 sp, 4 sc in next ch-3 sp;

ch 3, sl st in 3rd ch from hook for picot, ch 5, sl st in 5th ch from hook, ch 3, sl st in 3rd ch from hook; 4 sc in next ch-3 sp, 3 sc in next ch-2 sp; rep from * around; join. Fasten off. Block the edging.

FIG. I, 2A   STAINED GLASS AFGHAN: AFGHAN STITCH PANEL

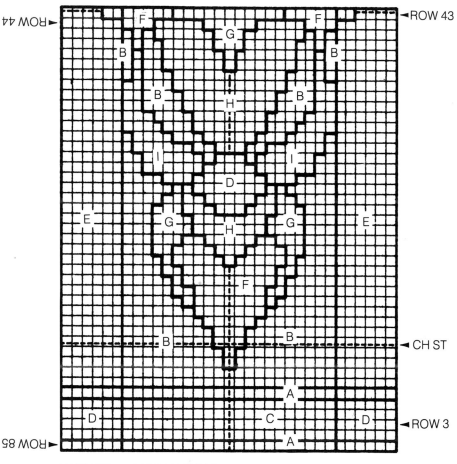

EACH SQ. = 1 UPRIGHT BAR
NOTE: BROKEN LINES ARE CHAIN STITCH
(EMBROIDERED AFTER PANEL IS COMPLETE)

FIG. I, 2B

SMALL SQUARE

COLD WEATHER CRAFTS

Now's the time to start crafting for the holidays. Make these projects for your own home, or to give as gifts.

Red Hot Flannel Quilt (directions, page 20)

RED HOT FLANNEL QUILT
(65 x 89 inches)

Average: For those with some experience in sewing.

Materials: 45-inch wide pre-shrunk cotton flannel: 7½ yards of red for patches, border and quilt back, 2⅝ yards of wide-striped for patches and binding, 1½ yards of narrow-striped for patches, and ½ yard of white for border; matching threads; 72 x 89 inches of synthetic batting; ruler; masking tape; scissors; darning needles; between needles *(optional)*; red quilting thread *(optional)*.

Directions
(½-inch seams allowed):
1. Cutting Borders: Across the 45-inch width of the fabric, cut the following strips: seven 2-inch-wide white and seven 5-inch-wide red strips for the borders, and eight 5-inch-wide strips from the wide-striped fabric for the binding. Stitch together the matching pieces at the short ends to make three continuous strips.

2. Cutting Patches: Draw, and then cut, the following 7¾-inch squares: 60 red, and 30 each of wide-striped and narrow-striped fabric. With a ruler, connect two opposite corners and draw a diagonal line across each red square. Cut on the drawn lines to make 120 triangles. Repeat with the narrow-striped squares, changing the direction of the diagonal on half of them *(see* FIG. I, 3A*)* to make 30 A triangles and 30 B triangles. The wide-striped squares should be cut in the same way as the narrow-striped.

3. Quilt Blocks: Following FIG. I, 3B, stitch the triangles into squares, and the squares into strips to make 27 each of A strips and B strips. Following FIG. I, 3C, stitch two strips together, turning one upside down, to make 12 A blocks and 12 B blocks. Each block will be 13 inches square (12 inches when finished). After making the blocks, you should have three A strips and three B strips remaining.

4. Quilt Top: Following the diagram in FIG. I, 3D, stitch four A and B blocks together, starting with an A block and alternating the blocks, to make Row 1. Add an A strip at the end. Make Rows 3 and 5 the same as Row 1. Make Rows 2, 4 and 6 starting with a B block and adding a B strip at the end. Press the seams open. Stitch the six rows together. Stitch together nine squares like the top half of Row 1 to make Row 7, and stitch it to Row 6. Press the seams open.

5. Borders: Stitch a white strip to one long edge of the quilt top, and trim the ends flush with the quilt top. Repeat at the opposite long edge, then at the top and bottom *(see* FIG. I, 3D*)*. Attach the red border the same way.

6. Quilt Back: Cut two 72 x 45-inch pieces from the red fabric, and stitch them together along the long edges to make a 72 x 89-inch quilt back. Press the seam open. Lay the quilt back on the floor, wrong side up, and tape down the corners. Place the batting on top, edges even. Place the quilt top, right side up and centered, on top. Using the darning needles, baste from the center outward diagonally to each corner and straight to each edge. Baste additional rows about 8 inches apart.

7. Quilting: Hand quilt with the between needles and quilting thread, or machine quilt, along the seamlines. Trim the edges of the quilt back and batting even with the quilt top.

8. Binding: Fold a binding strip in half lengthwise, stripes matching, and press. Pin the binding to one long edge of the quilt, right sides together and raw edges even. Stitch ½ inch from the edge, and trim the ends flush. Turn the binding to the wrong side of the quilt, and slipstitch the fold to the seamline *(see Stitch Guide, page 240)*. Repeat at the opposite long edge. Repeat at the top and bottom, turning in 1 inch at each end.

RED HOT FLANNEL QUILT

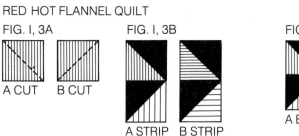

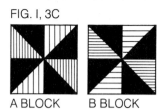

FIG. I, 3A   FIG. I, 3B   FIG. I, 3C

A CUT   B CUT   A STRIP   B STRIP   A BLOCK   B BLOCK

FIG. I, 3D

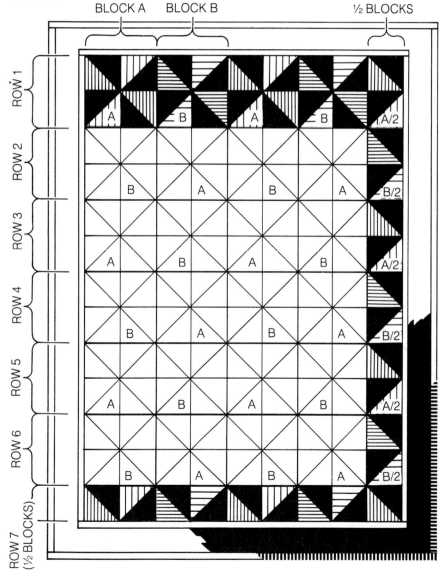

SCENTED SOAP BALLS

To make 2 soap balls, start with one 3½-ounce bar of unmilled, soft, unscented soap, ⅛-ounce of fruit- or flower-scented essential oil (available in specialty perfume or bath stores, see Note below), a grater, a saucepan and a fork.

✳

Coarsely grate the soap. Place the grated soap in the saucepan and add a tablespoon of hot tap water. Place the saucepan over low heat and stir the soap as it melts, adding water as needed, until the mixture is the consistency of mashed potatoes and leaves the sides of the pan.

✳

Remove the saucepan from the heat. Let the soap cool for a minute, and add a few drops of essential oil. Blend the soap and oil by mashing them with a fork.

✳

When the soap is cool enough to handle, knead it until it no longer sticks to your hands. Divide the soap in half, and shape each half into a ball.

✳

Place the soap balls in a bowl or basket and let them harden and cure, exposed to the air, for two weeks. When the balls are cured, wrap them individually in tissue paper or fabric tied with ribbon.

✳

Note: Do not use essential oils derived from spices, such as cloves and cinnamon, or herbs, as they are too strong for the skin.

WOOLLY BULLY PULLOVER

Average: For those with some experience in knitting.

This pullover is designed to be oversized. Directions are given for Child's Size 8. Changes for Sizes 10 and 12 are in parentheses.

Materials: Patons "Canadiana" 4-ply worsted weight yarn (3½-ounce skein): 5 (6, 7) skeins of No. 104 Natural; 1 pair each size 5 and size 8 knitting needles, OR ANY SIZE NEEDLES TO OBTAIN GAUGE BELOW; 1 pair size 5 double-pointed (dp) needles; 4 stitch holders; tapestry needle.

Gauge: On size 8 needles in Yarn-Over Mock Cable Pattern, 18½ sts = 4 inches; 23 rows = 4 inches.

Yarn-Over Mock Cable; Row 1 (wrong side): * K 3, sl 1, p 2, psso the 2 p sts; rep from * across, ending with k 3. **Row 2:** * P 3, k 1, yo, k 1; rep from * across, ending with p 3. **Row 3:** * K 3, p 3; rep from * across, ending with p 3. **Row 4:** * P 3, k 3; rep from * across, ending with k 3. **Row 5:** Rep Row 3. **Row 6:** Rep Row 4. Repeat Rows 1 to 6 for Yarn-Over Mock Cable pattern.

Measurements:

SIZES:	(8)	(10)	(12)
BODY CHEST:	27″	28½″	30″

Finished Measurements:

CHEST:	35″	37″	39″
WIDTH ACROSS BACK OR FRONT AT UNDERARMS:			
	17½″	18½″	19½″
WIDTH ACROSS SLEEVE AT UPPER ARMS:			
	14½″	15½″	16½″

Directions:

1. Back: Starting at the lower edge with size 5 needles, cast on 70 (76, 80) sts. Work in k 1, p 1 ribbing for 2 inches. **Next Row:** K across, increasing 11 (11, 13) sts evenly spaced across row—81 (87, 93) sts. Change to size 8 needles and beg Yarn-Over Mock Cable pat until total length is 15 (15½, 16) inches from beg, ending with a wrong-side row.

2. Raglan Armhole Shaping: Continuing in pat, bind off 4 (5, 5) sts at beg of next 2 rows. Work raglan decreases at each end as follows: **Row 1 (right side):** P 2; *depending* on whether next st is **k or p,** sl 1, k 1, psso **or** sl 1, p 1, psso; work across to last 4 sts; k 2 tog **or** p 2 tog; p 2. **Row 2:** K 2, work across row, k 2. Rep Rows 1 and 2, 21 (23, 25) times more, until 46 (50, 54) rows have been completed (including the 2 bound-off rows), and there are 29 (29, 31) sts on needle. Slip remaining sts onto a stitch holder for the Back Neckband.

3. Front: Work the same as the Back until there are 41 (41, 43) sts on needle after start of Raglan Armhole Shaping, ending with a wrong-side row.

4. Raglan Armhole and Neck Shaping, Row 1: P 2; sl 1, k 1, psso **or** sl 1, p 1, psso as for Back; work next 11 (11, 11) sts in pat. Slip center 11 (11, 13) sts onto a stitch holder for Front Neckband. Join 2d ball of yarn and work to last 4 sts; k 2 tog **or** p 2 tog as before; p 2. Continue in pat, working Raglan Armhole Shaping as established and, *at the same time*, bind off the following sts at each neck edge every *other* row: 3 (3, 3) sts, then 2 (2, 3) sts, 2 (2, 2) sts, and 1 (1, 0) st. When 46 (50, 54) rows have been worked and one st remains, bind off.

5. Sleeve: Starting at the lower edge with size 5 needles, cast on 36 (36, 38) sts. Work in k 1, p 1 ribbing for 2½ inches. **Next Row:** K across, increasing 3 (3, 7) sts evenly spaced across row—39 (39, 45) sts. Change to size 8 needles and beg Yarn-Over Mock Cable pat. Increase one st at each end every ¾ inch until there are 67 (71, 75) sts. Work even in pat until total length is 15½ (16, 16½) inches from beg, ending with a wrong-side row.

6. Raglan Sleeve Cap Shaping: Continuing in pat, bind off 4 (5, 5) sts at beg of next 2 rows. Work the Raglan Armhole decreases the same as the Back, **but** on the rows indicated below, work extra decreases as follows: **Row 13:** P 2, sl 1, k 1, psso **or** sl 1, p 1, psso as for Back; p 2 tog between next two cables, work to last two cables, p 2 tog between them, work to last 4 sts; k 2 tog **or** p 2 tog; p 2. **Row 27:** Rep Row 13. **Row 39:** Rep Row 13. **Row 45 (for Size 8 only):** Rep Row 13. When 7 (7, 7) sts remain and 46 (50, 54) rows have been completed, slip sts onto a stitch holder.

7. Finishing: Sew the Raglan Sleeve Caps to the Front and Back. **Neckband:** With the right side facing and dp needles, pick up 29 (29, 31) sts from the Back stitch holder, 7 (7, 7) sts from the left Sleeve stitch holder, 10 (11, 10) sts from the Neck edge, 11 (11, 13) sts from the Front stitch holder, 10 (11, 10) sts from the Neck edge, and 7 (7, 7) sts from the right Sleeve stitch holder—74 (76, 78) sts. Work in k 1, p 1 ribbing for 3 inches. Bind off sts loosely in ribbing. Fold the Neckband in half to the wrong side, and sew it to the inside of the sweater.

Woolly Bully Pullover

A single grateful thought raised to heaven is the most perfect prayer.

— GOTTHOLD EPHRAIM LESSING

Snow Bunny Suit and Hat

SNOW BUNNY SUIT AND HAT

Challenging: Requires more experience in knitting.

Directions are given for Child's Size 1. Changes for Sizes 2 and 4 are in parentheses.

Materials: Patons "Canadiana" 4-ply worsted weight yarn (3½-ounce skein): 3 (4, 5) skeins of No. 104 Natural for Sweater, 3 (4, 5) skeins for Pants, and 2 skeins for Hat; 1 pair each size 4 and size 6 knitting needles, OR ANY SIZE NEEDLES TO OBTAIN GAUGE BELOW; 1 size 6 double-pointed (dp) needle; stitch markers; stitch holders; tapestry needle; two ¾-inch-diameter buttons; size G crochet hook; 2-inch-wide piece of cardboard.

Gauge: On size 6 needles in Seed Stitch, 9 sts = 2 inches; 8 rows = 1 inch.

Measurements:

SIZES:	(1)	(2)	(4)
BODY CHEST:	20″	21″	23″

Finished Measurements:

CHEST:	22″	24″	26″
WIDTH ACROSS BACK OR FRONT AT UNDERARMS:			
	11″	12″	13″
WIDTH ACROSS SLEEVE AT UPPER ARMS:			
	10″	11″	12″
HIP:	26″	28″	30″
LENGTH OF LEG SEAM:			
	9¼″	12″	13½″

General Directions:

1. Seed Stitch, Row 1: * K 1, p 1; rep from * across. **Row 2:** K the p sts and p the k sts as they face you. Repeat Row 2 for Seed Stitch.

2. Cable, Row 1 (wrong side): K 1, p 8, k 1. **Row 2:** P 1, sl next 4 sts onto dp needle and hold in back of work, k next 4 sts, k 4 sts from dp needle, p 1. **Rows 3, 5 and 7:** Rep Row 1. **Rows 4 and 6:** P 1, k 8, p 1. Repeat Rows 2 to 7 for Cable.

3. Honeycomb, Row 1 (wrong side): K 1, * p 8; rep from * 2 times more, k 1. **Row 2:** P 1, * sl next 2 sts onto dp needle and hold in back of work, k next 2 sts, k 2 sts from dp needle — **Right Twist (RT) made**; sl next 2 sts onto dp needle and hold in front of work, k next 2 sts, k 2 sts from dp needle — **Left Twist (LT) made**; rep from * 2 times more, p 1. **Rows 3 and 5:** Rep Row 1. **Rows 4 and 8:** P 1, * k 8; rep from * 2 times more, p 1. **Row 6:** P 1, * LT, RT; rep from * 2 times more, p 1. **Rows 7 and 9:** Rep Row 1. Repeat Rows 2 to 9 for Honeycomb.

Sweater Directions:

1. Back: Starting at the lower edge with size 4 needles, cast on 44 (50, 56) sts. Work in k 1, p 1 ribbing for 2 inches, increasing 20 sts evenly spaced across last row — 64 (70, 76) sts. Change to size 6 needles and beg pattern as follows: **Row 1 (wrong side):** Following Row 1 of each pattern, work Seed Stitch over 6 (9, 12) sts, Cable over 10 sts, Seed Stitch over 3 sts, Honeycomb over 26 sts, Seed Stitch over 3 sts, Cable over 10 sts, Seed Stitch over 6 (9, 12) sts. Work pat as established until total length is 8 (8½, 9½) inches from beg, ending with a wrong-side row.

2. Armhole Shaping: Continuing in pat, bind off 4 (5, 5) sts at beg of next 2 rows. Dec one st each end every other row 1 (2, 2) times — 54 (56, 62) sts. Work even until armhole measures 5 (5½, 6) inches, ending with a wrong-side row.

3. Shoulder Shaping: Continuing in pat, bind off 15 (16, 19) sts at beg of next 2 rows. Bind off all sts.

4. Front: Work the same as the Back to Armhole Shaping, ending with a wrong-side row.

5. Armhole and Collar Shaping: Bind off 4 (5, 5) sts at beg of row, work across 16 (18, 21) sts in pat, then work in k 1, p 1 ribbing across 24 sts of Honeycomb for Collar, work in pat to end of row.

6. Right Front, Next Row: Bind off 4 (5, 5) sts at beg of row, work in pat across next 16 (18, 21) sts, work 24 sts in k 1, p 1 ribbing for right half of Collar, **do not** work remainder of row, **turn**. Continuing with Right Front **only**, work Armhole Shaping the same as the Back and Collar until Armhole measures the same length as the Back, ending at Armhole edge.

7. Shoulder Shaping: Bind off 15 (16, 19) sts for Shoulder, work 24 sts of Collar.

8. Collar: Working in k 1, p 1 ribbing, complete the right half of the Collar as follows: **Row 1 (right side):** Work 19 sts, **turn**. **Row 2:** Rep Row 1. **Row 3:** Work 24 sts, **turn**. **Row 4:** Rep Row 3. Rep Rows 1 to 4, 5 (6, 6) times. Bind off loosely in ribbing.

9. Left Front: With size 6 needles, cast on 24 sts for left half of Collar. Work in k 1, p 1 ribbing for 4 rows.

10. Attaching Collar to Left Front: Wrong side facing you, with size 6 needles work 24 sts of left half of Collar, then work in pat across the 16 (18, 21) sts of Left Front. Continuing on Left Front **only**, work to correspond to Right Front, reversing shaping.

11. Sleeve: Starting at the lower edge with size 4 needles, cast on 30 (32, 34) sts. Work in k 1, p 1 ribbing for 2 inches, increasing 20 (22, 24) sts evenly spaced across last row — 50 (54, 58) sts. Change to size 6 needles and beg pat as follows: **Row 1 (wrong side):** Following Row 1 of each pat, work Seed Stitch over 20 (22, 24) sts, Cable over 10 sts, Seed Stitch over 20 (22, 24) sts. Work pat as established until total length is 7 (9, 10½) inches from beg, ending with a wrong-side row.

12. Cap Shaping: Continuing in pat, bind off 4 (5, 5) sts at beg of next 2 rows. Dec one st each end every other row 10 (13, 14) times. Bind off 2 sts at beg of next 4 (2, 2) rows. Bind off rem 14 (14, 16) sts.

13. Finishing: Sew the Shoulder seams. Sew in the Sleeves. Sew the side and Sleeve seams. With the right half of the Collar overlapping the left half, sew the lower edge of the left half in place. Sew the center back seam of the Collar. Then sew the Collar to the Back neck edge.

Pants Directions:

1. Leg (Make 2): Starting at the lower edge of the Leg with size 4 needles, cast on 36 (40, 40) sts. Work in k 1, p 1 ribbing for 2 inches, increasing 24 (24, 28) sts evenly spaced on last row — 60 (64, 68) sts. Change to size 6 needles and work in Seed Stitch throughout until total length is 9¼ (12, 13½) inches from beg or desired length, ending with a wrong-side row.

2. Crotch Shaping, Next Row: Bind off 2 sts at beg of row for front edge, work to end. **Next Row:** Bind off 4 sts at beg of row for back edge, work to end. Work even in pat until total length is 16 (20, 22½) inches from beg, ending at back edge. **Rows 1 and 2:** Work across 27 (29, 31) sts; **turn. Rows 3 and 4:** Work across 17 (18, 20) sts, **turn. Rows 5 and 6:** Work across 8 (9, 10) sts, **turn. Rows 7 and 8:** Work across **all** sts. Place sts on a st holder. Sew Crotch and Leg seams. Divide sts of each Leg in half; place a marker in the middle — 27 (29, 31) sts on each side of marker.

3. Back Ribbing: With size 4 needles, work across sts for Back from both Legs — 54 (58, 62) sts. Continuing on Back sts **only**, work in k 1, p 1 ribbing for 1¼ inches. Bind off 15 (17, 19) sts at beg of next 2 rows — 24 sts.

4. Back Panel and Shoulder Straps: Continue in Seed Stitch on these 24 sts for 2½ inches.

5. Dividing for Straps: In Seed Stitch work across 7 sts for First Strap; join 2nd ball and bind off 10 sts, work across rem 7 sts for Second Strap. Work each strap separately until 14 inches long or desired length. Bind off sts of each strap.

6. Front Ribbing: Work the same as the Back Ribbing on 54 (58, 62) sts for 4 rows.

7. Buttonhole Row: Work in ribbing on 12 (13, 14) sts, yo, k 2 tog, work in ribbing on 26 (28, 30) sts, yo, k 2 tog, work to end. Work even in ribbing until it is the same length as the Back Ribbing. Bind off loosely in ribbing. Sew the side seams. Sew a button to the end of each Strap.

Hat Directions:

1. Starting at the brim of the Hat with size 4 needles, cast on 90 sts. Work in k 1, p 1 ribbing for 3 (3, 3½) inches. Change to size 6 needles and beg pat as follows:

Row 1 (wrong side): Following Row 1 of each pat, work Seed Stitch over 2 (2, 2) sts, Cable over 10 sts, * Seed Stitch over 5 (5, 5) sts, Cable over 10 sts; rep from * 4 times more, ending with Seed Stitch over 3 (3, 3) sts. Work pat as established until total length is 9½ (9½, 10½) inches from beg.

2. Top Shaping, Row 1: K 2 tog across row. **Row 2:** P 2 tog across row, leaving a 16 inch length of yarn. Thread the tapestry needle with this 16-inch length. Pull through rem sts on knitting needle tightly to close the opening and secure it. Sew the side seam.

3. Ear Flaps (make 2): With size 4 needles, cast on 22 (22, 26) sts. Work in k 1, p 1 ribbing for 10 rows. Dec one st each end every other row until 2 sts rem. Slip these 2 sts onto the crochet hook, yo, draw through both lps on hook. Make a 12-inch chain. Fasten off. Add a fringe to the end. Turn back the brim. Sew the Ear Flaps to the inside of the Hat.

4. Pompon (make 1): Wind yarn around the piece of cardboard 100 times. Slip a strand under the yarn at one end, and knot it securely. Cut the yarn at the other end and trim the ends evenly. Sew the pompon to the top of the Hat.

The Perfect Gift

Chances are, you're stumped by some of the people on your gift list. You can't possibly buy another tie for Uncle Jim, and your nephew won't be pleased with a gift of socks and underwear. Then there's your daughter's teacher, your hairdresser, and your brother's new girlfriend—she's joining the family celebration this year, and you haven't even met her yet. Don't worry! Here are a few ideas for those tough-to-tackle gifts.

Women

—A pretty, fabric cosmetic bag filled with travel-size bottles of shampoo, conditioner, body lotion, nail polish remover, and so on.
—Inexpensive knitted gloves you dress up with stitched-on sequins or pearl beads.
—A pretty mug filled with a selection of herbal teas.
—An "office emergency" kit with needle and thread, clear nail polish (to mend small hosiery runs), an extra pair of panty hose, aspirin, emery board, packages of non-dairy creamer and a pocket pack of tissues.

Men

—An athlete's bonanza package of sweat bands, athletic socks (some companies offer padded socks specially designed for different sports), a can of tennis or racquet balls, a tube of wintergreen muscle ointment.
—A miniature eyeglass repair kit or small screwdriver set (for tinkering with stereo equipment and computers).

—A beer mug emblazoned with the logo of his favorite football or baseball team.

Teenage Girls

—A subscription to her favorite magazine.
—A gift certificate from the local record store.
—Colorful socks or patterned tights.
—A fabric-covered "blank book" to use as a journal.

Teenage Boys

—A book about his favorite sport or rock band.
—A grooming kit with shaving cream, aftershave or cologne, hairbrush, comb and extra razor blades.
—A gift certificate from the local record store.
—New headphones for his portable stereo.

Kids

—A big box of crayons (they get lost or broken, and kids always can use more), plus a coloring book.
—Puppets.
—Novelty keychains.
—A personalized Christmas ornament.

Teachers

—Pretty magnets for filing cabinets and metal chalk boards.
—A brightly colored clip board, memo holder, or desk organizer for paper clips, rubber bands, and so on.
—Big memo cubes for little notes.
—A plant to brighten the teacher's desk all year.

COME HOME TO THE HARVEST— JUST FOR KIDS

Get your children involved in decorating the house for the fall. Give them each a big paper bag (preferably with handles) and send them out on a natural "treasure hunt." Pretty fall foliage, pine cones, nuts, colorful rocks, empty bird's nests, dried thistles, dried corn stalks, dried wheat stalks, dried sunflowers, and so on, are all beautiful symbols of the season. Then decorate the house together, finding the best place for each treasure.

Buy a bushel of small pumpkins and let your kids decorate them with faces and fancy designs. Place the decorated pumpkins throughout the house.

✳

Colorful construction paper turkeys, festooned with tissue paper feathers, can be taped onto windows, tacked onto doors or used to set a gobblin' good tone to the Thanksgiving table. If you have any real feathers around, add these to the supply table.

*C*ome, ye thankful
people come,
Raise the song of
Harvest-home;
All is safely gathered in,
Ere the winter storms begin.

— HENRY ALFORD

Roast Turkey with Wild Rice, Pecan and Apple Stuffing (recipes, pages 32 and 35); Creamy Corn Casserole with Jalapeños (recipe, page 35); Steamed Vegetables with Cheddar Cheese Sauce; Sour Cherry Cranberry Sauce (recipes, page 36)

GIVING THANKS

Menu for 8

Chestnut Soup with Brandy

Roast Turkey
*with Wild Rice, Pecan and Apple Stuffing**

*Creamy Corn Casserole With Jalapeños**

*Steamed Vegetables with Cheddar Cheese Sauce**

*Sour Cherry Cranberry Sauce**

Baked Sweet Potatoes, Whipped Honey Butter

Parker House Rolls

Perfect Pecan Pie, Pumpkin Pie**

*Recipe follows

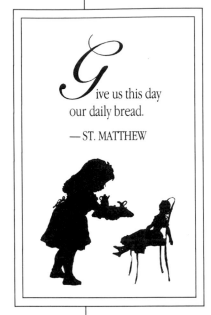

*G*ive us this day
our daily bread.

— ST. MATTHEW

Perfect Pecan Pie and Pumpkin Pie (recipes, page 37)

Giving Thanks — Countdown

UP TO ONE MONTH AHEAD:
—Prepare and freeze the Perfect Pecan Pie.
—Line the pie plate with the pastry for the Pumpkin Pie; wrap the pie plate tightly and freeze it.
—Prepare the Chestnut Soup with Brandy, and freeze it.

UP TO A WEEK AHEAD:
—Prepare and refrigerate the Sour Cherry Cranberry Sauce.

UP TO SEVERAL DAYS AHEAD:
—Prepare the Perfect Pecan Pie, if it was not prepared ahead and frozen. Refrigerate the pie for up to 2 days.
—Prepare and refrigerate the Whipped Honey Butter for the sweet potatoes.
—Prepare the Chestnut Soup with Brandy, if it was not prepared ahead and frozen. Refrigerate the soup for up to 3 days.

THE DAY BEFORE:
—Assemble and refrigerate the vegetables for Steamed Vegetables with Cheddar Cheese Sauce.
—Prepare and refrigerate the Wild Rice, Pecan and Apple Stuffing.

—Thaw the Perfect Pecan Pie, if it was prepared ahead and frozen.
—Prepare the pumpkin filling, pour it into the frozen pastry shell and bake the Pumpkin Pie.
—Thaw the Chestnut Soup with Brandy, if it was prepared ahead and frozen.

FIVE HOURS BEFORE:
—Stuff the turkey and *immediately* start roasting it.

ONE HOUR BEFORE:
—Bake the Sweet Potatoes.

JUST BEFORE DINNER (AFTER THE TURKEY IS ROASTED):
—Bake the Steamed Vegetables with Cheddar Cheese Sauce and the Creamy Corn Casserole with Jalapeños.
—Prepare the Giblet Gravy *(see Roast Turkey, page 32, Step 4).*
—Start heating the Chestnut Soup with Brandy.
—Heat the Parker House Rolls.

DURING DINNER:
—Heat the Perfect Pecan Pie, if you wish.

ROAST TURKEY WITH WILD RICE, PECAN AND APPLE STUFFING

A delicious Roast Turkey stuffed with all the goodness of the harvest.

Roast at 400° for 15 minutes, then at 325° for 3¼ hours. Makes 10 servings with leftovers.

Wild Rice, Pecan and Apple Stuffing (recipe, page 35)

Roast Turkey:
- 1   *turkey (about 12 pounds), thawed if frozen*
- ¾   *teaspoon salt*
- ½   *teaspoon freshly ground pepper*
- 2   *cups water*
- 2   *carrots, peeled and cut into 1-inch pieces*
- 2   *stalks celery, cut into 1-inch pieces*
- 2   *medium-size onions, peeled and quartered*
- 4   *parsley sprigs*

Giblet Gravy:
-     *Turkey giblets*
- 1   *can (13¾ ounces) chicken broth*
- 1   *bay leaf*
- 2   *cups defatted pan drippings*
- 2   *tablespoons butter or margarine*
- ¼   *cup all-purpose flour*
-     *Salt and freshly ground pepper, to taste*

Garnish (optional):
-     *Cranberries, sautéed green and red apple wedges, and sprigs of fresh sage*

1. Prepare the Wild Rice, Pecan and Apple Stuffing *(recipe, page 35)*. The stuffing can be prepared one day in advance and refrigerated. The stuffing, whether made in advance or not, should be brought to room temperature before stuffing the turkey.

2. Prepare the Roast Turkey: Preheat the oven to hot (400°). Remove the neck and giblets from the turkey and reserve them. Rinse the turkey well inside and out with cold water, and pat it dry with paper toweling. Sprinkle the body and neck cavities with ½ teaspoon of the salt and ¼ teaspoon of the pepper. Spoon the stuffing loosely into both cavities. Transfer any remaining stuffing to a baking pan and cover it. Place the pan in the oven with the turkey for the last 30 minutes of roasting time, to heat the stuffing through. Tie the turkey legs to the tail with string, and skewer the neck skin to the back. Place the turkey, breast side up, on a rack in a roasting pan with a tight-fitting cover. (If no cover is available, make a cover of aluminum foil to be sealed tightly around the pan.) Add the water, carrots, celery, onions and parsley to the pan. Sprinkle the turkey with the remaining ¼ teaspoon each of salt and pepper.

3. Roast the turkey, uncovered, in the preheated hot oven (400°) for 15 minutes. Reduce the temperature to slow (325°). Cover the pan with the tight-fitting lid or aluminum foil. Roast the turkey for 2½ hours. Uncover the pan and roast for 45 minutes more, or until a meat thermometer inserted in the thickest part of the thigh, without touching the bone, registers 180° to 185° and the center of the stuffing registers 160° to 165°, or the drumstick moves up and down freely, or the thick part of the thigh feels soft when pressed, or the juices are yellow or almost colorless when the inner thigh is pierced with a fork tine. Remove the turkey from the oven. Let it stand for 15 to 30 minutes before carving. Reserve the drippings in the roasting pan.

4. Meanwhile, prepare the Giblet Gravy: Combine the reserved neck and giblets (except the liver) with the broth and the bay leaf in a medium-size saucepan. Bring the mixture to boiling. Lower the heat, cover the saucepan and simmer the mixture for 1 hour, or until the giblets are tender. Add the liver and simmer for 15 minutes more. Drain the mixture, reserving the broth. Discard the bay leaf and the neck. Finely chop the giblets and reserve them.

5. When the turkey is done, strain the drippings from the roasting pan into a 4-cup glass measure. Skim off the fat and discard it. You should have at least 2 cups of drippings without fat. Add enough of the giblet broth to make a total of 3¾ cups. Melt the butter or margarine in a small saucepan. Stir in the flour and cook the mixture for 2 minutes. Gradually whisk in the broth mixture. Cook over medium heat, whisking constantly, until the mixture thickens and boils. Skim the foam from the top of the gravy. Lower the heat, add the reserved giblets and simmer for 5 minutes. Add the salt and pepper. Pour the gravy into a gravy boat.

6. If you wish, garnish the turkey with cranberries, sautéed green and red apple wedges, and sprigs of sage. To store, remove the stuffing from the turkey. Refrigerate the turkey and the stuffing separately.

Turkey Talk

CONVENTIONAL OVEN:
Timetable for Roasting Turkey (325°)

Weight (pounds)	Stuffed (hours)	Unstuffed (hours)
6 to 8	3 to 3½	2½ to 3½
8 to 12	3½ to 4½	3 to 4
12 to 16	4 to 5	3½ to 4½
16 to 20	4½ to 5½	4 to 5
20 to 24	5 to 6½	4½ to 5½

✸

Testing for Doneness
A meat thermometer inserted in the meatiest part of the thigh, without touching the bone, reads 180° to 185°F. If the thermometer is inserted in the center of the stuffing, it reads 160° to 165°F.

✸

The turkey juices run clear.

✸

The drumsticks move up and down easily

✸

Resting Period
Let the turkey stand at room temperature for 15 to 30 minutes. This allows the juices to settle and the meat to firm up for easier carving.

✸

Storing
Fresh Turkey: Keep refrigerated at all times. Cook within 1 to 2 days of purchase.
Frozen Whole Turkey: Store it in its original wrapper for up to 12 months at 0°F or lower.

Thawing
Note: *Never thaw a turkey at room temperature. Once thawed, cook or refrigerate the turkey immediately.*

✸

Conventional (long) Method
Thawing time—3 to 4 days, or about 24 hours for each 5 pounds of whole frozen turkey.
1. *Leave the turkey in its original wrapper.*
2. *Place the frozen turkey on a tray in the refrigerator.*

✸

Cold Water (short) Method
Thawing time—about 30 minutes per pound of whole frozen turkey.
1. *Leave the turkey in its original wrapper.*
2. *Place the turkey in a sink or large pan.*
3. *Cover the turkey completely with cold water.*
4. *Change the cold water every 30 minutes, but refill the sink or pan immediately so the turkey is immersed continuously.*

✸

Turkey Hotlines
U.S.D.A. Meat and Poultry Hotline (1-800-535-4555) will answer questions about turkey (and other meat and poultry products) from 10 A.M. to 4 P.M. (EST) Monday through Friday, no weekends or holidays.

✸

The Butterball Turkey Talk-Line (1-800-323-4848) will answer questions about preparing turkey and trimmings. It will operate from November 1 to November 23, Monday through Friday from 8 A.M. to 8 P.M. (CST); November 19 to 20 from 8 A.M. to 6 P.M. (CST); November 24 from 6 A.M. to 6 P.M. (CST); and November 25 through December 23, Monday through Friday, from 8 A.M. to 6 P.M. (CST).

WILD RICE, PECAN AND APPLE STUFFING

Makes 10 servings.

- ¾ cup wild rice
- 3 cups chicken stock OR: canned chicken broth
- 1 cup white wine
- 8 tablespoons (1 stick) butter
- 1 cup pecans, chopped
- ½ cup finely chopped cooked ham
- 2 Granny Smith apples, cored, seeded and chopped
- ¼ teaspoon ground cinnamon
- 2 tablespoons orange-flavored liqueur
- ½ teaspoon salt
- ¼ teaspoon freshly ground pepper
- ¾ cup pecan rice* OR: white rice

1. Pick over the wild rice and remove any stones or grit. Rinse the rice in a bowl of cold water. Drain the rice in a fine-mesh sieve and rinse it again.
2. Combine the wild rice, stock or broth, wine and 2 tablespoons of the butter in a large saucepan. Bring the mixture to boiling. Lower the heat and simmer the mixture, covered, for 40 minutes.
3. While the wild rice is cooking, melt the remaining 6 tablespoons of butter in a large skillet over medium heat. Add the pecans and sauté until they are lightly browned, for 3 to 4 minutes. Add the ham, apples and cinnamon, and sauté until the apples are almost cooked, for about 5 minutes. Add the liqueur, salt and pepper, and cook for 3 minutes more. Set aside the ham mixture.
4. Add the pecan rice or white rice to the wild rice. Simmer the mixture, covered, until the rice is done, for 20 minutes more.
5. Drain the remaining liquid from the rice. Return the rice to the saucepan. Stir in the ham mixture. Heat over medium-low heat, stirring, until the stuffing is heated through. The stuffing can be prepared 1 day in advance and refrigerated. Bring the stuffing to room temperature before stuffing the turkey.

*__Note:__ Pecan rice is a long-grain rice with a pecan-like flavor, grown in Louisiana. It can be found in the rice section of some supermarkets or in specialty food stores. If it is unavailable, substitute white rice.

CREAMY CORN CASSEROLE WITH JALAPEÑOS

Bake at 350° for 30 minutes.
Makes 8 servings.

- 2 cans (16 ounces each) white corn OR: yellow corn, drained
- 1 container (8 ounces) cream cheese with chives and onion
- 3 to 4 fresh jalapeño peppers, seeded and chopped (wear gloves) OR: 1 can (4 ounces) chopped jalapeño peppers

1. Preheat the oven to moderate (350°).
2. Combine the corn, cream cheese and fresh or canned jalapeño peppers in a 1½-quart casserole dish. Cover the dish.
3. Bake in the preheated moderate oven (350°) until the casserole is heated through, for about 30 minutes.

STUFFING THE TURKEY

When? Just before roasting the turkey is the time to stuff it. You run the risk of getting food poisoning if this is done earlier.
How much? Allow ¾ cup of stuffing per pound of bird for turkeys weighing more than 10 pounds, ½ cup of stuffing per pound for smaller turkeys.
Note: *Never freeze stuffing that is in a cooked or raw bird. Remove all the stuffing from the bird after it is roasted, wrap both separately and refrigerate them.*

STEAMED VEGETABLES WITH CHEDDAR CHEESE SAUCE

Bake at 325° for 20 to 40 minutes.
Makes 8 servings.

1   small head cauliflower, stems trimmed and head
    cut into flowerets (about 4 cups)
1   small head broccoli, stems trimmed and head cut
    into flowerets (about 4 cups)
6   large carrots, trimmed, peeled, halved and cut
    lengthwise into thick sticks (about 2½ cups)

Cheddar Cheese Sauce:
¼   cup (½ stick) butter
¼   cup all-purpose flour
2½ cups milk
½   cup dry white wine
2   teaspoons Dijon-style mustard
¼   teaspoon freshly ground white pepper
1   package (10 ounces) yellow sharp Cheddar
    cheese, grated
⅛   teaspoon ground hot red pepper

1. Steam the cauliflower in a large pot just until it is
tender, for about 4 minutes. Remove the cauliflower
with a slotted spoon to a bowl of ice water to stop the
cooking. Then remove the cauliflower with the slotted
spoon to paper toweling. Repeat with the broccoli,
steaming it for about 4 minutes, and with the carrots,
steaming them for about 4 minutes.
2. Prepare the Cheddar Cheese Sauce: Melt the butter
in a medium-size saucepan over medium heat. Whisk
in the flour until it is well mixed. Cook the mixture,
whisking, for 1 minute. Slowly whisk in the milk until
it is combined. Whisk in the wine. Bring the mixture to
boiling. Lower the heat to medium and cook, whisking
occasionally, until the mixture is smooth and thick, for
3 to 4 minutes. Whisk in the mustard and the white
pepper. Reduce the heat to low. Gradually whisk in the
Cheddar cheese and ground hot red pepper until they
are well mixed and the cheese has melted. Do not let
the sauce boil. (The vegetables and the cheese sauce
can be prepared ahead to this point and refrigerated.)
3. When ready to bake, preheat the oven to slow (325°).

4. Arrange the vegetables in a 13 x 9 x 2-inch baking
dish. Pour the sauce over the vegetables to cover them.
5. Bake in the preheated slow oven (325°) until the
sauce and vegetables are heated through, for 20 to
25 minutes. (If the vegetables and the sauce have been
refrigerated, add 10 to 15 minutes to the heating time).

SOUR CHERRY CRANBERRY SAUCE

Makes about 5 cups.

¼   pound dried sour cherries, pitted*
    OR: 1 can (1 pound) sour cherries
    in water, drained
    Warm water
1   pound whole cranberries
2   cups water
1½ cups sugar
    Fresh mint sprigs, for garnish (optional)

1. If using the dried cherries, place them in a small
bowl with just enough warm water to cover them. Let
the cherries stand until they are plump, for about
10 minutes. Drain the cherries.
2. Rinse the cranberries and drain them. Pick over the
cranberries, discarding any stones or grit.
3. Combine the 2 cups of water with the sour cherries,
cranberries and sugar in a medium-size, nonaluminum
saucepan. Bring the mixture to boiling, stirring to
combine the ingredients thoroughly. Cook until the
cranberry skins pop, for about 5 minutes. Remove the
saucepan from the heat. Skim and discard any froth
from the top of the sauce. Cool the sauce and
refrigerate it, covered. Garnish with fresh mint sprigs,
if you wish.
***Note:** Dried sour cherries usually are available in
health food stores. If canned cherries are substituted,
the yield of the cranberry sauce will increase to about
6 cups.*

PERFECT PECAN PIE

Bake at 350° for 40 to 45 minutes.
Makes one 9-inch pie (12 servings).

1 cup pecan halves
1 unbaked 9-inch pie shell with high fluted edge
3 eggs
1 cup firmly packed light brown sugar
  OR: ½ cup each firmly packed light and dark
  brown sugars
1 cup light corn syrup
1 teaspoon lemon juice
1½ teaspoons vanilla
6 tablespoons (¾ stick) butter or margarine, melted
  Whipped cream (optional)

1. Preheat the oven to moderate (350°). Sprinkle the pecans over the bottom of the pie shell and set aside.
2. Beat together the eggs, sugar, corn syrup, lemon juice and vanilla in a small bowl just until the ingredients are combined. Beat in the butter, one tablespoon at a time. Pour the mixture over the pecans in the pie shell.
3. Bake the pie in the preheated moderate oven (350°) until the filling is puffed and moves slightly when the pan is shaken gently, for about 40 to 45 minutes. Cool the pie on a wire rack to room temperature; the filling will fall as the pie cools. Serve the pie cut in slim wedges, topped with whipped cream if you wish.

PUMPKIN PIE

Bake at 375° for 10 minutes, then at 325° for 1 hour and 10 to 15 minutes.
Makes one 10-inch pie (10 servings).

3 eggs
1½ cups firmly packed, mashed cooked pumpkin,
  OR: 1 can (16 ounces) solid-pack pumpkin
  (not pumpkin pie mix)
½ teaspoon ground cinnamon
¼ teaspoon ground nutmeg
2 cups milk
¾ cup sugar
¼ teaspoon salt
1 unbaked 10-inch pie shell
  Whipped cream (optional)

1. Preheat the oven to moderate (375°).
2. Beat together the eggs, pumpkin, cinnamon, nutmeg, milk, sugar and salt in a large bowl until all the ingredients are combined thoroughly and the mixture is smooth. Pour the filling into the pie shell.
3. Bake the pie in the preheated moderate oven (375°) for 10 minutes. Reduce the oven temperature to low (325°). Bake for 1 hour and 10 to 15 minutes more, or until the pie is almost set in the center.
4. Cool the pie on a wire rack to room temperature. If you wish, garnish the top of the pie with whipped cream, or spoon a dollop on each serving.

COME HOME TO THE HARVEST—EVOCATIVE TOUCHES

For a centerpiece that's straight from the hearth, braid bread dough and shape it into a basket. Bake the basket until it is golden brown, and use it as a centerpiece or lined with a linen napkin to hold your dinner rolls.

✳

Use a spicy, simmering potpourri to fill your home with delicious fragrance. Simmering potpourri is available at many card or drug stores, or you can make your own.

Place apple, pear and orange wedges in a pan. Sprinkle cranberries, sugar and cinnamon over the top, then drizzle melted butter and white wine over all. Cover and bake until the fruits are tender but not mushy.

✳

Stir-fry shredded carrots, leeks, cabbage, turnip and parsnips in a mixture of butter, minced shallots and caraway seeds. Serve the mixture hot.

COZY MEALS FOR CHILLY DAYS

Two soul-warming meals guaranteed to banish the chill and satisfy the appetite.

Fava Bean Soup (recipe, page 40)

SOUP AND SALAD ITALIAN-STYLE

Menu for 8

*Fava Bean Soup**

*Prosciutto Bread**

*Sicilian Salad**

*Amaretti Ricotta Mousse**

✳

*Recipe follows

Soup and Salad Italian-Style — Countdown

UP TO ONE MONTH AHEAD:
— Prepare and freeze the Fava Bean Soup.
— Prepare and freeze the Prosciutto Bread.

UP TO THREE DAYS AHEAD:
— Prepare the Fava Bean Soup up through Step 3, and refrigerate it, if it was not prepared ahead and frozen.

THE NIGHT BEFORE:
— Prepare the Prosciutto Bread, if it was not prepared ahead and frozen.
— Thaw the Fava Bean Soup and Prosciutto Bread, if they were prepared ahead and frozen.

ONE HOUR BEFORE:
— Prepare and refrigerate the Amaretti Ricotta Mousse.

20 MINUTES BEFORE DINNER:
— Prepare the oranges, vinaigrette and salad greens for the Sicilian Salad, but do not toss them together.

JUST BEFORE DINNER:
— Heat the Prosciutto Bread.
— Heat the Fava Bean Soup.
— Toss the Sicilian Salad.

FAVA BEAN SOUP

Makes 8 servings.

1 *pound dried fava beans**
4 *ounces salt pork*
1 *large onion*
2 *cloves garlic*
¼ *cup Italian flat-leaf parsley, chopped*
11 *cups chicken or beef stock*
      OR: canned chicken or beef broth
1 *cup peeled, crushed tomatoes (canned or fresh)*
¼ *cup olive oil*
2 *bay leaves*
      Salt and freshly ground pepper, to taste
½ *pound tubular pasta such as ziti, mostaccioli or penne*

1. Place the fava beans in a large saucepan with enough cold water to cover the beans by 2 inches, and soak the fava beans overnight. Or, place the fava beans in a large saucepan with enough water to cover the beans by 2 inches. Bring the water to boiling. Boil the beans for 2 minutes. Remove the saucepan from the heat, cover it and let the beans stand for 1 hour.
2. Drain the fava beans. Slit the sides of the beans and pop them out of their skins. Set aside the fava beans.
3. Place the salt pork, onion, garlic and parsley in the container of a food processor, and pulse until all the ingredients are finely chopped. Place the mixture in a large saucepan or Dutch oven and cook it over low heat, stirring often, until most of the fat is rendered and the onion is tender.
4. Add the reserved fava beans and the chicken or beef stock or broth to the saucepan and bring the mixture to boiling. Lower the heat, cover the saucepan, and simmer the mixture for 45 minutes, stirring occasionally. Add the tomatoes, olive oil, bay leaves and the salt and pepper. Simmer the mixture until the fava beans are tender, for 30 minutes more.
5. Cook the pasta, following the package directions, until it is al dente, tender but firm to the bite. Drain the pasta, reserving one cup of the cooking water. Stir the pasta into the soup. Add the reserved cooking water as needed to adjust the consistency.
****Note:** If fava beans are not available, substitute lima beans or red or white kidney beans.*

AGED TO PERFECTION

Most soups improve in flavor if made a day or two before serving. To make Fava Bean Soup in advance, prepare it through Step 3. At serving time, reheat the soup, then cook the pasta in it.

PROSCIUTTO BREAD

Bake at 375° for 45 minutes.
Makes 1 loaf.

2   packages (¼ ounce each) active dry yeast
1   cup warm water (105°-115°)*
1½ cups whole wheat flour
2½ cups unbleached all-purpose flour
1   teaspoon salt
1½ teaspoons olive oil
4   ounces prosciutto, cubed

1. Sprinkle the yeast over the water in a bowl. Let the mixture stand until it is foamy, for about 10 minutes.
2. Combine the whole wheat and all-purpose flours with the salt in a large bowl. Make a well in the center of the flour mixture. Add the olive oil and the yeast mixture to the bowl. Stir until the wheat-yeast mixture forms a rough dough.
3. Turn out the dough onto a floured surface and knead until the dough is smooth, for about 10 minutes. Place the dough in a large, lightly oiled bowl and turn the oiled side up. Cover the bowl with plastic wrap and let the dough rise in a warm place, away from drafts, until it is doubled in size, for about 1 hour.
4. Punch down the dough and turn it out onto a lightly floured surface. Add the prosciutto and knead it into the dough for about 3 minutes.
5. Generously grease a 9 x 5 x 3-inch loaf pan. Shape the dough into a loaf and place it in the prepared loaf pan. Cover the pan with plastic wrap. Let the dough rise in a warm place, away from drafts, until it is doubled in size, for about 30 to 45 minutes.
6. Meanwhile, preheat the oven to moderate (375°).
7. Bake the loaf on the middle shelf of the preheated moderate oven (375°) until it is golden brown and sounds hollow when lightly tapped with your fingertips, for 45 minutes. Let the bread cool slightly and remove it from the pan.
__Note:__ Warm water should feel tepid when dropped on your wrist.

SICILIAN SALAD

Makes 8 servings.

2   large oranges, peeled and sliced into rounds
2   cloves garlic, crushed
6   tablespoons fruity olive oil
3   tablespoons vinegar
2   bunches curly chicory OR: escarole OR: 1 bunch
    of each, tender parts only, washed and dried

1. Quarter the orange rounds and place them in a large salad bowl. Add the garlic, oil and vinegar to the bowl. Toss the mixture well and set it aside.
2. Wrap the chicory and/or escarole in paper toweling, and refrigerate the greens until they are chilled.
3. At serving time, add the greens to the salad bowl and toss to mix all the ingredients well.

AMARETTI RICOTTA MOUSSE

Makes 8 servings.

2   tablespoons chopped candied fruit
3   tablespoons raisins
2   tablespoons chopped walnuts
2   ounces rum
1½ pounds ricotta cheese
¾   cup sugar
¼   teaspoon vanilla
2   ounces semisweet chocolate, chopped
4   amaretti cookies, crumbled

1. Place the candied fruit, raisins and walnuts in a bowl. Pour the rum over the mixture, and set it aside.
2. Place the ricotta cheese in the container of a food processor fitted with a plastic blade. Process the ricotta cheese for 30 seconds. With the motor running, add the sugar and the vanilla until they are blended. Add the chocolate and the reserved fruit mixture, and pulse the machine on and off to combine all the ingredients.
3. Spoon the mousse into 8 individual dessert dishes and sprinkle the amaretti crumbs over each serving. Chill the mousse for at least 1 hour before serving.

MICROWAVE MEXICAN FIESTA

Menu for 6

Frozen Margaritas

*Tortilla Chips with Nacho Cheese Sauce
and Spicy Tomato Salsa*

Enchiladas Olé (Chicken or Beef)*

Spanish Rice*

Pinto Beans Picante*

Flan*

*Recipe follows

Microwave Mexican Fiesta — Countdown

UP TO THREE DAYS BEFORE:
— Prepare the Shredded Beef or Chicken Filling for the Enchiladas Olé.

THE NIGHT BEFORE:
— Prepare the Enchilada Sauce. Assemble the Enchiladas Olé, cover the casserole dish and refrigerate it.
— Prepare and refrigerate the Pinto Beans Picante.
— Prepare and refrigerate the Flan.

30 MINUTES BEFORE DINNER:
— Prepare the Spanish Rice.
— Reheat the Enchiladas Olé. Reheat the Pinto Beans Picante.
— Unmold the Flan onto individual dessert plates and refrigerate them.

JUST BEFORE DINNER:
— Make the Frozen Margaritas.

ENCHILADAS OLÉ

Microwave at full power for 15 to 16 minutes.
Makes 8 enchiladas (4 to 6 servings).

¹/₂	*cup vegetable oil*
8	*corn tortillas (6-inch)*
1¹/₂	*cups hot Enchilada Sauce (recipe, page 44)*
2	*cups Shredded Beef Filling OR: Shredded Chicken Filling (recipes, page 44)*
1	*cup thinly sliced green onions*
24	*pitted ripe olives*
1	*cup shredded mild Cheddar cheese (4 ounces)*
1	*cup shredded Monterey Jack cheese (4 ounces)*
1	*cup dairy sour cream*
8	*radishes*

1. Place the oil in a shallow 7- or 8-inch round microwave-safe casserole dish.
2. Microwave at full power for 5 minutes, or until the oil is hot.
3. Remove the casserole dish from the oven. Using tongs, dip a tortilla in the hot oil, turning it once, until the tortilla is light golden brown in color and is soft and pliable, for about 30 seconds on each side. Place the tortilla on paper toweling. Repeat with a second tortilla. (The oil usually will remain hot enough to cook two tortillas.) Reheat the oil in the microwave for 2 minutes, and repeat the dipping process, until all of the tortillas are done, stacking them between paper

toweling as each tortilla is finished to absorb the excess oil.
4. If the Enchilada Sauce has cooled, heat it for about 1 minute at full power (it should be in a container wide enough to dip a tortilla into). Dip a tortilla into the sauce and place it in a microwave-safe shallow, rectangular casserole dish.
5. Arrange ¼ cup of the Shredded Beef Filling or Shredded Chicken Filling along the lower third of the tortilla. Add 2 tablespoons of the green onion and 2 olives to the Filling. Roll up the tortilla to enclose the Filling. Repeat the process with each tortilla, placing the filled enchiladas side by side in the casserole dish. Top the enchiladas with the Cheddar and Monterey Jack cheeses.
6. Microwave at full power for 4 minutes, or until the enchiladas are hot and the cheeses have melted.
7. Garnish the enchiladas with the remaining olives, the sour cream and radishes. Serve the enchiladas hot.
Note: *To prepare Enchiladas in a conventional oven: Heat the oil for the tortillas in a heavy skillet. Heat the Enchilada Sauce in a second skillet or small saucepan. Arrange the filled enchiladas in an ovenproof casserole dish, top with the Cheddar and Monterey Jack cheeses and cover the dish with aluminum foil. Bake the enchiladas in a preheated hot oven (400°) for 20 minutes, uncovering the dish during the last 5 minutes of cooking time.*

SHREDDED BEEF FILLING

Microwave at full power for 5 minutes, then at half power for 55 minutes.
Makes 2 cups.

1¼ pounds beef chuck, cut in 1½-inch cubes
1   cup beef stock OR: canned beef broth
1   bay leaf
2   cloves garlic, finely chopped

1. Place the beef in a microwave-safe 2-quart casserole dish. Add the beef stock or broth, bay leaf and garlic.
2. Microwave at full power for 5 minutes. Reduce the power to half and microwave for 30 minutes, stirring every 10 minutes. Let the beef mixture stand for 10 minutes. Microwave at half power for 15 minutes more. Let the beef mixture stand for 10 minutes.
3. When it is cool enough to handle, shred the beef with your fingers and return it to the broth. Cover the dish and microwave at half power for 10 minutes.

SHREDDED CHICKEN FILLING

Microwave at full power for 7 minutes.
Makes 2 cups.

1½ pounds boned, skinless chicken breast halves
¾   cup chicken stock OR: canned chicken broth
1   bay leaf
2   cloves garlic, finely chopped
    Pinch of salt, to taste

1. Place the chicken in a microwave-safe 1- or 2-quart casserole dish. Add the chicken stock or broth, bay leaf and garlic. Cover the dish with microwave-safe plastic wrap, slightly vented in one place.
2. Microwave at full power for 5 minutes. Uncover the dish and turn over the chicken. Re-cover the dish and microwave for about 2 minutes more, or until the chicken is done. Let the chicken stand for 5 minutes.
3. When it is cool enough to handle, shred the chicken with your fingers and return it to the broth. Add the salt to taste.

ENCHILADA SAUCE

Microwave at full power for 7 minutes.
Makes 1½ cups (enough for 8 enchiladas).

1½ tablespoons vegetable oil
2   tablespoons all-purpose flour
1   clove garlic, finely chopped
3   tablespoons chili powder
1   teaspoon ground cumin
½   teaspoon leaf oregano, crumbled
¼   teaspoon salt
1½ cups chicken stock OR: canned chicken broth

1. Combine the oil, flour and garlic in a microwave-safe 1-quart casserole dish, and stir to combine all the ingredients.
2. Microwave at full power for 1 minute, or until the oil mixture is hot.
3. Add the chili powder, cumin, oregano, salt and chicken stock or broth to the casserole dish, and stir to combine the ingredients.
4. Microwave at full power for 6 minutes, or until the enchilada sauce has thickened, stirring the sauce every 2 minutes.

SPANISH RICE

Microwave at full power for 21 minutes.
Makes 4 cups (6 to 8 servings).

1   tablespoon vegetable oil
1   cup long-grain white rice
1   sweet red pepper, cut into ¼ x 2-inch strips
1   medium onion, chopped (½ cup)
1   clove garlic, finely chopped
2   tablespoons chili powder
½   teaspoon ground cumin
½   teaspoon salt
¼   cup tomato sauce
1¾ cups chicken stock OR: canned chicken broth

1. Stir together the oil and rice in a microwave-safe 2-quart casserole dish.

2. Microwave at full power for 2 minutes. Stir the rice mixture and microwave for 2 minutes more, or until the mixture is golden brown. Stir in the red pepper, onion and garlic and microwave for 2 minutes.
3. Stir in the chili powder, cumin, salt, tomato sauce and chicken stock or broth. Cover the dish with microwave-safe plastic wrap.
4. Microwave at full power for 10 minutes. Uncover the casserole dish and stir the rice mixture. Re-cover the dish and microwave for about 5 minutes more. Let the rice mixture stand, covered, for about 5 minutes.

PINTO BEANS PICANTE

Microwave at full power for 1 hour and 22 minutes.
Makes 8 servings (about 8 cups).

½   pound sliced lean bacon
1   pound dried pinto beans
8   cups water
3   cloves garlic, finely chopped
1   teaspoon salt

1. Cut the bacon into ½-inch squares. Place the bacon squares in a microwave-safe 3-quart casserole dish.
2. Microwave at full power for 7 minutes, stirring after 5 minutes. If the bacon was fatty, pour off and discard all but 3 to 4 tablespoons of the fat.
3. Rinse the pinto beans, picking them over for any discolored ones. Add the beans to the casserole dish along with the water and the garlic.
4. Microwave at full power for 15 minutes. Stir the bean mixture and microwave for 1 hour more, stirring every 15 minutes. Add the salt during the last 15 minutes of cooking time. Let the bean mixture stand for at least 10 minutes before serving.

FLAN

Microwave at full power for 14½ minutes, then at one third power for 23 to 25 minutes.
Makes 6 servings.

Caramel:
1¼   cups sugar
⅓   cup water
*   Unsalted butter*

Custard:
3   whole eggs
3   egg yolks
¾   cup sugar
2   cups half-and-half
1   cup heavy cream OR: whipping cream
1½   teaspoons vanilla extract
3   cups very hot tap water

1. Prepare the Caramel: Combine the sugar and water in a microwave-safe 4-cup measure.
2. Microwave, uncovered, at full power for 8½ minutes, or until the caramel is a rich, golden brown.
3. Lightly grease six 6-ounce glass custard cups. Divide the hot caramel among the cups and set them aside.
4. Prepare the Custard: Whisk together the eggs, egg yolks and sugar in a bowl. Set aside the egg mixture.
5. Combine the half-and-half with the heavy or whipping cream in a microwave-safe 6-cup measure. Microwave at full power, uncovered, for 6 minutes, or until bubbles appear at the edges of the cream mixture. Add the vanilla to the cream mixture.
6. Whisk ⅓ cup of the cream mixture into the egg mixture. Whisk in the remaining cream mixture. Divide the custard between the prepared cups. Place the cups in a large microwave-safe dish and pour the hot water into the dish around the cups.
7. Microwave at one third power for 23 to 25 minutes, or until the flans are slightly firm and a knife inserted in the centers comes out clean. Refrigerate the flans.
8. To serve, run a thin knife around the edge of each flan to loosen it. Place a dessert plate on top of the cup, and quickly invert the dishes. Jiggle the cup until the flan falls free. Scrape any remaining caramel from the cup over the flan.

'Most all the time, the whole year round, there ain't no flies on me, But jest 'fore Christmas I'm as good as I kin be!

— EUGENE FIELD

A Cotton Christmas

CHAPTER 2

COUNTRY CELEBRATIONS

Come home to a real country Christmas!

For a touch of Americana, trim the tree in calicos and rickrack, and dress up the mantle with a pair of adorable calico dolls. Most of our quick country-style trims can be whipped up in an evening. Even more challenging projects, such as our exquisite "Stained Glass" Triptych, take only a few days. Many of these projects are perfect for the church bazaar; some are great to craft along with your kids.

We've also assembled a collection of country-style gifts for the home. Use your woodcrafting skills to make our Window Box Mirror or Street Scene Coat Rack. After the holiday rush, you can even make one of each for yourself! For the kids, we offer fun fashions to keep them warm and toasty at school and at home. These great knitted garments for toddlers and the elementary school set are perfect for those all-important holiday portraits. And even if you've tough-to-please people on your gift list, our tips for gift baskets make present planning easy.

The essence of country is a celebration of the home and an expression of individual style. When you combine country charm with Christmas, the result is a holiday filled with a special exuberance that will be woven into the fabric of your family traditions for years to come.

A HEARTLAND HOLIDAY

Pretty gingham checks recall our pioneer ancestors, celebrating the heart of our country. These yuletide trimmings can be made in a matter of days—some take only an evening.

Calico Corner Ornaments

CALICO CORNER ORNAMENTS
(4 inches in diameter)

Average: For those with some experience in crafting.

Materials for Five Ornaments:
¼ yard each of blue clover, white clover, blue dot, overall blue print calico, and white solid fabrics; cardboard; fusible interfacing; 2 yards of blue and white rickrack; white glue; ⅛ yard of polyester fleece interlining; 3 yards each of blue and white ⅜-inch-wide ribbon; tracing paper for patterns.

Directions:
1. Cut one 3⅝-inch-diameter circle each from the cardboard and fleece for each ornament. Using the fabric key in Fig. II, 1, cut a 3⅝-inch-diameter fabric circle for each background, and a 4⅞-inch-diameter fabric circle for each lining.
2. Pin each remaining piece of fabric to a piece of fusible interfacing, and fuse the pieces together.
3. Trace the full-size appliqué patterns in Fig. II, 1 onto tracing paper, and cut apart the tracings to use as patterns for the appliqué pieces. Using the fabric key in Fig. II, 1, cut the appliqués from the fused fabrics (you also can vary the fabrics used for each motif). Glue the appliqués to the center of the background fabric circles, using the diagrams in Fig. II, 1 as placement guides.
4. Place a fleece and cardboard circle over each lining circle. Finger-fold the lining up over the edges of the cardboard, and glue the lining flat. Glue the appliquéd background circles over the cardboard circles, inserting the ends of a 4½-inch-long loop of blue or white ribbon between the layers at the top of each design for a hanger *(see photo).*
5. Glue the blue or white rickrack over the outer edge of each ornament to cover the raw edges. Tie a matching bow around the base of each hanger.

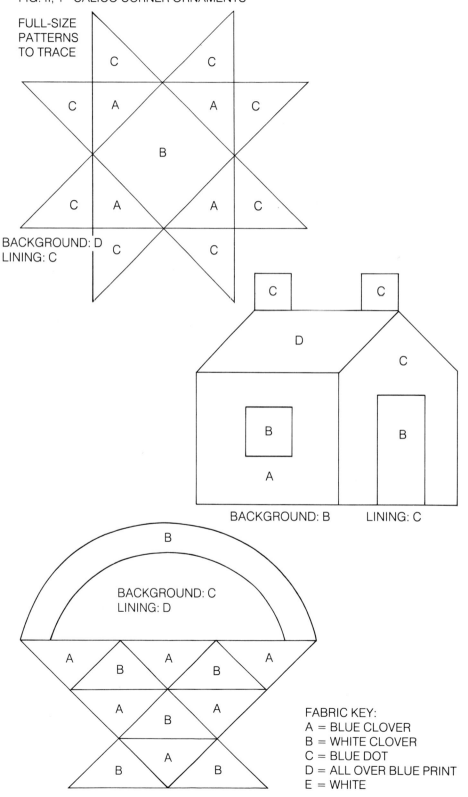

FIG. II, 1 CALICO CORNER ORNAMENTS

FULL-SIZE PATTERNS TO TRACE

BACKGROUND: D
LINING: C

BACKGROUND: B   LINING: C

BACKGROUND: C
LINING: D

FABRIC KEY:
A = BLUE CLOVER
B = WHITE CLOVER
C = BLUE DOT
D = ALL OVER BLUE PRINT
E = WHITE

THE CALICO KIDS

Average: For those with some experience in sewing and doll making.

Materials: 1 yard of unbleached muslin; ½ yard of white clover calico fabric; ¼ yard each of blue clover and blue dot calico fabrics; two 9 x 12-inch pieces of blue felt; knitting worsted (4-ounce-skein): 1 skein each of Rust and Brown; ¼ yard of interfacing; synthetic stuffing;

star and house ornament appliqués *(see Calico Corner Ornaments, page 48, and the photo above for color guide)*; fusible webbing; embroidery floss: Red, Blue, White and Black; embroidery needle; ⅓ yard of ⅛-inch-wide elastic; 1 yard of ¼-inch-wide elastic; ¼ yard of ¾-inch-wide elastic; ⅞ yards of gathered lace; 1⅔ yards of ⅝-inch-wide blue satin ribbon; four ⅝-inch-diameter buttons; rouge; white glue; paper for patterns.

DOLLS
Directions
(¼-inch seams allowed):

1. Enlarge the pattern in Fig. II, 2A *(page 52)* onto paper, following the directions on page 241. Cut out the paper pattern.
2. Cut four body pieces from the muslin. Cut four interfacing pieces *(see interfacing line in Fig. II, 2A)*.
3. Transfer the face and joint stitching lines onto two of the body pieces; omit the eyelashes on the boy doll.

4. Baste an interfacing piece to the wrong side of each body piece. Using the embroidery needle and floss, and the photo as a guide, embroider the faces in satin stitch *(see Stitch Guide, page 240)*. Lightly dust the rouge on the cheeks.

5. Pin the body fronts to the body backs right sides together. Stitch, leaving an opening in each doll for turning. Stitch again to secure. Trim the seams, turn the dolls right side out, and press them.

6. Stuff the arms and legs. Using a zipper foot, stitch the joint lines *(see broken lines in* Fig. II, 2A*).* Stuff the heads and bodies, turn in the open edges, and slipstitch the openings closed *(see Stitch Guide)*.

7. *Girl's Hair:* Cut a ½ x 8-inch muslin strip. Cut one hundred 30-inch strands each of the Rust and Brown yarns. Combine the strands to mix the colors. Center the strands crosswise over the muslin strip. Baste the strands down the center of the muslin. Machine-stitch the yarn to the muslin strip to anchor it and form the center part. Center and glue the muslin strip to the doll's head, beginning on the forehead about 2 inches from the seam. Glue the strip down the center of the back of the head. Let the glue dry. Smooth the hair to the sides of the head. Spot glue the hair as needed. Arrange the front of the hair as shown in the photo, and spot glue it in place. Braid the hair, and tie the ends with lengths of the ⅝-inch-wide blue ribbon.

8. *Boy's Hair:* Prepare the muslin strip following the directions in Step 7, and using 9-inch strands of the yarns. Center and glue the muslin strip over the seam of the head. Comb the hair, and spot glue it in place. Trim the hair into a bowl haircut.

CLOTHES:
Directions
(¼-inch seams allowed):
1. *Patterns:* Enlarge the patterns in Fig. II, 2B onto paper, following the directions on page 241. Make separate patterns for the Overalls and Bloomers, and for the Shirt and Dress. Cut out the patterns.
2. *Cutting:* From the blue felt, cut four

pairs of Shoe pieces. For the girl, from the white clover calico, cut one pair each of Dress and Bloomers pieces. From the blue dot calico, cut two 3½ x 4¾-inch pinafore bibs, two 2½ x 7½-inch pinafore straps, one 1½ x 38-inch pinafore waistband with the tie ends, one 6 x 32-inch pinafore skirt, and one 12 x 13½-inch bonnet. For the boy, from the blue clover calico cut a Shirt back on the fold, and two Shirt fronts. From the white clover calico, cut a pair of Overalls pieces, two 3¾ x 4¼-inch overalls bibs, two 2½ x 7½-inch overalls straps, and one 2½ x 16½-inch overalls waistband.

3. *Dress:* Sew the two Dress pieces, right sides together, at the sleeve/side seams and shoulder neck seams. Turn right side out and press. Fold the neck and sleeve ruffles at the fold line. Make neck and sleeve casings for ¼-inch-wide elastic. Cut an 8½-inch length of the ¼-inch-wide elastic for the neck, and two 4½-inch lengths for the sleeves. Insert the elastics into the casings. Hem the Dress.

4. *Bloomers:* Sew the two Bloomers pieces, right sides together, at the side and inner leg seams. Turn the Bloomers right side out, and press them. Make a waist casing for ¼-inch-wide elastic. Cut the elastic 11½ inches long, and insert it. Make leg casings for ⅛-inch-wide elastic. Hand stitch lengths of the gathered lace to the legs under the casings. Cut two 5-inch lengths of ⅛-inch-wide elastic, and insert them into the leg casings.

5. *Pinafore:* Fold each strap in half lengthwise, right sides together. Stitch along the long edge and one short end. Trim the seams, turn the straps right side out, and press them. Work a buttonhole in the finished end of each strap. Baste the straps to one bib piece at the corners along a 4½-inch edge, right sides together and raw edges even. Stitch the two bib pieces, right sides together with the straps in between, around the two short ends and the edge with the straps. Trim the seams, turn the bib right side out, and press it. Hem one long edge and

the two short ends of skirt. Gather the remaining raw edge to 10 inches. Fold the waistband lengthwise, right sides together, and stitch along the long edge. Turn the waistband right side out, and press the seam at the center back. Center the raw edge of the bib on one edge of the waistband, right sides together, and stitch in place. Center the gathered edge of the skirt on the opposite edge of the waistband, right sides together, and stitch. Turn in the open ends and stitch them closed. Fuse the star appliqué pieces to the bib following the fusible webbing manufacturer's directions. Sew two of the buttons to the back of the pinafore.

6. *Bonnet:* Sew a 13½-inch length of gathered lace to the right side of the bonnet piece, 5½ inches in from one 13½-inch edge. Fold the bonnet piece in half lengthwise, right sides together, and stitch along the long edge, leaving an opening for turning. Stitch along the short ends, leaving ½ inch open above the long edge seam on each end. Trim the seams, turn the bonnet right side out, and press it. Turn in the open edges on the long seam, and slipstitch the opening closed. Stitch a ½-inch casing above the long seam, and insert a 26-inch length of the ⅝-inch-wide blue satin ribbon. Pull the ribbon ends to gather the back of the bonnet to fit the doll's head. Tie the ribbon in a bow and trim the ends. Cut two 13-inch lengths of the blue ribbon, and sew them to the flat corners of the bonnet on top of the gathered lace.

7. *Shirt:* Sew the two Shirt front pieces right sides together along the CF seam to the mark. Sew the Shirt front and Shirt back right sides together at the sleeve/side seams. Sew the shoulder/neck seams to the dot. Fold the collar on the fold line, right sides together, and stitch the front edges to the opening mark. Trim the seams. Turn the collar facing to the inside, and tack it to the CF seam. Hem the sleeves and bottom edge of the Shirt.

8. *Overalls:* Sew the two Overalls pieces together following the directions in

Clothes, Step 4, but omitting the waist and leg casings. Hem the legs. Make the bib, straps and waistband, and attach the bib and Overalls to the waistband, following the directions in Clothes, Step 5. Insert the ¾-inch-wide elastic in the back of the waistband, pulling until the waist is 11 inches, and secure the elastic ends at the sides. Finish the waistband ends. Fuse the house appliqué to the bib following the fusible webbing manufacturer's directions. Sew the remaining two buttons on the back of the Overalls.

9. Shoes: Sew each pair of Shoe pieces right sides together, stopping at the dot. Stitch again. Clip to the dot on the line. Trim the seams to ⅛ inch. Turn the Shoes right side out, and press them. Fold the Shoes ½ inch to the outside at the ankles.

FIG. II, 2A   CALICO KIDS   1 SQ. = 1″

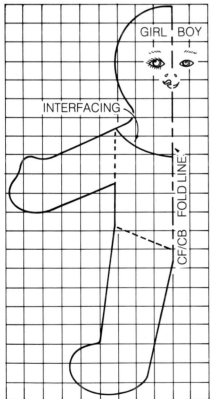

FIG. II, 2B   CALICO KIDS   1 SQ. = 1″

SHOE — CUT 4

CLIP

CUT — SHIRT

SHIRT — CUT 1
BACK ON FOLD
CUT 2 FRONTS

COLLAR
FACING

CUT — DRESS
FOLD LINE — DRESS
RUFFLE AND
SHIRT COLLAR

RUFFLE
FACING

CASING — DRESS, RUFFLE

CUT DRESS

FOLD DRESS

DRESS CASING

CUT — SHIRT

HEM — SHIRT

DRESS —
CUT 2
ON FOLD

CF/CB CUT SHIRT BACK ON FOLD

CUT — SHIRT FRONT

CUT — BLOOMERS
CASING — FOLD

HEM — SHIRT

CUT — SHIRT

OVERALLS CUT LINE
CASING FOLD

HEM — DRESS

CUT — DRESS

OVERALLS —
CUT 2

BLOOMERS —
CUT 2

CASING — FOLD

CUT — BLOOMERS

HEM — OVERALLS

CUT — OVERALLS

CF/CB   FOLD LINE

GIRL   BOY

INTERFACING

CF/CB   FOLD LINE

CALICO CHRISTMAS STOCKINGS

Average: For those with some experience in sewing.

Materials: ½ yard of background fabric; ½ yard of lining fabric; ⅜ yard of contrasting fabric; matching threads; 2 packages of rickrack; fleecy interlining; paper for patterns.

Directions
(⅝-inch seams allowed):

1. Enlarge the stocking pattern in Fig. II, 3 onto paper, following the directions on page 241.

2. Cut two stockings each from the background fabric, fleece and lining. Also cut a 4½ x 6-inch fleece strip. From the contrasting fabric, cut two toes and two heels, adding a seam allowance at their inner edges, a 9 x 16-inch cuff, and a 2 x 5-inch strip for a hanger.

3. Baste each fleece stocking to a background fabric stocking, and the fleece strip to the contrasting fabric and cuff.

4. Fold under the seam allowances on the straight edges of the heels and toes.

5. Position a heel and toe on each background fabric stocking, inserting rickrack under the folded edges. Edgestitch the heels and toes in place.

6. Baste rickrack around the edges of the front stocking piece, omitting the straight top edge.

7. Stitch the front stocking to the back stocking, right sides together. Trim the seams, turn the stocking right side out, and press it.

8. Stitch together the lining pieces, right sides together. Place the lining stocking inside the fabric stocking, wrong sides together. Baste the lining to the stocking at the top straight edges.

9. Fold the cuff lengthwise, right side out, raw edges even. Sew the rickrack to the cuff along the bottom fold. Stitch the short ends of the cuff together. Fold the hanger strip in half lengthwise, right sides

together, and stitch it along the long edge. Turn the hanger strip right side out. Fold it in half and baste it to the inside of the stocking back seam, raw edges even. Place the cuff inside the stocking, raw edges even. Sew the cuff to the stocking, easing in the cuff as needed. Trim and overcast the seam. Turn the cuff to the outside.

FIG. II, 3 CALICO CHRISTMAS STOCKINGS

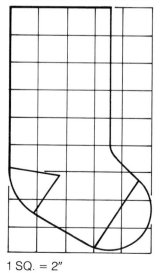

1 SQ. = 2"

SILENT NIGHT CHRISTMAS STOCKING

(about 8 x 18 inches)

Average: For those with some experience in needlepoint.

Materials: 14 x 22 inches of 10-mesh-to-the-inch needlepoint canvas; tapestry wool or Persian yarn: Red, Aqua, White, Brown, Green, Medium Green, Dark Green, Light Avocado, Metallic Gold, Yellow, Blue, Magenta, Wine and Pink; tapestry needle; ¾ yard each of corduroy or velveteen for stocking back, and lightweight fabric for lining; matching threads; paper for pattern; black ballpoint pen.

Directions
(½-inch seams allowed):

1. Enlarge the stocking pattern in Fig. II, 4A onto paper, following the directions on page 241. Go over the outline with the black ballpoint pen. Against a bright light, center the canvas over the pattern, and trace the pattern onto the canvas.

2. Thread the tapestry needle with the tapestry wool, or use 3 full strands of the Persian yarn. Work the design in Fig. II, 4B in Continental stitch *(see Stitch Guide, page 240).*

3. Block the finished work *(see How To Block Like A Pro, page 239),* and cut the canvas ½ inch outside the stitching for the stocking front. From corduroy or velveteen, cut a stocking back the same size. From the lining fabric, cut a stocking front and back. Turn over the pattern when you cut the back pieces.

4. Stitch the stocking back to the stocking front, right sides together, around all edges except the top. Turn the stocking right side out. Stitch the lining back to the lining front the same way. Turn in ½ inch at the top edge of both. Slide the lining, wrong side out, inside the stocking. Fold in the top edges ½ inch, and slipstitch them together *(see Stitch Guide).*

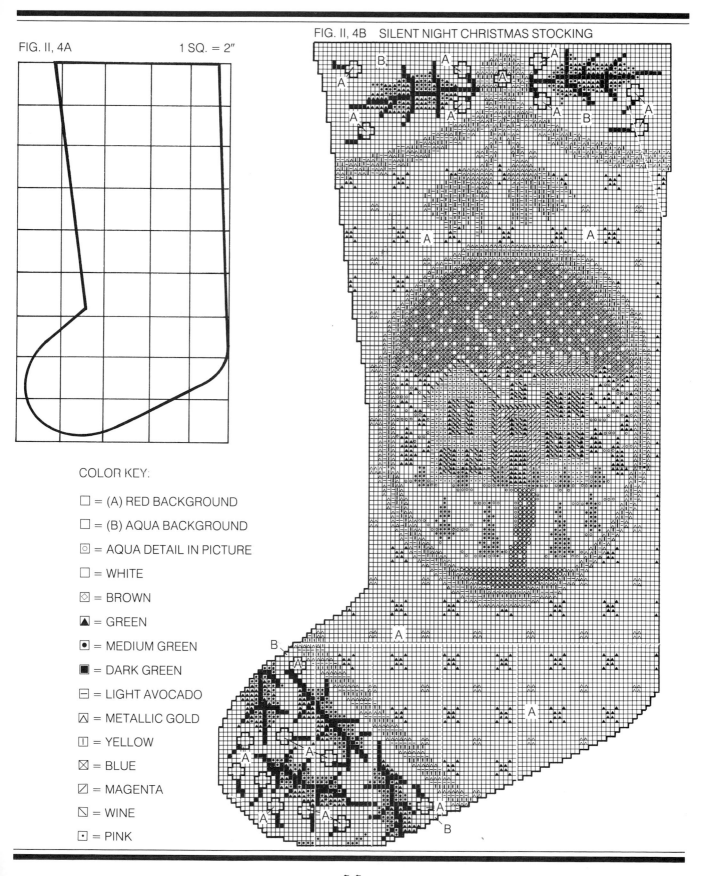

FIG. II, 4A   1 SQ. = 2″

FIG. II, 4B   SILENT NIGHT CHRISTMAS STOCKING

COLOR KEY:

☐ = (A) RED BACKGROUND

☐ = (B) AQUA BACKGROUND

◎ = AQUA DETAIL IN PICTURE

☐ = WHITE

⊠ = BROWN

▲ = GREEN

● = MEDIUM GREEN

■ = DARK GREEN

⊟ = LIGHT AVOCADO

◺ = METALLIC GOLD

Ⅱ = YELLOW

⊠ = BLUE

◿ = MAGENTA

◹ = WINE

• = PINK

ROCKING HORSE
(about 5½ inches high)

Easy: Achievable by anyone.

Materials: Craft felt: 1 square each of red, white and green; embroidery floss: Red, Green and Black; embroidery needle; white glue; synthetic stuffing; pinking shears; paper for patterns.

Directions:

1. Enlarge the patterns in FIG. II, 5 onto paper, following the directions on page 241. Use the outside lines for the red pinked pieces, the inside lines for the white and green pieces.

2. Cutting: From the white felt, cut a horse. From the red felt, using the pinking shears, cut a horse, a rocker and two saddles. From the green felt, cut a saddle and a rocker.

3. Assembly: Center and glue the green rocker over the red rocker. Glue the red saddles together, and glue the green saddle over the red saddles. Glue the combined saddles to the white horse, using the photo as a placement guide. Using the embroidery needle, work Red lazy-daisy stitches for the saddle and eye, a Red French knot for the nose and saddle center, a Black French knot for the eye center, and Red stem stitches around the saddle. Work the bridle in Green stem stitches *(see Stitch Guide, page 240).*

4. Following the arrows on the inside of the red horse piece, baste twelve 2-inch lengths of Green floss for the tail, and thirty 1-inch lengths for the mane. With wrong sides together, center and pin the white horse over the red horse, then the feet over the rocker. Cut a 9-inch length of Red floss, and knot the ends to make a

FIG. II, 5   ROCKING HORSE

1 SQ. = 1"

loop for a hanger. Using Red floss and beginning at the front of the saddle, work an outline stitch around the horse, through all thicknesses, stuffing the horse lightly as you stitch, and catching in the knotted end of the hanger loop at the front of the saddle.

COUNTRY CELEBRATIONS — EVOCATIVE TOUCHES

Patchwork quilts make wonderful, country-style tablecloths. Look for inexpensive, slightly worn quilts at tag sales. Just treat the quilts with fabric stain repellent before using them. Do not use a quilt that is an heirloom or has personal value on a table.

✳

Old-fashioned pomanders are a lovely way to add a sweet scent to your holiday home. Pierce oranges all around with a skewer. Insert a whole clove into each hole, using a light tack hammer. Roll the fruit in orris root powder to preserve it. Arrange pomanders in baskets or bowls, or tuck them into drawers and onto closet shelves.

Make gingerbread place cards for your Christmas Dinner table: Prepare the gingerbread dough following your favorite recipe directions, and roll it out. Cut out 3 x 5 rectangles for the place cards, and squares or smaller rectangles for card stands. After baking the gingerbread pieces, let them cool completely. Pipe out the names on the place cards with white decorator frosting, and decorate the cards with frosting flowers or holly leaves. Let the frosting dry completely. Attach the stands to the backs of the place cards at an angle with more frosting, and let the frosting dry completely.

CALICO CAT ORNAMENT

Easy: Achievable by anyone.

Materials: 12-inch square of print cotton or polyester/cotton fabric; matching thread; ½ yard of ¼-inch wide red satin ribbon; embroidery floss: scraps of Blue and Red; embroidery needle; synthetic stuffing; paper for pattern; scissors.

Directions:
1. Enlarge the pattern in FIG. II, 6 onto paper, following the directions on page 241.
2. Cut two cat pieces from the fabric, reversing the pattern to make the cat front and cat back.
3. Place the fabric pieces right sides together and stitch around the edges, leaving a 3½-inch opening at the bottom edge. Turn the cat right side out, and stuff it. Turn in the open edges, and slipstitch

the opening closed *(see Stitch Guide, page 240).*
4. Embroider the eyes with Blue French knots, and the mouth with two Red straight stitches of unequal length *(see Stitch Guide).*
5. Fold the tail toward the front of the body, and tack it in place *(see photo).* Make a ribbon bow, and sew it to the cat using the photo as a placement guide. Make a loop from the Red floss, and sew it to the cat where the left ear and body join, for a hanger.

PLAID RIBBON PINWHEEL

Easy: Achievable by anyone.

Materials: 1 yard of 3-inch-wide plaid ribbon; compass; cardboard; pencil; white tailor's chalk; white glue; glue stick; thread for hanging; sewing needle.

Directions:
1. Using the compass, draw and cut out a 2½-inch-diameter cardboard circle for the ornament backing.
2. Starting at one end of the ribbon, measure 3 inches in from the corner of the top edge, and mark with the tailor's chalk. Measure 6-inch increments on the same edge five more times. Measure 6 inches in from the corner of the bottom edge of the ribbon, and mark. Continue marking 6-inch increments for the length of the ribbon (six marks).

3. With the chalk, draw a diagonal cutting line from the corner of the bottom edge to the 3-inch mark on the top edge. Connect the 3-inch mark with the first 6-inch mark on the bottom. Continue drawing connecting lines to make 10 triangles. Cut the triangles on the lines, and discard the first half-triangle.
4. For each triangle, overlap the two edges adjacent to the point. Glue the edges together with the glue stick to form a cone.
5. Cover one side of the backing cardboard with white glue. Place the cones on the cardboard over the glue, with the points touching at the center. Using the needle and a 5-inch length of thread, take a stitch at the top of one of the points. Tie off the thread for a hanger.

FIG. II, 6   CALICO CAT ORNAMENT   1 SQ. = 1"

"STAINED GLASS" TRIPTYCH
(19 x 31 inches)

Challenging: Requires more experience in crafting.

Materials: Clear acrylic sheets: two ⅛ x 9 x 19-inch sheets, and one ⅛ x 12 x 19-inch sheet; two pairs of 1½ x 1¾-inch acrylic hinges; small bottle of acrylic glue (acetone); Great Glass color stains: 1 jar each of light blue, light orange, kelly green, royal blue, red, peach, wine, rose, white, brown, purple, yellow and orange; 14 eyedroppers; 4 large bottles and 2 small bottles of Liquid Leading; cotton swabs; facial tissue; paper toweling; paper for patterns.

Note: *For a more rustic look, craft this project using wood and wood paints with ordinary hinges. Follow the Directions using the same dimensions.*

Directions:

1. Lay the 12 x 19-inch acrylic sheet on a flat, clean surface, flanked by the two 9 x 19-inch sheets. Space the sheets ¼ inch apart.

2. Place the hinges ½ inch from the outer edges of the sheets, with the hinge pins centered on the ¼-inch space between the sheets. Press the hinges down, and apply acrylic glue on the hinge edges with an eyedropper. Hold the hinges in place for a moment until the bond is achieved. Glue each hinge in turn, aligning the sheet edges.

3. Enlarge the patterns in Fig. II, 7 *(page 60)* onto paper, following the directions on page 241. Turn the hinged acrylic sheets so the hinges are face down. Place a full-size pattern drawing under each sheet. Be sure the acrylic sheets are clean and free of dust.

4. Apply Liquid Leading lines over the drawing lines, following the manufacturer's directions. Use the small bottles for delicate shapes, such as the stars and clothing details. Let the leading dry for about 8 hours.

5. Clean the areas to be painted with the cotton swabs. Using the photo as a guide and following the color key below, apply the color stains within the appropriate areas, using a different eyedropper for each color. Read the manufacturer's directions before starting, and work in a well-ventilated area. To achieve a gradation of color in areas such as the sky, robes and ox, tilt the acrylic sheet slightly while the stain is still wet. Let the stain dry completely, for 8 hours or more depending on the humidity. Stain the following areas with the following colors:

Sky — light blue, more color at the top, and using the tilting technique to achieve a lighter effect at bottom

Stars — light orange

Mountains — yellow, light orange and kelly green

Perimeter — royal blue

Mary — peach on the face, red, royal blue, light blue and yellow

Joseph — peach on the face, brown on the hair and beard, wine, rose, white and yellow

Christ Child — white, peach and orange

Kings — purple, red, wine, yellow and orange

Doves — white

6. The side panels of the triptych can be folded back completely for storage. The forward tilt is limited by the hinges to about 45° to the center panel plane. This is sufficient to give the triptych stability when it is displayed. The side panels can be adjusted to any angle in between.

"Stained Glass" Triptych

FIG. II, 7   "STAINED GLASS" TRIPTYCH   1 SQ. = 1"

Here Comes Santa Claus

Collectibles, knickknacks, wonderful "found" treasures from another time . . . no country home would be complete without them. This year, why not begin a country Christmas collection of Santa Claus figures?

✳

Santa is enormously popular on the collectibles market. You'll find all sorts of St. Nick figures, drawings and other items at gift shops, flea markets and antique stores. As you hunt for your own Santa collectibles, you'll discover that Santa is a man of many faces.

✳

History tells us that Saint Nicholas was a kind-hearted bishop who lived in Asia Minor (now Turkey) in the fourth century A.D. He is said to have distributed sweets to children and gifts to the poor. Over hundreds of years and thousands of miles, the Saint Nicholas character and legend have changed dramatically.

✳

Today in many European countries, Saint Nicholas is pictured as a tall, thin, white-bearded man in ornate bishop's robes and mitre. He visits houses openly by day to deliver gifts and blessings.

✳

In Holland, Christmas Day itself is a quieter celebration, devoted to church services. According to legend, Saint Nicholas came riding up from Spain on a white horse to deliver presents on the Epiphany, December 6. Saint Nicholas brought with him a servant, Black Peter, who carries a switch to beat naughty children. If a child has been particularly bad, there is talk of stuffing him into a sack and carrying him off to Spain (this was considered a serious punishment centuries ago, when Holland was fighting for its independence from Spain). The American "Santa Claus" is derived from the Dutch "Sinter Claes."

In England, many of the Christmas traditions celebrated today were made popular by Queen Victoria and her husband, Prince Albert. Albert was from the German royal house of Saxe-Coburg Gotha, and brought many Germanic Christmas traditions with him upon his marriage to Victoria, including the Christmas tree and St. Nicholas. Known in England as Father Christmas, this giver of gifts is pictured as a white-bearded, warm-hearted gentleman dressed in scarlet robes trimmed with white fur.

✳

The rotund, jolly, white-bearded Santa Claus truly is an American creation. In 1853, Baldwin, Adams & Co. published an engraving of a big-bellied St. Nick with a scraggly beard driving a team of equally ragged reindeer. The roly-poly version of Santa gained wider acceptance in the 1860's when the famous cartoonist Thomas Nast began drawing the apple-cheeked old gentleman for magazine covers and bookplates. With the publication of Clement Clarke Moore's "A Visit From St. Nicholas," the transformation of the dignified bishop into a "chubby and plump — right jolly old elf" was complete.

✳

Over the years, the image of Santa Claus has appeared in virtually every shape and form imaginable, from candy molds to cast iron doorstops to classic Coca-Cola advertisements. No wonder Santa Claus items are so popular with collectors!

✳

Use your Santa collection to decorate the mantel, or place it under the tree. Put some Santas in the powder room, kitchen and dining room. And remember, even though he does his best work at Christmas time, folks display their Santa collections all year round.

COUNTRY GIFTS FROM THE HEART

A selection of country-style presents for family and friends that are sure to please.

Holiday Home Sampler

HOLIDAY HOME SAMPLER

Challenging: Requires more experience in counted cross stitch.

Materials: Embroidery floss: 1 skein each of White, Blue, Green, Dark Red, Terra Cotta, Gray, Brown and Bright Green; tapestry needle; 8- or 10-inch embroidery hoop; embroidery scissors; even-weave fabric *(the more threads or squares per inch, the smaller the cross stitches and sampler)*: Aida cloth, monk's cloth, or country gingham with a printed weave that is at least 131 squares wide and 100 squares long; masking tape; brightly colored sewing thread; picture frame; cardboard to fit picture frame opening; sawtooth hanger, or picture wire and 2 screw eyes.

Directions:
1. Cut the floss into 18- to 20-inch lengths. Do not make knots on the back of the work. Instead, leave about 3 inches of floss at the back, and work stitches over it. Finish each length of floss by running it through stitches on the back of the work.
2. Cut the fabric 6 inches wider and 6 inches longer than the design in Fig. II, 8 *(page 64).* Tape all four edges to prevent fraying.
3. Before starting the sampler, use a single strand of the brightly colored sewing thread to stitch two perpendicular guide lines *(see photo).* This will help position the design, lettering and border.
4. Each square on the chart represents one *stitch* and *not* one thread or hole. Using the diagram and color key in Fig. II, 8, cross stitch: ***Blue*** on the window and door trim; ***Gray*** to fill in the windows and checks on the foundation; ***Dark red*** on the front door, roof and the pots for the small trees; ***Green*** on the wreath, small trees, and to add the open-work for the large trees on each side of the house; the blank spaces in the large trees are left open; ***White*** to fill in the house; ***Terra cotta*** to fill in all the blank spaces on the roof; ***Brown and dark red*** on the chimney; ***Bright green*** for side of house and the word "Christmas."
5. To block the finished sampler, place it face down on a towel and press it lightly. Center the sampler on the cardboard, fold the fabric edges to the back of the cardboard, and tape them down. Insert the sampler in the picture frame, and tape it to the back of the frame with masking tape. Attach the sawtooth hanger, or picture wire and screw eyes, to the back of the frame for a hanger.

*C*hristmas won't be Christmas without any presents.

—LOUISA MAY ALCOTT

FIG. II, 8 HOLIDAY HOME SAMPLER

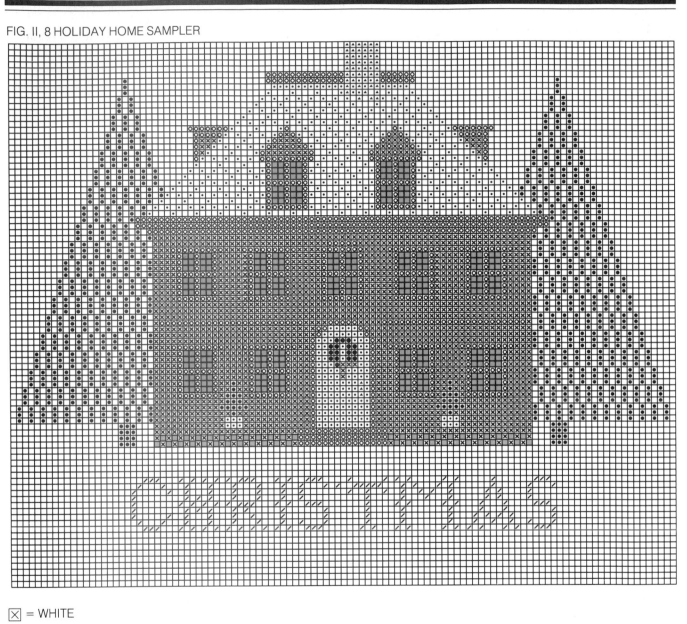

☒ = WHITE
☐ = BLUE
⦿ = GREEN
⊙ = DARK RED
☐ = TERRA COTTA
■ = GRAY
╱ = BRIGHT GREEN
▲ = BROWN

BEAUTIFUL BASKETS

Average: For those with some experience in sewing and/or crafting.

General Materials: New or used baskets, with or without handles.

General Directions:

1. Dress up the baskets by lining them with fabric, slipcovering them or dyeing them.

2. Fill the gift baskets following the suggestions in the tip box on page 67, or using your own gift themes.

FABRIC-LINED BASKET

Materials: Print fabric; matching thread; paper for pattern; bias binding, or trim of your choice *(optional: for the basket in the photo below, we used quilted fabric for the lining and eyelet beading threaded with red satin ribbon for the trim)*; General Materials.

Directions:

1. Make a paper pattern of the basket's inside bottom. Measure the basket's inside depth and add 2 inches if you want a cuff to extend outside the basket. Measure the basket's circumference.

2. Cut a fabric strip whose measurements are as follows: the basket depth by the circumference, with a ½-inch seam allowance added to all sides. Cut a fabric bottom piece using the paper pattern, adding a ½-inch seam allowance.

3. Sew together the short ends of the fabric strip to form a loop. Stitch a gathering row along the loop's bottom edge. Gather the bottom of the strip to fit the bottom piece and pin them right sides together. Sew together the strip and bottom piece, and remove the pins.

4. Hem the strip's raw upper edge, or if you wish, bind or trim the raw edges. Slip the lining into the basket.

SLIPCOVERED BASKET

Materials: Print fabric; matching thread; polyester fleece interlining; pre-gathered lace trim *(optional)*; ribbon *(optional)*; General Materials.

Directions:

1. Measure the basket (#1) from one end of the rim, down along the inside bottom, up to the other end of the rim, and (#2) from one outside end of the rim, down along the outside bottom, up to the other end of the rim.

2. Cut two fabric circles, the first with a diameter of measurement #1 plus a ½-inch seam allowance, and the second with a diameter of measurement #2 plus a ½-inch seam allowance.

3. If the basket has a handle, measure the handle's length and circumference. Cut one strip each from the fleece and the fabric whose measurements are the handle length by the circumference, with a ½-inch seam allowance added to all the edges. Wrap the fleece strip around the handle, and whipstitch the long edges together *(see Stitch Guide, page 240)*. Press under ½ inch on one long edge of the fabric strip. Wrap the fabric strip around the fleece, and slipstitch the fabric strip in place *(see Stitch Guide)*.

4. Sew a gathering row ½ inch from the edge of each fabric circle. Place the larger circle on the outside of the basket, and the smaller circle on the inside. Pin the edges together, turning in the seam allowances, and pulling up the gathers to ease in the fullness evenly. Slipstitch the edges together.

5. If you wish, slipstitch purchased gathered lace around the edge of the slipcover, and add a ribbon bow at each base of the handle *(see photo, page 66)*.

Fabric-Lined Basket

Slipcovered Basket (directions, page 65)

DYED BASKET

This technique adds a simple, rustic beauty to a gift basket.

Average: For those with some experience in crafting.

Materials: Unpainted and unvarnished wicker basket; powdered or liquid fabric dye; paintbrush; newspaper; clear polyurethane, varnish or shellac.

Note: *To protect your hands, wear rubber gloves when working with permanent dye.*

Directions:

1. Remove any dirt or grease from the basket with a warm, sudsy cloth. Rinse the basket well, and let it dry completely.

2. Dissolve the powdered dye in hot, not boiling, water in a saucepan, following the manufacturer's directions. Or combine ¼ cup of liquid dye with ¼ cup of hot water in a cup.

3. Cover your work surface with the newspaper. Test the dye color on the underside of the basket by dipping the paintbrush into the dye solution and stroking the dye onto the wicker. If the color is too dark, add more hot water. If the color is too light, add more dye. Remember that the color looks darker when it is wet than it will look after it has dried.

4. Using even strokes, brush the warm dye over the entire basket, or paint only selected loops on the basket to create a design. Let the basket dry completely on the newspaper.

5. Seal the color by covering the entire basket with one or two coats of clear polyurethane, varnish or shellac.

Dyed Basket

Merry Christmas

BASKETS FULL OF LOVE
Fill a basket for a special person.

For a Christmas Baby:
Line a shallow basket with quilted cotton fabric with a bright print and trim it with beaded eyelet lace and ribbons (directions, page 65). Fill the basket with baby "musts": powder, lotion, moist baby wipes, a baby hair brush, a cushion with extra diaper pins, cotton balls and a rattle to occupy the little one at changing time.

✳

For a Winter Bride:
Fill a Dyed Basket (directions above) with a variety of kitchen gadgets — cheese grater, garlic press, ice cream scoop, mushroom brush — and a selection of favorite recipes, for which each gadget is to be used. Cover the contents of the basket with a pretty tea towel, and tie a big bow on the handle.

For a Special Friend:
Make a Slipcovered Basket (directions, page 65) to match a friend's bathroom decor, and fill it with a selection of sweet-smelling soaps. For fun, add a bottle of bubble bath, a romantic novel, a small box of chocolates and after-bath lotion in her favorite scent. Encourage her to pamper herself after a hard day.

✳

For a Far-Away Loved One:
When a friend or relative has to spend the holidays far from home, send him or her a Christmas "care" basket filled with homemade cookies or fruitcake, a pretty ornament, simmering potpourri with an evergreen or spicy scent, a photo, and a tape-recorded message or videotape from the whole gang.

STREET SCENE COAT RACK

Average: For those with some experience in woodworking.

Materials: 1 x 10 x 20 inches of pine; 5/4 x 5/4 x 30 inches of baluster pine lattice; four 6½-inch-long cast metal hooks; eight 1½-inch flathead wood screws; 2 screw eyes; picture wire; red, yellow, blue, black, white and olive green glossy paints; wood glue; paintbrush.

Code	Pieces	Size
A (1 x 10)	(1)	¾" x 9" x 20" Street
B (LAT)	(4)	⁵⁄₄" x ⁵⁄₄" x 7½" Spacers
C	(4)	6½" Hooks

Directions:

1. Following the specifications in FIG. II, 9, cut the 1 x 10 pine into the row of buildings.

2. Following the Cutting Directions, cut the lattice into spacers. Glue and screw the spacers to the back of the street ¾ inch from the bottom, with each spacer centered on a house.

3. Using the photo as a guide, paint the houses with the glossy paints.

4. Screw the cast metal hooks into the bottom of the houses, with each hook centered on a house. To hang the coat rack, attach the screw eyes and picture wire between the center two spacers, as shown in FIG. II, 9.

FIG. II, 9 STREET SCENE COAT RACK
BACK VIEW   (2" D. x 13½" H. x 20" L.)

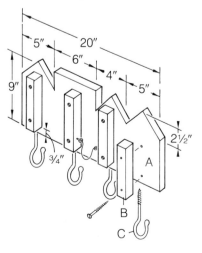

LOG CARRIER

(carrier: about 22½ x 17 inches; handles: about 44 inches each.)

Easy: Achievable by anyone.

Materials: Aunt Lydia's 100% Kodel polyester Rug Yarn (60-yard skein): 12 skeins of Red and 4 skeins of Teal; size K and size Q crochet hooks, OR ANY SIZE HOOK TO OBTAIN GAUGE BELOW; tapestry needle.

Gauge: With size Q hook, 4 sc = 3½ inches.

Note: *The carrier is worked with 6 strands of yarn held together throughout. The handles are worked with 2 strands held together throughout.*

Directions:

1. Carrier: With size Q hook and Red, ch 22, turn. Work sc for 19½ inches. Fasten off. With Teal, sc 2 rows at the beginning and end of the piece. Fasten off.

2. Handles (make 2): With size K hook and Teal, ch 100, turn. Sc 1 row around each side of ch, ending with 3 sc at each end. Fasten off.

3. Finishing: Fold the carrier in half. Fold one handle in half, and attach it to the bottom of one side of the carrier 4½ inches in from each edge. Sew the ends of the handle in place. Repeat for the second handle.

Dad's Denim Apron; Child's Apron

DAD'S DENIM APRON

Average: For those with some experience in sewing.

Materials: 1 yard of 45-inch-wide striped denim; 3¼ yards of 1-inch-wide navy twill tape; matching threads; tailor's chalk; 1 pair of 1¼-inch-wide D-rings.

Directions:

1. Cutting: Straighten the cut ends of the denim. Cut an apron rectangle, 28 inches wide and 36 inches long, with one long side along the selvage edge. Cut a pocket rectangle, 9 x 17 inches, with one long side along the other selvage.

2. Bib Shaping: Fold the apron piece in half lengthwise to 14 x 36 inches, edges even, and pin. Measuring from the top raw-edged corner, mark 9 inches in toward the fold on the top edge, and 10 inches down on the side edge. With the tailor's chalk, mark a bib edge horizontally for about 3 inches in from the side mark, then sloping gradually up to the top mark. Cut through both layers along the mark, and unpin.

3. Pocket: Turn under ½ inch along the three raw edges, and press. Pin the pocket to the apron starting about 4 inches below the bib, lengthwise centers matching. Edgestitch the pocket to the apron, then stitch on the vertical center to divide it into two pockets.

4. Hem: Turn ¼ inch twice to the wrong side at all raw apron edges, and stitch.

5. Ties: Cut 50 inches of twill tape. Fold the tape in half, and edgestitch. Pin the raw ends under the apron at the right-hand top of the bib, and stitch. Cut an 8-inch length of tape, fold it in half, and edgestitch. Fold the tape over the pair of D-rings, raw ends even. Stitch the raw ends. Stitch again just below the rings. Pin the raw ends under the left-hand top of the bib, and stitch. Cut another 50-inch piece of tape, cut it in half, and fold each half in half again to make two 12½-inch ties; edgestitch. Stitch the raw ends under the apron just below the bib.

CHILD'S APRON

(20 to 24 inches long)

Average: For those with some experience in sewing.

Materials: ½ yard of red-checked tablecloth fabric; 3½ yards of fold-over braid; matching threads; 1¼ yards of 1-inch-wide embroidered braid trim *(optional)*.

Note: *The bib and skirt are made separately, then overlapped. This enables you to lengthen the bib up to 2 inches, to keep up with your child's growth. In addition, a 2-inch hem has been allowed.*

Directions
(½-inch seams allowed):

1. Cut an apron skirt 29 inches wide and 17 inches long. Cut a bib 7½ inches wide and 9 inches long. Repeat for the bib facing. Cut two 4½-inch square pockets.

2. Skirt: At each 17-inch edge, turn ¼ inch twice to the wrong side, and stitch. At the bottom, turn 2½ inches to the wrong side, turn under the raw edge, and stitch the hem. At the top of the skirt, sew two gathering rows ¼ inch and ½ inch from the raw edge, using the longest machine stitch.

3. Skirt Binding: Cut a 27-inch strip of fold-over braid, and press it open. Fold it in half crosswise to 13½ inches, pin-mark the center, and open the piece again. Mark 8 inches on each side of the center. Gather the top of the apron skirt to 16 inches, pin the braid to the wrong side of the skirt along the gathered edge, centers matching, and edgestitch; the braid's top edge will extend upward. Stitch another 27-inch strip, pressed open, to the right side of the skirt, braid edges even. Edgestitch all the braid edges together, enclosing the skirt edge. The braid ends will form the apron ties.

4. Pockets: Turn under ½ inch along each edge, and press. If you wish, stitch 1-inch-wide embroidered braid trim to the top edge of each pocket, turning the raw ends of the trim to the wrong side of the pockets. Stitch the pockets 4 inches to each side of the apron center, starting about 3½ inches below the gathering.

5. Bib: Pin the bib and bib facing right sides together. Stitch along one short end and two long edges. Turn the bib right side out, and press.

6. Shoulder Ties: Cut two 15-inch strips of fold-over braid. Edgestitch each strip at its three open edges. Pin an end of one strip under one end of the bib top edge, and stitch. Repeat with the other strip and bib top edge end.

7. Braid Trim: If you wish, sew 1-inch-wide embroidered braid trim across the top edge of the bib, folding the raw ends of the trim over to the wrong side of the bib. Stitch braid trim to the gathered top edge of the skirt, placing the piece of trim over the braid binding between the edges of the skirt. Turn under the raw ends of the trim and stitch.

8. Assembly: Pin the skirt over the bib, overlapping them 1 to 3 inches at the bib's lower edge, according to the child's height. Topstitch the skirt to the bib across the top edge of the braid.

Window Box Mirror

WINDOW BOX MIRROR
(26½ x 19 x 5¼ inches)

Average: For those with some experience in woodworking.

Materials: Pine: ¾ x 1⅝ x 72 inches, 1 x 6 x 16 inches, and 1 x 4 x 8 inches; lattice: ½ x ¾ x 36 inches, ¼ x 1⅝ x 84 inches, and ¼ x ¾ x 40 inches; two ⅝ x 2-inch mending plates; ⅛ x 16 x 20-inch mirror; ⅛ x 16 x 20 inches of corrugated cardboard; two 1¾-inch flathead wood screws; ¾- and 1-inch brads; clamps; wood glue; white paint; green wood stain; rope or heavy picture wire.

Cutting Directions:

Code	Pieces	Size
A (PINE)	(2)	¾ x 1⅝ x 26⅜ Stiles
A1 (PINE)	(1)	¾ x 1⅝ x 15½ Rail
A2 (1 x 6)	(1)	¾ x 5½ x 15½ Rail
A3 (LAT)	(1)	½ x ¾ x 15½ Mullion
A4 (LAT)	(1)	½ x ¾ x 19¼ Mullion
B (1 x 4)	(2)	¾ x 3½ x 4 Sides
B1 (LAT)	(2)	¼ x 1⅝ x 18⅞ Bottom
C (LAT)	(2)	¼ x ¾ x 18⅞ Fence rail
C1 (LAT)	(7)	¼ x 1⅝ x 5 Pickets
D	(1)	⅛ x 16 x 20 Mirror
E	(1)	⅛ x 16 x 20 Cardboard

Directions:

1. Cut out the pine and lattice pieces following the Cutting Directions.
2. Cut a ¼ x ⅜-inch rabbet in the ¾ x 1⅝ x 72-inch and the 1 x 6 pine. Cut parts A, A1 and A2 to length.
3. Cut the A3 and A4 mullions to size, and cut the dado at the center *(see the detail in* FIG. II, 10*)*.
4. Glue and clamp the A1 and A2 rails, A3 and A4 mullions and one A stile together, with the rabbets up. Slide the mirror and cardboard into place *(see* FIG. II, 10*)* before attaching the other A stile. Attach the mending plates to the back of the window assembly, at the top corners across the rabbets *(see* FIG. II, 10 *detail)*.
5. Cut the B sides and the B1 bottom slats

to size. Glue and nail with ¾-inch brads, the B1 bottom slats to the B sides *(see* FIG. II, 10*)*. Using glue and one screw in each side, attach the B/B1 piece to the window front at the bottom corners, rabbets at the back. Stain the window assembly green.
6. Cut the C1 pickets and C fence rails to size, and paint them white.
7. When the paint is dry, glue and nail, using ¾-inch brads, the C fence rails to the edges of the B sides, with the bottom C rail ¾ inch up from the bottom of the B sides, and the second C rail 1 inch above the first *(see* FIG. II, 10*)*. Glue the C pickets to the C1 rails, one picket at each corner, one in the center, and two equally spaced between the corners and the center.
8. Knot one end of the rope or picture wire. Slip the unknotted end through one mending plate from below *(see* FIG. II, 10 *detail)*, through the other plate from above, and knot the end for a hanger.

FIG. II, 10   WINDOW BOX MIRROR

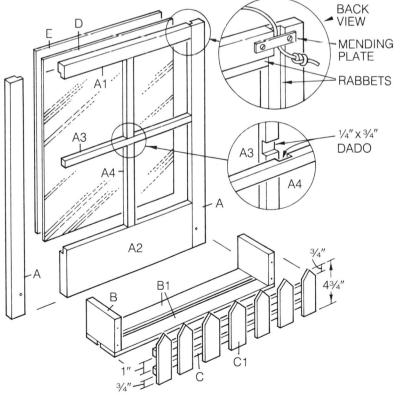

BACK VIEW

MENDING PLATE

RABBETS

¼" x ¾" DADO

JUST FOR KIDS
Warm and Woolly
Fun fashions your little ones can snuggle into.

Snow Country Cap; Snowflake Mittens (directions, page 77)

SNOW COUNTRY CAPS

Crown the season with adorable knitted caps for your little ones. The hat shown at left is the Girl's Cap, directions for which are in parentheses below.

Challenging: Requires more experience in knitting and crocheting.

Directions are given for boy's hat. Changes for girl's hat are in parentheses.

Materials: 3-ply sport-weight yarn (1¾-ounce skein): 1 skein each of White (MC) and Scarlet (CC); 1 pair each sizes 4 and 5 knitting needles, OR ANY SIZE NEEDED TO OBTAIN GAUGE BELOW; size 5 or F crochet hook *(optional)*; tapestry needle.

Gauge: On size 4 needles in Stockinette stitch (st st), 11 sts = 2 inches; 7 rows = 1 inch.

Directions:

1. With size 4 needles and MC, cast on 110 sts. **Row 1:** Purl. **Rows 2 to 14:** Working in st st (k on right side, p on wrong side), follow the chart in FIG. II, 11 *(page 76)* and use CC for the design. Carry the CC yarn along the wrong side of the work, twisting it with MC every fourth or fifth stitch. **Row 15:** Cut off CC, and p with MC across row. **Rows 16 to 32 (31):** Change to size 5 needles and reverse st st (p on right side, k on wrong side). **Row 33 (32):** P across row. **Row 34 (row 33, inc 2 sts):** Begin working the design on the wrong side, carrying the yarn across the right side of the work; the first 15 rows will turn up for a cuff so that both areas with the design will be on the same side. **Rows 35 to 64 (rows 34 to 65; dec 2 sts at beginning of row 53):** Follow the chart in FIG. II, 11 *(page 76)* to work the design.

Row 65 (66): P 2 tog across row. Break off yarn, leaving an 18-inch length. Using the tapestry needle, draw the length through the sts rem on the needle, pulling tightly to gather the top. Fasten off, and weave or sew the seam together. Turn up the first 15 rows, and slipstitch the cuff in place *(see Stitch Guide, page 240)*. Make a pompon in CC, and sew it to the top of the hat.

2. Ear Flaps (optional; make 4): See the diagram in FIG. II, 11 *(page 76)* for the shape of the ear flaps. With size 4 needles and MC, cast on 10 sts. * P 1 row. On next row, k 1, k 1 in front and k 1 in back of next st, k to last 2 sts, k 1 in front and k 1 in back of next st, k 1 (12 sts). Repeat from * two times (16 sts). Work in st st until 20 rows are completed. Bind off.

Finishing: Place two ear flaps wrong sides together. With the crochet hook and MC, sc through both flaps from one top edge to the center bottom. Chain 6 inches, turn, and sc in each st of chain. Continue sc up the remaining side of the flap. Repeat with the remaining two flaps. Sew the double flaps securely at the center sides of the hat.

*H*ere a little
child I stand,
Heaving up my either hand;
Cold as paddocks though
they be,
Here I lift them up to thee,
For a benison to fall
On our meat, and on us all.
Amen.

— ROBERT HERRICK

FIG. II, 11   SNOW COUNTRY CAPS

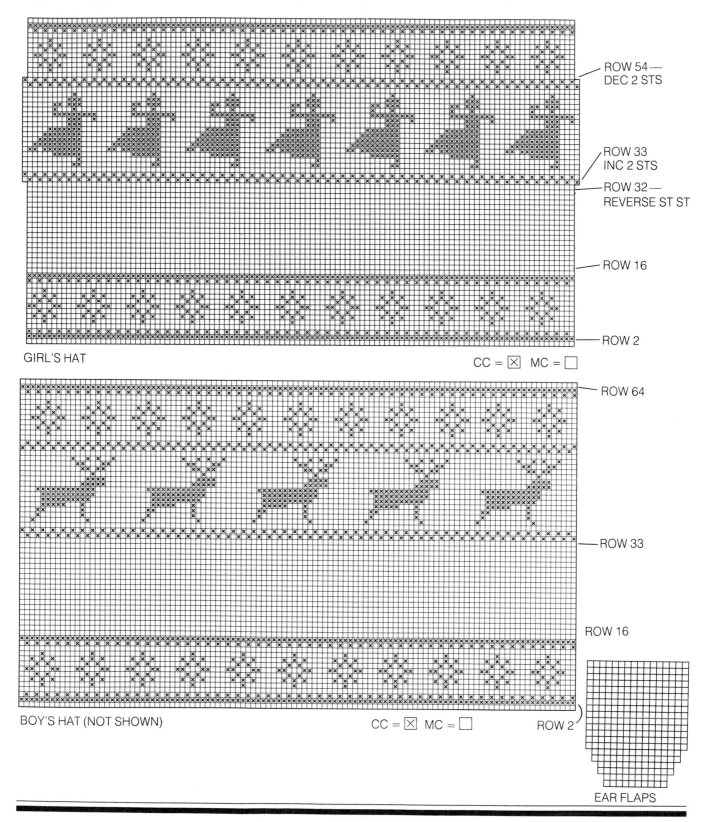

ROW 54 — DEC 2 STS

ROW 33 INC 2 STS

ROW 32 — REVERSE ST ST

ROW 16

ROW 2

GIRL'S HAT

CC = ☒   MC = ☐

ROW 64

ROW 33

ROW 16

ROW 2

EAR FLAPS

BOY'S HAT (NOT SHOWN)

CC = ☒   MC = ☐

SNOWFLAKE MITTENS

Average: For those with some experience in knitting.

Directions are given for girl's mittens. For boy's mittens, reverse the colors. Or, make a mitten in each color scheme, as we show in the photo on page 74. Directions are given for Child's Size 2-3. Changes for Sizes 4-5 and 6-6X are in parentheses.

Materials: 3-ply sport-weight yarn (1¾-ounce skein): 1 skein each of White (MC) and Scarlet (CC); 1 pair size 2 (4, 6) knitting needles, OR ANY SIZE NEEDLES TO OBTAIN GAUGE BELOW; stitch markers; tapestry needle.

Gauge: In Stockinette Stitch (st st), 7 sts = 1 inch, 8 rows = 1 inch (11 sts = 2 inches, 7 rows = 1 inch; 9 sts = 2 inches, 6 rows = 1 inch).

Finished Measurement: Length of the hand above the cuff is 4 inches (4¾-5 inches, 5½-5¾ inches).

Directions:

1. Right Mitten: With MC cast on 32 stitches. Work in k l, p l ribbing for 17 rows.

Row 18: Start st st (k 1 row, p 1 row) and the design, following the chart in FIG. II, 12 and working from left to right on the even numbered rows, right to left on the odd numbered rows. Work through Row 19. ***Mark Thumb Gusset, Row 20:*** K 15 following the chart, put a marker on the needle, k 2, put a second marker on the needle, k 15. Work three more rows, placing markers as you work.

2. Thumb Gusset, Row 21: Work 15 sts following the chart, inc 1 st in each of next 2 sts (4 sts between markers), work to end of row. ***Row 22:*** Purl, keeping in pat. ***Row 23:*** Work 15 sts following the chart, slip marker, inc 1 st in next st, k to 1 st before second marker, inc 1 st in next st (6 sts), k 15. Repeat Rows 22 and 23 for 8 sts between markers, ending with a p row. ***Next Row:*** K 15 sts following the chart, k to second marker, turn.

3. Thumb: Increase 1 st in first st, p to 1 st before marker, inc 1 st in next st, turn. Work in st st on 10 sts for 2¼ inches (2½, 2¾ inches), ending with a p row.

Next Row: K 2 tog across row. Break off yarn, leaving a 12-inch length. Using the tapestry needle, draw the length through the 5 sts rem on the needle, fasten off, and sew the Thumb seam.

4. Hand: Join MC to last st in pattern on the right side of the work. Pick up 2 sts over the Thumb, k to end of row. Continue in st st until the design has been completed. If more length is needed, add more rows in st st at this point until ¾ inch from the desired length.

5. Top, Row 43: K 2, k 2 tog across row. ***Rows 44 and 46:*** Purl. ***Row 45:*** K 1, k 2 tog across row. ***Row 47:*** K 2 tog across row. Break off yarn, leaving a 12-inch length. Draw the length through the rem sts on the needle, and fasten off. Sew the seam, and steam the mitten lightly.

6. Left Mitten: Position the design on the last 15 sts by reversing the direction for the Right Mitten. Work from right to left on the even numbered rows, and left to right on the odd numbered rows.

FIG. II, 12 SNOWFLAKE MITTENS

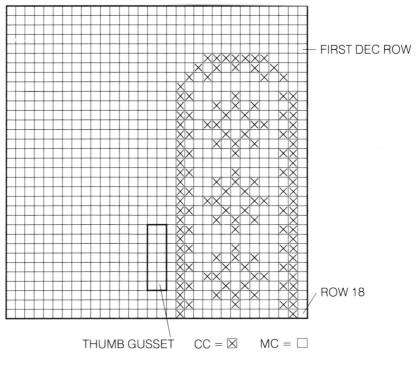

FIRST DEC ROW

ROW 18

THUMB GUSSET   CC = ☒   MC = ☐

"WASHING DAY" SWEATER

Average: For those with some experience in knitting.

Directions are given for Size 6 Months. Changes for Sizes 1, 2 and 3 are in parentheses.

Material for Sweater: 3-ply sport-weight yarn (3-ounce skein): 2 (2, 2, 2) skeins of Light Blue; 1 pair each size 4 and size 6 knitting needles, OR ANY SIZE NEEDLES TO OBTAIN GAUGE BELOW; stitch holders; tapestry needle. *Materials for Clothesline and Clothes:* Yarn: 2 yards of Beige; size E crochet hook; Brown embroidery floss; White and Red cotton thread; size 1 knitting needles; denim and floral print fabric scraps; red and white felt; orange and yellow rickrack; paper for patterns; sewing machine.

Gauge: On size 6 needles in Stockinette Stitch (st st), 11 sts = 2 inches; 7 rows = 1 inch.

Measurements:

SIZES:	6 mos.	1	2	3
BODY CHEST:	19″	20″	21″	22″

Finished Measurements:

CHEST:	21″	22″	23″	24″

WIDTH ACROSS BACK OR FRONT AT UNDERARMS:

	10½″	11″	11½″	12″

WIDTH ACROSS SLEEVE AT UPPER ARMS:

	7½″	8″	9″	9½″

Directions:

1. Back: Starting at the lower edge with size 4 needles and Blue Jewel, cast on 56 (60, 64, 68) sts. Work in k 1, p 1 ribbing for 1½ inches. Change to size 6 needles and st st (k 1 row, p 1 row) until the total length is 6 (7, 8, 9) inches from beg or desired length, ending with a p row.
2. Armhole Shaping: Bind off 5 (6, 6, 6) sts at beg of next 2 rows — 46 (48, 52, 56) sts. Work even in st st for 12 (14, 16, 18) rows more, ending with a k row.
3. Neck Shaping: P 15 (16, 17, 18) sts, slip next 16 (16, 18, 20) sts onto a st

holder for center Neck, join new ball of yarn and p rem sts. Working both sides at the same time, dec 1 st at each Neck edge on next row, then every other row until there are 4 sts on needle. Bind off.
4. Front: Work the same as the Back.
5. Sleeves: Starting at the lower edge with size 4 needles and Blue Jewel, cast on 34 (38, 42, 46) sts. Work in k 1, p 1 ribbing for 1½ inches, 6 sts evenly spaced across last row — 40 (44, 48, 52) sts. Change to size 6 needles and work in st st until length is 7 (7½, 8½, 9½) inches from beg or as desired. Bind off all sts.
6. Front Neckband: With right side facing, using size 4 needles and Blue Jewel, pick up and k 24 (25, 26, 27) sts along left Neck edge, k 16 (16, 18, 20) sts from st holder. Pick up and k 24 (25, 26, 27) sts along right Neck edge — 64 (66, 70, 74) sts. Work in k 1, p 1 ribbing for 5 rows. Bind off loosely in ribbing.
7. Back Neckband: Work the same as the Front Neckband.
8. Assembling Sweater: Pin the pieces to finished measurements on a padded flat surface, cover with a damp cloth, and let dry. *Do not press.* Place the Back over the Front so the shoulder seams are 3 rows below the neckline. Insert and pin Sleeves to armhole edges. Sew Sleeves, stitching through the double thickness at

the shoulders. Sew side and Sleeve seams.
9. Tiny Clothesline Sweater: With size 1 needles and Red thread, cast on 13 sts. Work in k 1, p 1 ribbing for 3 rows. Change to st st, and work in the following striped pattern: * 2 rows with White, 2 rows with Red; rep from * until total length is 2 inches from beg, ending with a p row. *Neck Shaping:* K first 4 sts, join a new ball of thread and bind off center 5 sts, k rem 4 sts. Working both sides at the same time, work even for 2 rows more. Bind off. *Sleeves:* Mark each side edge 1 inch from the top for the armholes. With the right side facing and Red, pick up 7 sts along the armhole edge. Work in striped pat for 16 rows. Change to Red and work in k 1, p 1 ribbing, dec 1 st each end of next row. Work even in ribbing for 2 rows more. Bind off.
10. Clothesline and Clothes: Enlarge the patterns in FIG. II, 13 onto paper, following the directions on page 241. Using the photo as a guide, cut and sew the Clothes. With the crochet hook and Beige yarn, work a chain about 11 inches long for the clothesline. Sew the clothesline, Tiny Sweater and Clothes onto the Front of the sweater, using the photo as a guide. With the tapestry needle and Brown floss, work two long stitches for each clothespin.

FIG. II, 13 "WASHING DAY" SWEATER   1 SQ. = ½″

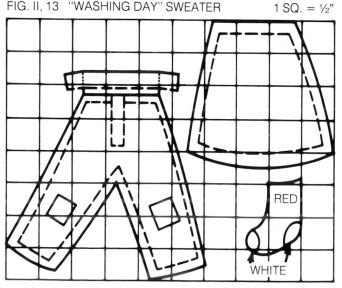

"Washing Day" Sweater

BABY'S ARGYLE SWEATER

Challenging: Requires more experience in knitting.

Directions are given for Size 6 Months. Changes for Sizes 1 and 2 are in parentheses.

Materials: 3-ply sport-weight yarn: 2 (2, 3) skeins of Heather Blue (A), and 1 skein each of Heather Green (B) and Off White (C); 1 pair each size 4 and size 6 knitting needles, OR ANY SIZE NEEDLES TO OBTAIN GAUGE BELOW; 3 stitch holders; four ½-inch-diameter buttons; size F crochet hook; 3 bobbins; stitch markers; tapestry needle.

Gauge: On size 6 needles in Stockinette Stitch (st st), 11 sts = 2 inches; 7 rows = 1 inch.

Notes: *The sweater buttons are at the shoulders. The diagonal lines are embroidered in duplicate stitch (see FIG. II, 14B) with C (Off White) when the sweater is finished. Wind the three bobbins with B (Green), and join as needed. When changing colors, pick up the new color from under the color previously used, twisting the yarns on the wrong side to prevent holes in the work. Carry the unused color loosely on the back.*

Measurements:

SIZES:	6 mos.	1	2
BODY CHEST:	19″	20″	21″

Finished Measurements:

CHEST:	20″	21″	22″
WIDTH ACROSS BACK OR FRONT AT UNDERARMS:			
	10″	10½″	11″
WIDTH ACROSS SLEEVE AT UPPER ARM:			
	7½″	8″	9″

Directions:

1. Back: Starting at the lower edge with size 4 needles and A, cast on 56 (58, 60) sts. Work in k 1, p 1 ribbing for 2 inches, inc 1 st at end of last row—57 (59, 61) sts. Change to size 6 needles and purl 1 row. Work in st st (k 1 row, p 1 row) for 28 (32, 36) rows more, ending with a p row.

2. Armhole Shaping: Bind off 2 sts at beg of next 2 rows—53 (55, 57) sts. Work even in st st for 21 (23, 25) rows more, dec 1 st at end of last row—52 (54, 56) sts. Change to size 4 needles and work in k 1, p 1 ribbing for 6 rows. Bind off loosely in ribbing.

3. Front: Starting at the lower edge with size 4 needles and A, cast on 56 (58, 60) sts. Work in k 1, p 1 ribbing for 2 inches, inc 1 st at end of last row—57 (59, 61) sts. Change to size 6 needles and purl 1 row. Now start Row 2 of Diamond Pattern *(see* FIG. II, 14A*),* working in st st as follows: With A k 2 (3, 4), place a marker on the needle, with A k 8, with B k 1, with A k 17, with B k 1, with A k 17, with B k 1, with A k 8, place a marker, with A k 2 (3, 4). Place markers on every row, working the sts outside the markers with A. Follow the chart in FIG. II, 14A back and forth for the size indicated, working Size 6 Months from a to b, Size 1 from c to d, and Size 2 from e to f. Work until Row 19 is completed (first group of Diamonds), then repeat Rows 2 to 11 (2 to 15, 2 to 19) once, ending with a p row.

4. Armhole Shaping for 6 Months and Size 1:
Bind off 2 sts at beg of next 2 rows, and continue to follow the chart for the Diamond pat until Row 19 is completed. Then repeat Rows 2 to 7 (2 to 13) once (third group of Diamonds).

Armhole Shaping for Size 2:
Bind off 2 sts at beg of next 2 rows, and continue to follow chart (Rows 2 to 19) once until third group of Diamonds is completed.

5. Neck Shaping, Next Row:
Continue in Diamond pat, k 19 (20, 21), slip next 15 sts onto a st holder for Front Neck, join 2nd ball of yarn and k 19 (20, 21). Working each side with a separate ball, dec 1 st at Neck edge on next row, then every other row 4 times. Slip rem 14 (15, 16) sts on each side onto st holders for Shoulders.

6. Front Neck Ribbing:
With size 4 needles and A, from right side pick up 8 sts along left Neck edge, k 15 sts from st holder, pick up 9 sts along right Neck edge — 32 sts. Work in k 1, p 1 ribbing for 6 rows. Bind off loosely in ribbing.

7. Front Shoulder Ribbing:
With size 4 needles and A, k 14 (15, 16) sts from the left Shoulder st holder, pick up 4 (5, 4) sts along the side of the Neck ribbing. Work in k 1, p 1 ribbing for 6 rows. Bind off in ribbing. Work the right Shoulder ribbing to correspond to the left Shoulder ribbing. From the right side of the work, sew the Shoulders tog ¾ inch in from the Shoulder edge; the remainder of the Shoulders is left open.

8. Sleeves:
With size 6 needles and A, from right side of work pick up 42 (45, 48) sts along Armhole edge. Work in st st for 6½ (7, 7½) inches, ending with a p row. **Next Row:** * K 1, k 2 tog; rep from * across — 28 (30, 32) sts. Change to size 4 needles and work in k 1, p 1 ribbing for 2 inches. Bind off loosely in ribbing.

9. Duplicate Stitch:
With the tapestry needle and C, work duplicate stitches diagonally across the Front of the sweater (*see* FIGS. II, 14A *and* B).

10. Finishing:
Pin the sweater to the finished measurements on a padded surface, cover with a damp cloth, and allow the sweater to dry; *do not press the sweater*. Sew the side seams. Sew the Sleeve seams, starting at the ribbing and sewing the last ¼ inch to the bound-off sts at the underarm. Sew 2 buttons onto each Front Shoulder ribbing, with the first at the Neck edge and the second at the center of the Shoulder ribbing.

11. Button Loops:
With right side facing, and using the crochet hook, sl st across the Back Neck ribbing, working a ch-6 for a button loop opposite each button.

FIG. II, 14B
DUPLICATE STITCH

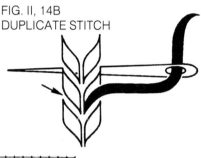

FIG. II, 14A BABY'S ARGYLE SWEATER

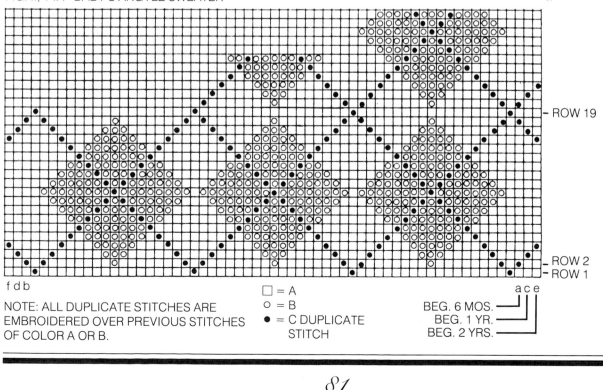

- ROW 19

- ROW 2
- ROW 1

f d b

NOTE: ALL DUPLICATE STITCHES ARE EMBROIDERED OVER PREVIOUS STITCHES OF COLOR A OR B.

□ = A
○ = B
● = C DUPLICATE STITCH

a c e

BEG. 6 MOS.
BEG. 1 YR.
BEG. 2 YRS.

DARLING DOLLS

Little girls will treasure these dolls all their lives.

LITTLE WOMEN DOLLS

(about 16 and 17 inches tall)
Looking as though they'd stepped out of the pages of Louisa May Alcott's novel, these pretty girls, and their handsome neighbor Laurie (shown on page 84), will thrill any girl on your gift list.

Average: For those with some experience in sewing and doll making.

Materials To Make One Woman and One Man Doll: ⅓ yard of 44-inch-wide fabric for woman's dress; scrap of striped fabric for man's shirt; scraps of flesh and white fabrics; scrap of black fabric for woman; tapestry or worsted yarn for hair; matching threads; synthetic stuffing; embroidery floss: Pink and Dark Brown;

embroidery needle; rouge; light brown indelible marking pen; fancy button for woman; 20 inches of ⅝-inch-wide white ribbon and scraps of lace trims for woman *(optional)*; scrap of striped ribbon for man; ½ yard of ¼-inch-wide dark plaid grosgrain ribbon for man; miniature straw hats *(optional)*; paper for patterns.

Directions
(¼-inch seams allowed):
1. Patterns: Enlarge the patterns in FIG. II, 15 *(page 85)* onto paper, following the directions on page 241.
2. Cutting: For both dolls, from the flesh fabric, cut one pair each of Head pieces and two pairs of Hand pieces. From the white fabric, cut one pair of Knickers pieces. For the woman, from the dress

fabric cut one pair each of Blouse and Sleeve pieces and a 10½ x 32-inch rectangle for the Skirt. From the black fabric, cut two pairs of Boot pieces. For the man, from the white fabric cut one pair of Slacks pieces, two pairs of Boot pieces and two 1¼ x 3-inch strips for the cuffs. From the shirt fabric, cut one pair each of Shirt and Sleeve pieces.

3. Head/Blouse or Shirt: Sew each Blouse or Shirt piece to a Head piece across the neck edge. Sew the two combined pieces together around the Head and across the shoulders. Sew the Blouse or Shirt side seams.
4. Sleeves: Fold one Sleeve in half lengthwise, right sides together and armhole edges matching, and stitch the

seam. Sew a gathering row as indicated on the pattern, around the top edge of the Sleeve, and pull the gathers until the Sleeve fits an armhole. Sew the Sleeve to the armhole. Repeat for the second Sleeve. Gather the lower edge of each Sleeve to fit the top edge of a woman's Hand or a man's cuff. Sew the Sleeve to the Hand over the gathered row, then sew around the Hand. Repeat for the second Sleeve. For the man's cuffs, fold both long raw edges of a cuff piece toward the center, and press. Place the bottom edge of the cuff over the top edge of a Hand, and at the bottom of a Sleeve. Slipstitch the cuff in place *(see Stitch Guide, page 240)*. Repeat for the second Sleeve.

5. Skirt: Sew the skirt along one short edge, right sides together. Hem one long edge of the skirt. On the other long (top) edge of the skirt, sew two gathering rows ¼ inch and ½ inch from the edge. Pin the Skirt to the Blouse, raw edges matching, pulling up the gathers to fit the doll's waist. Sew the skirt to the Blouse.

6. Knickers: Unfold the Knickers pieces, and sew the curved edges at the front crotch and back crotch. Refold the Knickers along the broken line on the pattern so the crotch seams match at the inner legs. Sew the inseam down each leg. At the lower edges, turn ½ inch to the wrong side and baste. Turn the Knickers right side out, and stuff them.

7. Boots: Sew around each pair of Boot pieces, right sides together, except along the top edges. Trim the seams to ⅛ inch, turn the Boots right side out, and stuff them. Tuck and pin a Boot ½ inch inside each lower edge of the Knickers. Securely slipstitch the Knickers over the Boots *(see Stitch Guide)*.

8. Waist Seam: For the woman and man, stuff the Hands, Sleeves, Head, and Blouse or Shirt. For the woman, pin the Knickers' raw edge to the doll's waist seam inside the Skirt, seams and centers matching. Stitch in place. For the man, turn under ½ inch at the Shirt's waist edge. Tuck and pin the Knickers' raw edge ½ inch inside

the Shirt, seams and centers matching. Slipstitch the Shirt over the Knickers.

9. Dress: Sew the button at the neckline for a brooch. If you wish, decorate the dress with scraps of lace trims, using the photo as a guide. Or make an apron: Cut a 1-inch square from the white fabric, and narrowly hem two side edges. Turn under the lower edge, lap it over a piece of lace trim, and stitch. Gather the top edge, and bind it with a 20-inch length of ⅝-inch-wide white ribbon, centers matching and fullness gathered to 1½ inches on each side of the center. The ribbon ends will form the apron ties. If you wish, make an apron bib from eyelet, and attach the bib to the ribbon binding *(see photo)*.

10. Slacks: Sew the Slacks pieces together following the directions in Step 6. Turn under ½ inch at the waist and ankle edges, and stitch. Pull the Slacks over the doll. Cut two 9-inch lengths of the plaid grosgrain ribbon. Slide their ends under the Slacks, crossing the ribbons in back, and sew them in place for suspenders. Tie the striped ribbon around the man's neck for a bow tie.

11. Woman's Hair: Arrange twelve 36-inch-long strands of yarn side by side, with the ends even, to make a bundle. Tie a piece of thread around the center of the bundle. Tack the center of the bundle to the doll's head behind one ear. Bring all the yarn up to the center front about ½ inch in front of the Head seam, and stitch the yarn to the Head across the bundle. Bring the yarn down the other side of the head and sew it behind the opposite ear. Dress the hair using the photos on pages 82 and 84 as a guide.

12. Face: Using the embroidery needle and six strands of the Brown floss, make a French knot for each eye. Using two strands of Pink floss, make a short straight stitch for the nose, and one or two straight stitches for the mouth *(see Stitch Guide)*. Dust rouge lightly over the woman's cheeks. The man's hair is drawn using the light brown pen. If you wish, add a straw hat on either the woman or man.

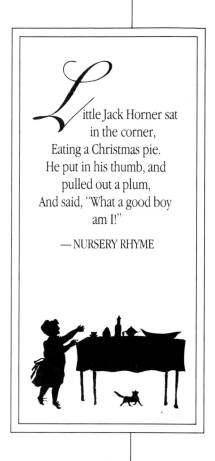

*L*ittle Jack Horner sat
in the corner,
Eating a Christmas pie.
He put in his thumb, and
pulled out a plum,
And said, "What a good boy
am I!"

— NURSERY RHYME

Little Women Dolls — Woman and Man (directions, page 82)

FIG. II, 15 LITTLE WOMEN DOLLS

1 SQ. = 1"

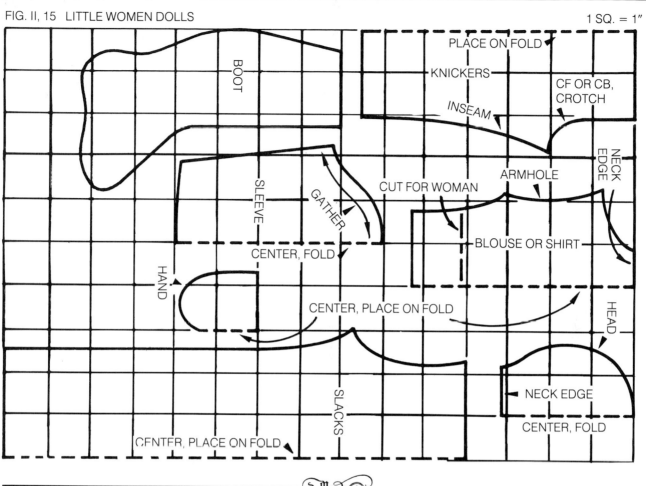

PLACE ON FOLD

KNICKERS

CF OR CB,
CROTCH

INSEAM

NECK EDGE

BOOT

ARMHOLE

CUT FOR WOMAN

SLEEVE

GATHER

BLOUSE OR SHIRT

CENTER, FOLD

HAND

CENTER, PLACE ON FOLD

HEAD

SLACKS

NECK EDGE

CENTER, FOLD

CENTER, PLACE ON FOLD

Christmas in the Country — Just for Kids

A traditional Christmas cookie from old Pennsylvania is great fun for children to make. Prepare a basic sugar cookie dough and separate the dough into four equal portions. Add a few drops of food coloring to each portion of dough to tint it. Roll out the dough on a lightly floured surface, and let the kids cut out different shapes with cookie cutters. Place the cookies on greased baking sheets. Use a drinking straw to cut out a hole at the top of each cookie for hanging. Bake the cookies following the directions in the recipe. Let the cookies cool completely, then decorate them with tinted icing. Thread ribbons through the holes, and hang the cookies on the Christmas tree or in windows.

Let the kids make cinnamon stick place cards: Use twelve 4-inch-long sticks for each place card. Wrap the cinnamon sticks together using floral tape, adding a few sticks at a time and wrapping with the tape to secure them. Try to keep one side flat so the bundle will not wobble. Dip the ends of dried flowers into white glue, and place the flowers among the cinnamon sticks. Wrap the bundle with 3/4-inch-wide ribbon to conceal the tape, and tie the ends in a big bow on top. Add a second bow of 1/4-inch ribbon on top of the first bow. Tuck the name cards between the cinnamon sticks.

Country Touches

Bring a wonderfully rustic texture to your table with woven place mats made of raffia or reeds. The natural fibers complement any color in your country palette. During December, finish each place setting with a nubby cotton napkin in jaunty red or green plaid.

✳

"Antique" a new basket by rubbing it with ashes or soaking it in tea. Fill a small basket with potted plants. Use a larger basket for firewood or kindling — just be sure to keep the basket far from the fireplace! *(For more basket ideas, see pages 65-67.)*

✳

Cheery red bandannas can be used to add a touch of color to your table: use them as napkins, place mats, bread basket liners or place them under centerpieces.

✳

If you chill your rolling pin before using it, the dough will roll out more easily. During the holidays, when you're baking often, just store your rolling pin in the refrigerator.

✳

Candles burn more slowly and evenly, with fewer wax drippings, if you place them in the freezer for several hours before using them.

Pamper yourself with a holiday soak in the tub. Place ¼ pound each of chamomile and linden (available in herb shops and health food stores) in a pan with hot water and let the herbs brew for about 15 minutes. Add the herbal brew to a tub of warm (not hot) water for a relaxing bath. For extra-tired muscles — a seasonal hazard after a long day Christmas shopping or cleaning for the holidays — add ½ cup of epsom salts or witch hazel to your bath water.

Make your own fire starters. You'll need pine cones and a collection of candle ends — the stubs that are too short to burn. Dry the pine cones, and remove any grass or weeds clinging to them. Melt the candle ends in an aluminium foil-lined saucepan over low heat. Using long-handled tongs, dip the pine cones, one at a time, into the melted wax. Place the wax-covered pine cones on paper toweling, and let them sit until the wax cools and hardens. These fire starters make great hostess gifts when they're arranged in a basket.

Make your own simmering potpourri: Place orange and apple peel on a baking sheet, and bake in a slow oven (200°) until they are dry, for about 4 to 5 hours. Mix the dried peel with crushed cinnamon sticks, whole nutmeg and a few whole cloves. Simmer the potpourri on the stove in one quart of water. If you wish, the potpourri can be cooled, dried and used again.

✳

Dress up your country collections for the holidays. Fill your antique tins with pine cones, sprigs of holly or small glass ball ornaments. Display a collection of perfume bottles, adorned with red ribbon bows, set on a bed of evergreens. Use your imagination to give your favorite collectibles a touch of Christmas magic.

✳

Create a Christmas kitchen by filling ceramic mixing bowls with wooden fruit or nuts and tying a big bow around them. Replace your regular dish towels with towels that have a seasonal motif, or red and white towels. Place poinsettias in groups on your kitchen table, on the counters, a sideboard or the window sills. Frame your kitchen windows with miniature white lights or multi-colored lights. Hang seasonal cookie cutters from ribbons in doorways or windows.

Fill a wooden bowl with assorted nuts and place it on your coffee table. Add a nutcracker and nut picks. The beautiful browns, red-browns and yellow-browns of the nuts make a warm arrangement, and your decorative accent will be a welcome snack at your Christmas gatherings.

✳

When you do your holiday cooking, make a little extra and freeze it in single-serving, microwave-safe containers. These special frozen dinners can bring the holiday spirit to your office lunch, or make delicious treats for the kids on those nights you'll be out late shopping.

✳

An aluminum wash tub placed beside the fireplace makes a sturdy country container for firewood. Place a few pine cones on top of the woodpile, and tie bright ribbon bows to the tub handles to dress it up.

✳

Need a quick holiday centerpiece or table decoration? A bunch of carnations or miniature carnations in all red, all white or a combination of both, does the trick beautifully. Or look for peppermint-striped carnations (white tipped with red). For a country look, place the flowers in a ceramic or pewter pitcher, an old milk bottle tied with ribbons or a grouping of Mason jars.

Camouflage old burn marks or stains on your holiday tablecloth with appliqués. Use lace flowers and leaves, or cut out seasonal motifs from a print fabric. If you're repairing a burn hole, cut away the burnt part with cuticle scissors. Back the hole with a small piece of thin fabric, and hand stitch the appliqué over it. If you're covering a stain, back the appliqué itself with a piece of fabric, cut to the same shape.

✳

Make "painted" candles for the holidays. Melt the stubs of colored candles in an aluminum foil-lined saucepan. Dip a paint brush in the melted colored wax, and paint designs on white candles.

Keep the kids busy making paper loop garlands for the tree. Give each child round-tipped scissors, a glue stick and a stack of construction paper, wrapping paper or craft ribbon. To add personal interest to the chain making, have each child make a garland that measures his or her height. The kids can team up to make garlands as tall as Mom and Dad. When you drape them on the tree, the smallest child's garland goes at the top, working on down to Mom and Dad. Save the garlands so the kids can see how much they've grown the following year.

✳

Put together a holiday powder room basket of hand towels, soaps and toiletries for your guests. Buy toothbrushes with Christmas designs, or paint your own (with water-resistant paints) on red, white and green toothbrushes.

✳

Don't spend a fortune on seasonal paper plates, cups and napkins. Instead, buy plain white, red or green paper goods. Decorate the cups and napkins with holiday theme stickers. If there are any solid color extras left, you can use them for entertaining any time of the year.

Hot Cereal with Raisins and Cinnamon; Spiced Christmas Brioche (recipe, page 92);
Cranberry Orange Braid (recipe, page 96); Bittersweet Candied Orange Peel
(recipe, page 93)

A COUNTRY CHRISTMAS BREAKFAST

Menu for up to 16

Hot Cereal with Raisins and Cinnamon

*Carrot Hazelnut Twist**

*Spiced Christmas Brioche**

*Bittersweet Candied Orange Peel**

*Streusel-Topped Kugelhopf**

*Cranberry Orange Braid**

*German Stollen**

Coffee, Spiced Tea, Hot Chocolate, Assorted Juices

✳

*Recipe follows

A Country Christmas Breakfast — Countdown

UP TO ONE MONTH AHEAD:
—Prepare, but do not glaze, the Carrot Hazelnut Twist, Spiced Christmas Brioche, Streusel-Topped Kugelhopf, Cranberry Orange Braid and German Stollen. Freeze the breads and cakes following the directions on page 93.
—Prepare the Bittersweet Candied Orange Peel.

THE DAY BEFORE:
—Remove all the breads and cakes from the freezer, and let them thaw.

THE NIGHT BEFORE:
—Glaze the Spiced Christmas Brioche and the Cranberry Orange Braid.

JUST BEFORE BREAKFAST:
—Prepare the hot cereal, adding some raisins to the cereal as it cooks. Sprinkle more raisins and some cinnamon over each individual serving.
—Prepare the coffee, spiced tea and hot chocolate. Set out the assorted juices.
—Warm the Carrot Hazelnut Twist, Streusel-Topped Kugelhopf and German Stollen. Dust the twist and the stollen with 10X (confectioners' powdered) sugar.

COUNTRY CELEBRATIONS — SPICE IS NICE
The words country and spice seem to go hand in hand.

Place whole cinnamon sticks and strips of orange peel in a saucepan filled with water on the stove, and let the mixture simmer to perfume the air with spicy goodness.

✼

Add a dollop of spicy sweetness to holiday pies by flavoring whipped cream with honey, cinnamon, ginger and nutmeg. Beat the cream just until it forms soft, billowy mounds.

✼

For a hearty holiday breakfast to feed a crowd, bake 3 pounds of Canadian bacon in a preheated moderate oven (350°) until a meat thermometer inserted in the center registers 150°, for about ½ hour. Combine 1 cup of apricot preserves, 2 teaspoons of coarse mustard and 1 teaspoon of ground ginger in a small bowl. Spoon the apricot mixture over the bacon. Continue baking until the meat registers 165°, for about 15 minutes more. The bacon may be served hot, warm or at room temperature.

Spice and simmer canned pears, peaches or apricots into a wonderfully scented side dish for roast ham. Combine your choice of fruit with its syrup with one cinnamon stick, 2 whole cloves, the zest from one lemon (yellow part of rind only) and 2 tablespoons of lemon juice (remove the zest from the lemon before juicing it). Bring the mixture to a gentle simmer and cook for about 5 minutes, just long enough to infuse the fruit with the spicy syrup. Serve the fruit mixture warm.

✼

Let your fireplace mantel overflow with natural beauty. Arrange pine boughs in abundance, then tuck in clusters of whole nuts, cinnamon sticks, cranberries and generous bundles of dried herbs and dried flowers for a sweetly scented decoration. This arrangement works equally well on a sideboard or coffee table.

CARROT HAZELNUT TWIST

Bake at 350° for 35 to 45 minutes.
Makes 2 large loaves.

¾   pound carrots, sliced
2   packages (¼ ounce each) active dry yeast
½   cup firmly packed light brown sugar
1   cup warm water (105° to 115°) *
½   cup (1 stick) unsalted butter, melted and cooled
      to room temperature
¼   cup golden rum
2   eggs
6   to 7½ cups unbleached all-purpose flour
⅓   cup buttermilk powder
2   teaspoons salt

Hazelnut Filling:
2   cups hazelnuts OR: pecans
¾   cup firmly packed light brown sugar
2   teaspoons ground cinnamon
¼   cup (½ stick) unsalted butter, softened
1   egg
      10X (confectioners' powdered) sugar, for dusting
      (optional)

1. Place the carrots in a medium-size saucepan and add enough water to cover them. Bring the water to boiling over medium heat. Lower the heat and simmer for 25 minutes, or until the carrots are tender. Drain the carrots, place them in the container of a food processor or electric blender, and whirl until the carrots are puréed. Cool the carrot purée to room temperature. You should have 1 cup of carrot purée.
2. Combine the yeast, 1 tablespoon of the brown sugar and the 1 cup of warm water in a large bowl. Let the mixture stand until it is foamy, for about 5 minutes.
3. Add the ½ cup of melted butter, the rum, eggs, carrot purée and the remaining brown sugar to the yeast mixture, beating until all the ingredients are blended. Beat in 3 cups of the flour, the buttermilk powder and the salt. Beat the flour mixture with an electric mixer at medium speed for 2 minutes. Turn the mixer speed to low and beat in 1 cup of the flour just until it is blended. Stir in 2 cups of the flour with a wooden spoon until all the ingredients are blended.

4. Turn out the dough onto a lightly floured surface. Knead the dough until it is smooth and elastic, for 5 minutes, adding more flour as needed to prevent the dough from sticking. Sweet doughs tend to be very sticky, so do not add too much flour.
5. Place the dough in a greased bowl and turn the greased side up. Cover the bowl with plastic wrap and let the dough rise in a warm place, away from drafts, until it is doubled in size, for 2 to 2½ hours.
6. Meanwhile, prepare the Hazelnut Filling: Combine the hazelnuts or pecans, the ¾ cup of brown sugar and the cinnamon in the container of a food processor. Whirl until the nuts are finely ground. Add the butter and the egg and whirl until all the ingredients are evenly blended.
7. Punch down the dough and divide it in half. Pat or roll out each dough half into a 14 x 12-inch rectangle. Using a sharp knife, cut each rectangle in half lengthwise, making four 14 x 6-inch rectangles. Spoon one-fourth (6 tablespoons) of the Hazelnut Filling down the center of each rectangle to within ¾ inch of the edges. Roll up each rectangle, jelly-roll style, along a long side and pinch the edges and the ends to seal the roll.
8. Lightly grease a large baking sheet. Place a roll, seam side down, on the baking sheet. Place a second roll at an angle across the first roll to form an "X" shape. Working from the center, twist the rolls loosely around each other. Repeat with the remaining two rolls.
9. Cover the twists loosely with lightly greased plastic wrap. Let the twists rise in a warm place, away from drafts, until they are doubled in size, for about 1 hour.
10. Preheat the oven to moderate (350°).
11. Bake the twists in the preheated moderate oven (350°) until they are golden and sound hollow when tapped with your fingertips, for 35 to 45 minutes. Tent the twists with aluminum foil during the last 15 minutes of baking time if they brown too quickly. Remove the twists to wire racks to cool. If you wish, dust the twists with the 10X (confectioners' powdered) sugar before serving them.
*****Note:** Warm water should feel tepid when dropped on your wrist.*

SPICED CHRISTMAS BRIOCHE

Bake at 375° for 30 to 35 minutes.
Makes 3 brioches.

Spiced Brioche Dough:
- 2   packages (¼ ounce each) active dry yeast
- ¼   cup sugar
- ½   cup warm water (105°-115°) *
- 6   eggs, at room temperature
- 4½ cups unbleached all-purpose flour
- 2   teaspoons ground cinnamon
     OR: pumpkin pie spice
- 2   teaspoons salt
- 1   cup (2 sticks) unsalted butter, softened
- ½   cup chopped crystallized ginger
- ½   cup chopped Bittersweet Candied Orange Peel
     (recipe, page 93)
- ½   cup golden raisins
- ½   cup orange-flavored liqueur
- ⅔   cup toasted pine nuts**
     Nonstick vegetable cooking spray

White Chocolate Glaze:
- 6   ounces white chocolate melting wafers
- 2   tablespoons vegetable shortening
     Bittersweet Candied Orange Peel, for garnish
     (optional; recipe, page 93)

1. Prepare the Spiced Brioche Dough: Combine the yeast, sugar and water in a large bowl. Let the yeast mixture stand until it is foamy, for about 5 minutes.
2. Add the eggs to the bowl and, using an electric mixture at medium speed, beat until all the ingredients are blended. Add 3 cups of the flour, the cinnamon or pumpkin pie spice and the salt, and beat for 2 minutes more. Blend in the butter, beating until the mixture is smooth. Reduce the mixer speed to low and blend in 1 more cup of the flour. Stir in the remaining ½ cup flour with a wooden spoon until all the ingredients are well blended.
3. Cover the bowl with greased plastic wrap. Let the dough rise in a cool place, away from drafts, until it is doubled in size, for 2½ to 3 hours. (If the dough is placed in too warm a spot, the butter in the dough will melt.)

4. Punch down the dough. Re-cover the bowl tightly with the plastic wrap and refrigerate the dough for 12 hours or overnight. (The dough can be prepared up to this point and refrigerated for up to 3 days.)
5. Combine the crystallized ginger, Bittersweet Candied Orange Peel, raisins and orange-flavored liqueur in a small saucepan. Heat the mixture over medium-low heat just until it is hot. Transfer the mixture to a small bowl and let it stand for at least 1 hour. Add the pine nuts to the bowl, and stir to coat them well. Drain the mixture, reserving the solids and discarding the liquid.
6. Trace the bottoms of three 1-pound coffee cans onto a sheet of wax paper, and cut out the traced circles. Spray the inside of the coffee can bottoms with the nonstick vegetable cooking spray. Place the wax paper circles in the bottom of the cans. Spray the wax paper circles and the sides of the coffee cans with the cooking spray. (Or line the bottoms of two 8-inch (5-cup) brioche pans, and spray the bottoms and sides of the pans with the cooking spray.)
7. Remove the dough from the refrigerator and let it stand for 1½ hours.
8. Turn out the dough onto a well-floured surface. Divide the dough in half, and roll out each half into a 15 x 10-inch rectangle, using additional flour as needed. Sprinkle the raisin-nut mixture over the surface of the dough to within ¾ inch of the edges. Roll up the dough, jelly-roll style, along a long side and pinch the edges and the ends to seal the roll.
9. Slice each roll crosswise into three 5-inch sections. Fold each section in half. With well-floured hands, mold each section into a teardrop-shaped ball. Place two balls in each prepared coffee can, rounded end up. To make traditionally-shaped brioches, cut off one-third of a roll. Form the larger piece into a ring-shape, and place it in the brioche pan. Shape the remaining small piece into a teardrop shape, and place it in the center of the larger ring so the rounded end is up. Repeat with the remaining roll. Cover the coffee cans or the brioche pans with greased plastic wrap. Let the dough rise in a cool place, away from drafts, until it is almost doubled in size, for 1½ to 2 hours.
10. Preheat the oven to moderate (375°).
11. Bake the brioches in the lower third of the preheated moderate oven (375°) for 15 minutes.

Tent each coffee can with aluminum foil. Bake the brioches until they are golden and sound hollow when tapped with your fingertips, and their internal temperature registers 185° on an instant-reading thermometer, for about 15 to 20 minutes. Cool the brioches in the coffee cans for 10 minutes, then remove them to wire racks to cool completely.

12. Prepare the White Chocolate Glaze: Place the chocolate and the shortening in the top of a double boiler set over boiling water. Heat the chocolate mixture, stirring until the chocolate is melted and the the mixture is smooth. Spoon the glaze over the cooled brioches, allowing some of the glaze to drip down the sides. Sprinkle with additional Bittersweet Candied Orange Peel, if you wish. Let the brioches stand until the glaze is hardened.

__Note:__ Warm water should feel tepid when dropped on your wrist.

*__*Note:__ Toast the pine nuts on a baking sheet in a single layer in a preheated moderate (350°) oven until they are lightly golden, for about 8 minutes.*

COLD STORAGE:
FREEZING BREADS AND MUFFINS

Allow freshly baked breads and muffins to cool completely before freezing them. Place the breads or muffins in freezer-safe plastic bags, or wrap them in heavy-duty aluminum foil. Label and date the packages, and freeze them.

✳

Remove the breads or muffins from the freezer and let them thaw at room temperature for 12 to 24 hours. Remove the breads or muffins from their wrappings, and place them on a baking sheet. Warm in a slow (325°) oven until the breads or muffins are heated through, for about 15 minutes.

✳

Glaze or ice the breads and muffins only after they have been thawed and warmed.

BITTERSWEET CANDIED ORANGE PEEL

Makes about 4½ cups.

> 3 large oranges (about 2¼ pounds)
> ¾ cup water
> 2 tablespoons light corn syrup
> 2¾ cups sugar

1. Cut each each orange into quarters, then remove the peel (orange part of the rind only) in sections. Slice the peel into ¼-inch-wide strips. You should have about 4 cups of orange peel.

2. Place the orange peel in a medium-size, nonaluminum saucepan with enough water to cover. Bring the mixture to boiling over medium heat, lower the heat and cover the saucepan. Cook the orange peel for 15 minutes. Drain the orange peel in a colander.

3. Boil the ¾ cup of water, the corn syrup and 2 cups of the sugar in a large saucepan over medium heat, stirring until the sugar is dissolved. Add the orange peel. Simmer, stirring occasionally, until the orange peel is translucent and tender, for 35 to 55 minutes.

4. Remove the orange peel from the saucepan with a slotted spoon, and place it on a wire rack set over a large baking pan. Let the peel drain for 5 minutes. Separate the orange peel and let it dry until it is tacky to the touch, for about 1 hour.

5. Place the remaining ¾ cup of sugar in a large bowl. Add the orange peel and toss it with the sugar until it is coated evenly.

6. Transfer the sugar-coated orange peel to wire racks and let it stand for about 2 hours to air-dry. Store the candied orange peel in an airtight container for up to 1 month. Or place the peel in a self-sealing plastic bag and freeze it.

STREUSEL-TOPPED KUGELHOPF

Bake at 350° for 40 to 50 minutes.
Makes 1 loaf.

Dough:
- 2   packages (¼ ounce each) active dry yeast
- 1   cup warm milk (105° to 115°) *
- ⅓   cup sugar
- 4   egg yolks
- 1   teaspoon vanilla
- 4   cups unbleached all-purpose flour
- 1   teaspoon salt
- ¾   cup (1½ sticks) unsalted butter, softened

Filling:
- ⅔   cup dried currants
- ⅓   cup cognac or brandy
- ⅓   cup sugar
- 2   teaspoons ground cinnamon

Streusel Topping:
- ½   cup sugar
- ⅓   cup unbleached all-purpose flour
- ⅛   teaspoon ground cinnamon
- ¼   cup (½ stick) unsalted butter, sliced

1. Prepare the Dough: Combine the yeast, the warm milk and 1 tablespoon of the sugar in a large bowl. Let the yeast mixture stand until it is foamy, for 5 minutes.
2. Add the egg yolks and the vanilla to the bowl, beating with a wooden spoon until they are well blended. Beat in 3 cups of the flour, the salt and the remaining sugar with an electric mixer at medium speed for 2 minutes. Add the butter and beat for 1 minute more, or until the ingredients are blended.
3. Stir in the remaining 1 cup of flour with a wooden spoon until it is well combined (the dough will be soft and sticky). Cover the bowl with lightly greased plastic wrap, and let the dough rise in the refrigerator for 4 hours, or overnight.
4. Meanwhile, prepare the Filling: Combine the currants and the cognac or brandy in a small bowl. Let the mixture stand for 4 hours, or overnight. Drain the currant mixture and discard the excess liquid. Combine the ⅓ cup of sugar and the 2 teaspoons of

cinnamon in a second small bowl.
5. Remove the dough from the refrigerator and let it stand for 1 hour.
6. Turn out the dough onto a well-floured surface (if necessary, scrape the bowl to remove the dough). With well-floured hands, pat the dough into a rectangular shape, then roll it into a 16 x 12-inch rectangle.
7. Sprinkle the currant mixture and the sugar-cinnamon mixture over the dough evenly to within ¾ inch of the edges. Roll up the dough, jelly-roll style, along a long side and pinch the edges and the ends to seal the roll.
8. Grease a 12-cup kugelhopf or tube pan, or a fluted ring mold. Place the roll in the pan, seam side down, stretching the roll to make a level ring. Cover the pan with lightly greased plastic wrap, and let the dough rise in a warm place, away from drafts, until it is doubled in size, for 1½ to 2 hours.
9. Preheat the oven to moderate (350°).
10. Meanwhile, prepare the Streusel Topping: Combine the ½ cup of sugar, the ⅓ cup of flour and the ⅛ teaspoon of cinnamon in a medium-size bowl. Cut in the butter slices with a pastry blender until the mixture resembles coarse meal. Sprinkle the topping over the dough in the pan.
11. Bake in the preheated moderate oven (350°) until a wooden pick inserted in the loaf comes out clean, or the internal temperature registers 185° on an instant-read thermometer, for 40 to 50 minutes. Cover the loaf with aluminum foil during the last 20 minutes of baking if it is browning too quickly. Cool the loaf in the pan on a wire rack for 5 minutes. Remove the loaf from the pan to the wire rack to cool completely.
***Note:** Warm milk should feel tepid when dropped on your wrist.*

RISE AND SHINE: YEAST BREAD BASICS

To Dissolve Yeast: *Combine the yeast with 1 teaspoon of sugar and warm water (warm water should feel tepid when dropped on your wrist).*

✳

Substitutions: *You can substitute 1 cake (0.6 oz.) of compressed yeast for each package of active dry yeast in most recipes. Use warm water to dissolve the fresh yeast.*

✳

To Heat Milk: *Place the milk with the other liquid ingredients in a small saucepan. Heat slowly until the milk is hot, not boiling.*

✳

To Knead Dough: *Turn out the dough onto a lightly floured surface. Knead the dough until it is smooth and elastic in texture.*

✳

Letting Dough Rise: *Place the dough in a large greased bowl and turn the greased side up. Cover the bowl with plastic wrap, and let the dough rise in a warm place, away from drafts, until it is doubled in size.*

Double-in-Size Test: *Before letting the dough rise, press it flat in the greased bowl. Mark the level of the flattened dough. Remove the dough from the bowl and fill the bowl with water to twice the level of the first mark; mark the second level. Return the dough to the bowl. When the dough has risen to the level of the second mark, it has doubled in size. Another quick test is to make a depression in the dough with a fingertip when you think the dough has doubled. If the depression remains, then the dough has indeed doubled in size.*

✳

Shaping Dough: *Punch down the dough in the bowl and turn it out onto a lightly floured surface. Follow the shaping directions of the individual recipes.*

✳

Testing for Doneness: *Bake the bread until it is golden and sounds hollow when lightly tapped with your fingertips.*

✳

Cooling Bread: *Place the bread in its pan on a wire rack for 5 minutes. Run a thin knife around the edges of the bread to loosen it from the pan and invert the bread onto the wire rack to cool completely.*

CRANBERRY ORANGE BRAID

Bake at 350° for 30 to 35 minutes.
Makes 2 loaves.

Dough:
- 2 packages (¼ ounce each) active dry yeast
- 1 cup warm milk (105° to 115°)*
- ¼ cup warm water (105° to 115°)*
- 1 tablespoon sugar
- ⅛ teaspoon ground ginger
- ⅓ cup unsalted butter, melted and cooled to room temperature
- ⅓ cup maple syrup
- 2 eggs
- Grated zest of 1 lemon (yellow part of rind only)
- 2 cups whole wheat flour
- 2 teaspoons salt
- 3 to 3½ cups unbleached all-purpose flour

Cranberry Orange Filling:
- 2 cups orange marmalade
- 4 cups fresh cranberries OR: frozen cranberries, coarsely chopped
- ½ teaspoon ground cinnamon
- 3 tablespoons cranberry liqueur OR: orange-flavored liqueur

Orange Glaze:
- 1 cup 10X (confectioners' powdered) sugar
- 2 tablespoons orange juice

1. Prepare the Dough: Combine the yeast, milk, water, sugar and ginger in a large bowl. Let the yeast mixture stand until is it foamy, for about 5 minutes.
2. Beat in the butter, maple syrup, eggs and lemon zest until all the ingredients are blended. Add the whole wheat flour, salt and 1 cup of the all-purpose flour. Beat the mixture with an electric mixer on medium speed for 2 minutes. Reduce the mixer speed to low and beat in 1 cup more of the all-purpose flour just until it is combined. With a wooden spoon, stir in the remaining 1 cup of all-purpose flour.
3. Turn out the dough onto a lightly floured surface. Knead the dough until it is smooth and elastic, for 5 minutes. Add flour as needed to keep the dough from sticking; be careful not to add too much flour.
4. Place the dough in a greased bowl and turn the greased side up. Cover the bowl with plastic wrap and let the dough rise in a warm place, away from drafts, until it is doubled in size, for 1½ to 2 hours.
5. Meanwhile, prepare the Cranberry Orange Filling: Combine the marmalade, fresh or frozen cranberries and the cinnamon in a saucepan, and bring the mixture to a boil over medium heat. Lower the heat, cover the saucepan and simmer, stirring occasionally, for 5 minutes. Remove the cover and simmer for 5 minutes more. Stir in the cranberry or orange-flavored liqueur. Spoon the Filling into a bowl and let it cool.
6. Punch down the dough and divide it in half. Turn out one half onto a floured surface, and pat out the dough into a 14 x 10-inch rectangle. Remove the rectangle to a lightly floured baking sheet, patting it back into shape, if necessary. Lightly score a border line 3 inches in from each long side of the rectangle.
7. Spoon 2 cups of the Filling onto the center of the rectangle, spreading the Filling out to the border lines and to within ¾ inch of the short ends.
8. Cut diagonal strips, 1½ inches wide and 2½ inches in from the edge of the rectangle, along one of the borders. Cut the opposite border in the same way, reversing the direction of the strips. Fold the strips over the filling, alternating the sides to create a braid effect. Pinch the dough at each end into points. Repeat with the remaining half of the Dough and Filling. Cover the braids loosely with greased plastic wrap and let them rise in a warm place, away from drafts, until they are almost doubled in size, for about 45 minutes.
9. Preheat the oven to moderate (350°).
10. Bake in the preheated moderate oven (350°) until the braids are golden brown and sound hollow when tapped with your fingertips, for 30 to 35 minutes. Tent the braids with aluminum foil during the last 10 minutes of baking time if they are browning too quickly. Remove the braids to wire racks to cool.
11. Prepare the Orange Glaze: Blend the 10X (confectioners' powdered) sugar with the orange juice in a bowl until it is a good drizzling consistency. Drizzle the glaze over the braids in a criss-cross pattern. Let the glaze harden before serving.
Note: *Warm milk and warm water should feel tepid when dropped on your wrist.*

GERMAN STOLLEN

Bake at 375° for 30 to 40 minutes.
Makes 2 loaves.

½	cup dried currants
½	cup dried cherries*
½	cup dried pineapple, chopped *
½	cup golden raisins
	Boiling water
2	packages (¼ ounce each) active dry yeast
1	cup warm milk (105° to 115°) **
½	cup granulated sugar
5	to 6 cups unbleached all-purpose flour
2	eggs
2	tablespoons brandy
	Grated zest of 1 lemon (yellow part of rind only)
1	teaspoon salt
½	teaspoon ground nutmeg
¾	cup (1½ sticks) unsalted butter, softened
2	tablespoons granulated sugar
½	teaspoon ground cinnamon
2	tablespoons butter, melted and cooled
	10X (confectioners' powdered) sugar, for dusting

1. Combine the currants, cherries, pineapple and raisins in a bowl. Add enough boiling water to cover the fruits. Let the mixture stand until the fruits are plumped, for 1 hour. Drain the fruits, return them to the bowl and set them aside.

2. Combine the yeast, warm milk and the ½ cup of sugar in a large bowl. Let the yeast mixture stand until it is foamy, for about 5 minutes. Beat in 1 cup of the flour until the mixture is smooth, for about 1 minute. Cover the bowl with plastic wrap and let the dough rise in a warm place, away from drafts, until it is doubled in size, for 45 minutes.

3. Add the eggs, brandy, lemon zest, salt, nutmeg and 2 cups of the flour. Beat with an electric mixer at medium-high speed for 2 minutes. Reduce the mixer speed to low, and beat in the ¾ cup of butter. Beat in 1 cup of the flour just until it is combined. Using a wooden spoon, stir in the reserved fruit and 1 cup of the flour until all the ingredients are combined.

4. Turn out the dough onto a lightly floured surface. Knead the dough until it is smooth and elastic, for

about 5 minutes, adding more flour as needed to prevent the dough from sticking. Sweet dough tends to be very sticky, so do not add too much flour. Cover the dough with a towel and let it rest for 10 minutes.

5. Combine the 2 tablespoons of sugar and the cinnamon in a small bowl.

6. Divide the dough in half. Turn out one half onto a lightly floured surface. Roll out or pat the dough into a 12 x 8-inch oval. Transfer the oval to a sheet of aluminum foil. Repeat with the other half of the dough. Brush both ovals with part of the 2 tablespoons of melted butter. Sprinkle the ovals with part of the sugar-cinnamon mixture. Fold each oval over lengthwise, to within ¾ inch of the opposite edge. Press the top edge lightly to seal the loaf.

7. Carefully transfer the loaves to a large baking sheet. Cover the loaves loosely with lightly greased plastic wrap, and let them rise in a warm place, away from drafts, until they are doubled in size, for about 1 hour.

8. Preheat the oven to moderate (375°).

9. Bake in the preheated moderate oven (375°) until the loaves are golden and sound hollow when lightly tapped with your fingertips, for 30 to 40 minutes. Tent the loaves with aluminum foil during the last 10 minutes if they are browning too quickly. Remove the loaves to wire racks to cool completely. Dust the stollen well with the 10X (confectioners' powdered) sugar before serving it.

*__*Note:__ Equal amounts of mixed candied fruit can be substituted for the dried cherries and pineapple in this recipe. Stollen keeps well for several days if it is wrapped in plastic wrap and stored at a cool room temperature.*

*__**Note:__ Warm milk should feel tepid when dropped on your wrist.*

*H*appy Christmas
to all, and to all a goodnight!

— CLEMENT CLARKE MOORE

CHAPTER 3

VICTORIAN SPLENDOR

Create holiday elegance—Victorian-style.

So many of our Christmas traditions are ones in which the Victorians reveled: caroling, mistletoe—even Christmas cards! But perhaps what most comes to mind is the opulence of the trims and decorations. In this chapter, you can make splendid tree trims by transforming plain silver glass balls with velvet ribbons and pretty beads. Add touches of Victoriana in your home with our glorious Angel Centerpiece, our Sugarplum Wreath or any of our beautiful Christmas stockings.

"It's the thought that counts" was practically the motto of Victorian gift-giving; a hand-made gift was treasured far more than something store-bought. Our selection of gifts to make include mother-daughter cardigans, darling dolls, a lovely christening gown, and more!

To create a lavish setting for your Victorian Christmas Dinner, drape floral chintz fabric over the dining table, tacking it evenly all around, and add complimentary bows. Use the same floral fabric, backed with a contrasting color, to make window swags. Truly authentic Victorian dinners would feature roast goose or roast turkey. Ours, with a Stuffed Crown Roast of Pork, holds true to the sumptuousness of the Victorian feast. Enjoy!

SPLENDID CHRISTMAS DECORATIONS

Trims for house and tree that recall the opulent Victorian era.

ANGEL CENTERPIECE
(15 inches tall)

Average: For those with some experience in sewing and crafting.

Materials: Doll kit *(available at craft stores)*; synthetic stuffing; doll stand; 1 yard of 24-inch mushroom-colored pleated polyester charmeuse; ¼ yard of mushroom-colored charmeuse without pleats; matching thread; bugle beads; pearl beads; white hat feathers *(available at millinery supply stores)*; 2 hat pins; thin sewing needle; paper for patterns; white glue.

Directions:

1. Assemble the doll, following the manufacturer's directions. Attach the doll to the doll stand.

2. Cut a Skirt from the pleated charmeuse, using the measurements in FIG. III, 1A.

3. Enlarge the patterns in FIG. III, 1B following the directions on page 241. Using the paper patterns, cut out the Bodice pieces from the unpleated charmeuse, and two Sleeves from the pleated charmeuse *(see FIG. III, 1A)*.

4. Stitch together the Bodice pieces, leaving the back open. Sew the two gathering rows on each Sleeve as indicated on the pattern in FIG. III, 1B. Pull the top gathers until the top of the Sleeve fits the Bodice armhole. Right sides together, stitch the Sleeve to the Bodice.

FIG. III, 1A
ANGEL CENTERPIECE

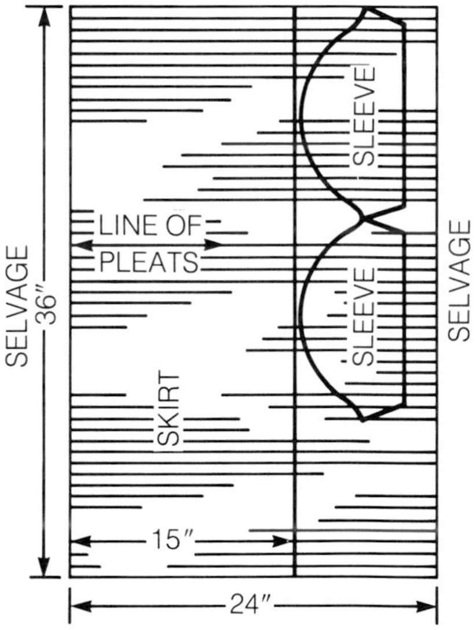

FIG. III, 1B   1 SQ. = 1"

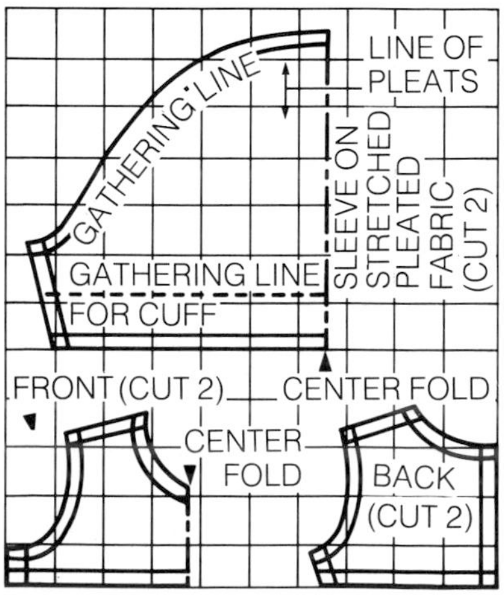

Repeat for the second Sleeve.

5. Sew a gathering row along a long edge of the Skirt piece. Gather the Skirt top to fit the bottom of the Bodice. Right sides together, sew the Skirt to the Bodice, leaving the back open. Stitch the back seam, leaving an opening at the neck.

6. Using the photo as a guide, stitch the bugle beads and pearl beads to the dress. Dress the doll, gently stretching the bottom of the skirt to achieve a graceful fall of fabric. Pull the second set of gathers on the Sleeves to fit the doll's arms. Slipstitch the neck opening closed *(see Stitch Guide, page 240)*.

7. Thread the needle with a 4-inch strand. Alternately thread bugle beads and pearl beads to make a halo. Glue the halo to the angel's head.

8. Glue the feathers to the hat pins in an attractive arrangement to make two wings. Begin by gluing the largest feathers, and gradually fill in with smaller feathers. When the glue is dry, lay one wing across the angel's back so that the wing extends beyond and slightly above her shoulder *(see photo)*. Securely stitch the wing to the back of the angel's dress. Repeat with the second wing.

Angel Centerpiece

Mandolin

MANDOLIN
(about 5¼ inches long)

Easy: Achievable by anyone.

Materials: 1½ x 7 inches of ³⁄₁₆-inch cedar or ¼-inch balsa; dark brown and antique white acrylic paints; artist's paintbrush; white glue; fine sandpaper; jigsaw or hobby scroll saw; 10¼ inches of ⅛-inch-wide orange satin ribbon; fine orange crochet thread; brown sewing thread; transparent tape; graphite paper; stylus or old ballpoint pen; heavy paper for pattern.

Directions:

1. Enlarge the pattern in FIG. III, 2 onto heavy paper, following the directions on page 241. Cut out the paper pattern.

2. Tape the paper pattern to the cedar or balsa. Draw around the mandolin shape, and cut it out from the wood with the jigsaw or scroll saw. To make the bridges, cut a ¼ x 1-inch piece and a ¼ x ⅝-inch piece. Saw three shallow grooves in each *(see* FIG. III, 2*)*. Sand all the wood pieces.

3. Mix two parts white glue with one part water. Brush a coat of the glue mixture on one side and the edges of the mandolin. Let dry, and repeat on the opposite side. When the glue mixture is completely dry, sand the sides and edges. Using the graphite paper and stylus or old ballpoint pen, trace the details from the pattern onto the front of the mandolin. Paint the large circle, bridges, and mandolin edges dark brown. Paint the small dots antique white using the tip of the stylus or ballpoint pen to achieve a fine dot. Glue the bridges in place, and let the glue dry.

4. For the mandolin strap, center and glue one end of an 8-inch length of the orange ribbon to the bottom edge of the mandolin, following the curve for ½ inch. Glue the other ribbon end to the center back of the mandolin ¼ inch from the top edge. Center dots of glue between the layers of a 2¼-inch-long orange ribbon double bow, and secure the bow at the center with a pin until the glue dries. Glue the bow over the strap end at the bottom of the mandolin. Wind the brown sewing thread above and below the top bridge, tie the thread at the back, and knot the ends to make a loop for a hanger. Wrap orange crochet thread around the mandolin through the grooves on the bridges. Knot the thread ends together at the back of the mandolin, clip the ends, and glue the knot to the wood.

'Twas Christmas broached the mightiest ale;
'Twas Christmas told the merriest tale;
A Christmas gambol oft could cheer
The poor man's heart through half the year.

— SIR WALTER SCOTT

FIG. III, 2 MANDOLIN   1 SQ. = ½"

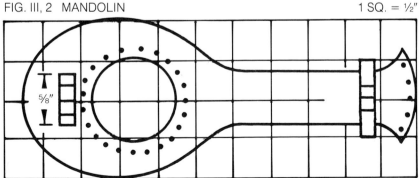

SILVER BALL WITH MAUVE FLOWERS

Easy: Achievable by anyone.

Materials: 1½ yards of ¼-inch-wide dark pink velvet ribbon; scraps of mauve taffeta and sheer polyester or nylon fabric; fine wire; small pearl and silver beads; white glue; 3-inch-diameter silver glass ball ornament; tracing paper for pattern.

Directions:

1. Starting at the neck of the ball ornament, glue a strip of ribbon around the ball, trimming the ribbon ends at the neck. Glue three more strips evenly spaced around the ball. Make a multi-loop bow and glue it to the top of the ball.

2. Trace the full-size petal pattern in FIG. III, 3 onto tracing paper. Cut five sheer and five taffeta petals. Bend a 2-inch length of wire in half loosely, and twist it tightly around the center of one taffeta petal. Twist a sheer petal, place it under the taffeta petal, and twist the wire around both. Twist and clip the wire ends. Make four more flowers. Glue the flowers to the top of the ball.

3. Glue a pearl bead to each flower. Using the photo as a guide, glue clusters of pearl and silver beads to the top of the ball.

SILVER BALL WITH PINK FLOWERS

Easy: Achievable by anyone.

Materials: 1 yard of ¼-inch-wide pink velvet ribbon; fine wire; iridescent beads; white glue; green floral tape; 3-inch-diameter silver glass ball ornament; scraps of sheer pink nylon fabric; votive candle; tracing paper for pattern.

Directions:

1. Starting at the neck of the ball ornament, glue a strip of ribbon around the ball, trimming the ribbon ends at the neck. Repeat with another ribbon strip at right angles to the first. Make a multi-loop bow and glue it to the top of the ball.

2. Trace the full-size pattern in FIG. III, 3 onto tracing paper. Cut two petals for each flower from the sheer nylon. Light the votive candle. Heat-seal the edges of the petals by holding the petals near the side of, but not touching, the candle flame and turning them slowly.

3. Wire the petals following the directions in Silver Ball with Mauve Flowers, Step 2, but do not clip the wire ends. Instead, wrap the ends with floral tape, and continue to twist the tape into a 3- or 4-inch-long stem. Glue a bead to the center of each flower.

4. Remove the hanger cap from the ball, and place the flower stems inside the ball. Replace the cap, and glue beads around it *(see photo)*.

FIG. III, 3   PETAL   FULL SIZE

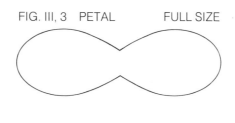

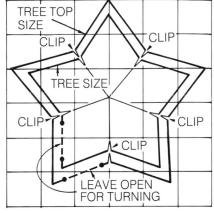

FIG. III, 4   SHINING STAR

TREE TOP SIZE

CLIP

CLIP

TREE SIZE

CLIP

CLIP

CLIP

LEAVE OPEN FOR TURNING

1 SQ. = 1"

angles and points as sharp as possible. Leave 2 inches of cording at the end, twist it into a loop, and glue it at the back of the star for a hanger *(see photo)*.

Note: *To make a Tree Top Star, make a large gold star using the Tree Top Size pattern in* Fig. III, 4, *and following Steps 1 through 3 at left. Glue cording to the radiating lines shown on the pattern in* Fig. III, 4. *Glue cording around the outside edges of the star, omitting the hanger loop. Form a loop of cording and glue it to the back of the star. Glue large gold beads to the center and at the ends of the star points. Put a dot of glue at the head of each bead, and insert a straight pin through the bead to secure it.*

SHINING STAR

Easy: Achievable by anyone.

Materials: Two 6-inch squares of red satin fabric, or silver or gold metallic fabric; matching thread; ½ yard of ⅛-inch-wide twisted gold cording; synthetic stuffing; hot glue gun or thick craft glue; small crochet hook; paper for pattern.

Directions:

1. Enlarge the tree size star pattern in Fig. III, 4 onto paper, following the directions on page 241. Cut out the paper pattern.

2. Pin the fabric squares right sides together, and cut out the star using the pattern. Stitch around the fabric stars,

using a ¼-inch seam allowance, and leave an opening between the dots for turning. Clip the inside angles, trim the points of the star, and turn the star right side out.

3. Using the crochet hook, carefully push the points of the star into shape. Stuff the star firmly, turn in the open edges, and slipstitch the opening closed *(see Stitch Guide, page 240)*.

4. Dip each end of the gold cording into a dot of glue to keep it from unraveling. Beginning at the end of one star point *(see photo)*, run a narrow line of glue along the seam. If you are using a hot glue gun, allow the glue to cool for a second or two. Carefully press the cording into the glue. Continue around the star, keeping the

O' CHRISTMAS TREE

One of the most cherished Christmas traditions is selecting and decorating the family tree. This primer will help you to pick out the perfect evergreen.

Selecting a fresh tree: Run your hand over a branch; very few or no needles should come off. Thump the tree on the ground; only a few outside needles should fall. Smell the tree; it should have a full, rich, fresh fragrance.

Making the tree last: Cut off 1 inch from the base of the tree, cutting on a diagonal, to allow the tree to absorb water more easily. Put the tree into water immediately after cutting it. When you are ready to set up the tree, make a second cut straight across the base of the stump. Use a 1- to 1½-gallon capacity tree stand, and maintain the water level above the cut base of the tree. Trees need 1 quart of water daily per inch of trunk diameter. Don't place the tree near a working fireplace, TV or other heat source.

For the best effect: Place the tree in the stand at least a day before decorating it, and untie the branches so they have a chance to spread. If the branches begin to droop after being decorated, move back the ornaments at the branch tips to redistribute their weight.

▲ **BALSAM FIR**
Fairly slender shape. Deep-green needles are banded with white on the underside for a beautiful silvery cast. Has been the most popular Christmas tree in this country for years. Holds needles well, but sheds them faster than the Douglas fir. Its sap causes dermatitis in some people.

▲ **DOUGLAS FIR**
Graceful pyramid of upswept branches. Long, deep-green needles have a slightly bluish cast. Holds its needles longer than most trees, even after the needles have turned brown.

◀ **SCOTCH PINE**
A full, slightly rotund shape that doesn't need loads of ornaments. Needles have a lovely gray-green tint; bark is orange brown. A showy tree in its own right. Has great needle retention.

◀ *WHITE PINE*
Bundles of feathery, soft
bluish-green to gray-
green needles create an
airy appearance. Long
branches sweep upward
a bit at the tips. Needles
remain on the tree for
quite a while, but tend to
get brittle. Generally one
of the least expensive
Christmas trees.

BLUE SPRUCE
Rigid needles create a
dense, compact shape.
Needles have a gorgeous
color ranging from blue-
green to grayish-blue.
Not as widely available
as other varieties, also it
is more expensive,
because usually it is
used for landscaping.
Has long-lasting needles.
▼

RED CEDAR ▶
A columnar shape; short
branches grow more
upright than horizontal.
Needles are dark green
or bluish. Was the
favorite Christmas tree
of 19th century America.
Sheds needles faster
than the other trees.

*NORWAY
SPRUCE*
Dark green, stiff, sharp
needles with four sides
(you can feel the sides if
you roll a needle
between your fingers)
create a very dense
shape; branches dip and
sweep upward
gracefully. Like the
Scotch pine, can take
fewer ornaments. Very
good needle retention.
▼

VISIONS OF VICTORIANA

Sugarplums, ribbons and froths of lace.

Lavender and Lace Wreath

LAVENDER AND LACE WREATH

Easy: Achievable by anyone.

Materials: Grapevine wreath; several yards of wide lavender satin ribbon; scraps of new or antique lace *(lace-trimmed handkerchiefs work well)*; dried flowers, such as larkspur or clusters of rose heads *(see How to Dry Flowers for Arrangements and Wreaths, at right; if you wish, substitute clusters of bay leaves, cinnamon sticks or mistletoe for the dried flowers)*; floral wire.

Directions:
1. Using the floral wire, attach small bunches of the dried flowers to the grapevine wreath.
2. Wrap the lavender satin ribbon around the wreath, and tie the ribbon ends into a large bow.
3. Tuck the lace scraps into the wreath at random *(see photos at left and above).*

HOW TO DRY FLOWERS FOR ARRANGEMENTS AND WREATHS

Easy: Achievable by anyone.

Materials for Hang Drying: Rubber bands; clothesline and clothespins, or drying rack and string or twine. *For Silica Gel Drying:* Large rectangular pan with airtight cover; silica gel *(available at florist shops and garden centers)*; floral wire *(optional)*; slotted spoon; soft brush. *For Air Drying:* Piece of window screen or cheesecloth stretched over a frame or tray.
For Oven Drying: Baking sheet.
Directions:
1. Use hang drying for flowers with stems, drying with silica gel for whole blossoms, petals and leaves, and air drying and oven drying for blossoms, petals and leaves. Use only flowers that are at their prime. Flowers are properly dried when the petals and leaves are not sticky to the touch, and are so brittle that they would crack rather than bend.
2. Hang Drying: Keep the stems as long as possible. Strip the leaves. Fasten the flowers together in bunches of three to five with a rubber band placed 1 inch from the stem ends. Hang the bunches from a clothesline with clothespins, or from a drying rack with string or twine. Do not let the flower heads touch each other. To preserve the flowers' colors and minimize mold growth, hang the flowers in a dry, well-ventilated area away from direct sunlight and heat. Check the flowers daily until they are dried.
3. Silica Gel: Silica gel, an absorbent powder, dries flowers in a few days and preserves their colors well. If you are going to use the flowers in arrangements, leave a 1½-inch-long stem on each flower head, and insert a 3-inch length of wire into the core of each stem. As the stem dries, it will shrink around the wire.

Fill the pan one third full with silica gel. Press the flower heads, face up, into the gel. Fill in gently with more gel around each flower head until the flower is covered completely. Cover the container, and store it in a cool, dry place. Remove the flowers from the gel as soon as they are dried, or they will become too brittle and shatter when you touch them. Lift out the flowers with the slotted spoon, and use the soft brush to remove any remaining gel. When the flowers are dried, wind a longer piece of floral wire around the first wire in each stem.
4. Air Drying: Arrange the flowers in a single layer on the window screen or cheesecloth. Dry the flowers in a well-ventilated area away from direct sunlight for two to three days.
5. Oven Drying: Spread whole buds, loose petals, and leaves in one layer on the baking sheet. Place the baking sheet in a preheated 100° oven, and leave the oven door slightly ajar. Check the flowers frequently until they are dried. Depending on the type of flower, drying will take a few minutes to several hours.

SUGARPLUM WREATH

Average: For those with some experience in crafting.

Materials: 16-inch-diameter wire-ring wreath form or twig wreath; firm fruits, such as apples, grapes, lemons, limes, kumquats, pears, miniature pears and lady apples; green floral wire; 30-gauge wire; ⅜-inch paintbrush; 4 lightly beaten egg whites; 1 box of granulated sugar; Styrofoam ® or floral foam block.

Note: *The fruit should last about a month outdoors, or two weeks indoors at 65° to 68°. Citrus fruits last the longest time, grapes the shortest time.*

Directions:

1. For better adhesion, wash the wax off the fruits with dishwashing liquid.

2. To wire large fruits, bend a 2½- to 3-inch length of floral wire into a hairpin shape. Stick the wire's prongs into the fruit on the side you will attach to the wreath; the fruit's best side should face outward. Push the hairpin about ¾ inch into the fruit, leaving about a ½-inch-long loop sticking out. Wrap a length of 30-gauge wire around the hairpin loop at the base. To wire small fruits, loop a length of 30-gauge wire directly through the fruit.

3. Using the paintbrush, brush a thin coat of the beaten egg white evenly over each fruit, and dust the fruit with the sugar, varying the thickness of the sugar to look like snow. The top of the fruit should be more heavily covered than the sides. After you finish dusting each fruit, stick its wires into the foam block and let the fruit air dry completely.

4. When the fruits are dry, use the 30-gauge wires attached to the fruits to wire them to the wreath form or twig wreath. Attach the larger fruits first, and fill in with the smaller fruits.

BURNISHED BEAUTY WREATH

Average: For those with some experience in crafting.

Materials: Plywood wreath form with an outside diameter of 20 inches and an inside diameter of 12 inches; 18-inch-diameter Styrofoam® wreath form; dark brown wood stain or paint; paintbrush; copper spray paint; about 200 pine cones; 30 to 36 eggs; 2 pounds of assorted nuts; sturdy picture hanger or wire loop; clear acrylic spray varnish; hot glue gun or fast drying glue; 34 x 23 inches of copper-color satin fabric; matching thread; 13½ x 9 inches of synthetic batting; darning needle or pointed tool; newspaper; floral wire.

Directions:

1. Attach the picture hanger or wire loop to the back of the plywood form.

2. Glue the Styrofoam wreath form to the plywood wreath form.

3. Paint the Styrofoam wreath with the dark brown wood stain or paint.

4. Glue pine cones along the inner and outer rims of the plywood wreath so that the ends of the pine cones touch the Styrofoam wreath. It will be easier to attach the pine cones if you first snip off their tiny stems. Then completely cover both the Styrofoam and plywood wreaths with pine cones.

5. To empty the eggshells, carefully make a small hole in both ends of each egg with the darning needle or pointed tool; be sure to pierce the membrane at both ends. Blow the contents of the egg into a bowl. Wash the eggshells, and blow out the excess water through the holes. Allow the eggshells to dry. Spray the dried shells with the copper spray paint.

6. When the paint has dried, glue the eggshells onto the wreath. Glue on the nuts and remaining pine cones to cover the blowholes in the eggshells, and to fill in any empty spaces. Try to keep the look of the decorated wreath balanced.

7. Lay the wreath on newspaper in a well-ventilated area. Spray the entire wreath with the clear acrylic spray varnish.

8. To make the bow, cut a 19 x 14-inch rectangle from the satin fabric. Fold the rectangle in half lengthwise, right sides together. Sew a ¼-inch seam along one short end and the long edge. Turn the rectangle right side out, insert the batting, turn in the open edges, and slipstitch the opening closed *(see Stitch Guide, page 240)*. Cut a second rectangle measuring 34 x 9 inches from the satin. Fold it in half lengthwise, right sides together, and trim the ends diagonally *(see photo)*. Sew a ¼-inch seam along one short end and the long edge. Turn the rectangle right side out, turn in the open edges, and slipstitch the opening closed. Tie the longer rectangle around the center of the stuffed rectangle *(see photo)*, and wire the bow to the wreath.

Red Velveteen Stocking

RED VELVETEEN STOCKING

Average: For those with some experience in sewing and embroidery.

Materials: ½ yard of red velveteen; ½ yard of polyester lining *(optional)*; ¼ yard of white satin; ¼ yard of thin white cotton fabric; 1 yard of 1¾- to 2-inch-wide heavy lace with 2 borders; 1½ yards of ¼-inch-wide flexible flat gold braid; matching sewing threads; embroidery floss: 2 skeins of Medium Green, and 1 skein each of Red and Dark Green; embroidery needle; dressmaker's carbon; tracing paper for pattern.

Directions:

1. Enlarge the pattern and embroidery design in FIG. III, 5 onto tracing paper, following the directions on page 241.

2. Cut two red velveteen stocking pieces following the directions on the stocking pattern. If you wish, cut two lining pieces following the directions on the pattern.

3. Mark the heel and toe outlines on the right sides of the stocking pieces, and sew the gold braid along the outlines. Cut a wide enough border from each side of one end of the heavy lace to sew as an outer border along the gold braid. Sew the lace in place.

4. Pin and stitch the stocking pieces right sides together, leaving the top edge open. Clip the seam allowances where indicated on the pattern. Turn the stocking right side out.

5. If you wish, stitch and clip two lining pieces the same way. Place the lining inside the stocking, wrong sides together. Baste the lining to the stocking along the top edge.

6. Cut one 18½ x 7-inch strip each from the white satin and the thin white cotton. Place the two strips right sides together, and sew along one long edge. Turn the cuff to the right side, and topstitch as close to the edge of the seam as possible. Pin the heavy lace to the stitched edge of the cuff, with one scalloped edge

extending beyond the seam edge. Place gold braid at the top edge of the lace, with the lace slightly overlapping the braid, and sew both to the cuff. Sew a second row of braid 3½ inches above the first row of braid. Cut off the thin cotton cuff lining just above the stitching line of the upper band of braid so only satin extends above that braid. Make a small rolled hem on the edge of the satin.

7. Using the dressmaker's carbon, transfer the enlarged embroidery design from FIG. III, 5 onto the satin cuff, centering the design between the gold braid lines. Embroider the stems with 2 strands of Dark Green floss using a whipped stem stitch *(see Stitch Guide, page 240).* Embroider the leaves with three strands of Medium Green floss using a lazy daisy stitch, and using a single straight stitch to fill each center open area. Embroider the buds with two strands of Red floss at the center, two strands of Medium Green floss on each side, and two strands of Dark Green floss at the bottom using a satin stitch *(see Stitch Guide).*

8. Turn the portion of the cuff that extends above the upper line of gold braid to the inside of the stocking, and sew the cuff to the stocking. Overlap the raw ends of the cuff in back, turn under the upper raw edge, and slipstitch it in place *(see Stitch Guide).*

FIG. III, 5   1 SQ. = 1"

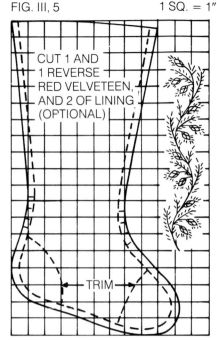

CUT 1 AND 1 REVERSE RED VELVETEEN, AND 2 OF LINING (OPTIONAL)

TRIM

RED VELVETEEN STOCKING

VICTORIAN STOCKINGS

All the stockings shown at right were made from this pattern, then trimmed as fancy dictated.

Average: For those with some experience in sewing.

Materials (for one stocking): ⅓ yard of velvet or brocade fabric for stocking; scraps of velvet or brocade for contrasting cuff; ½ yard of braid, ribbon, fringe or pompons for trim; matching threads; yarn for tassel *(optional)*; 3-inch-wide piece of cardboard *(optional)*; tapestry needle *(optional)*; paper for pattern.

Directions
(½-inch seams allowed):

1. Enlarge the stocking pattern in FIG. III, 6 onto paper, following the directions on page 241. Cut out the paper pattern.
2. Pin the pattern to the velvet or brocade, and cut out a stocking front and back; if using velvet, be sure the nap runs in the same direction on both pieces. Cut a 4½ x 13-inch cuff from contrasting fabric.
3. Hem one long edge of the cuff.
4. Place the stocking pieces right sides together, and sew the shin seam from toe to top. Right sides together, stitch the cuff to the top of the stocking, raw edges even. Turn the cuff up and, right sides facing, stitch the foot, back and cuff seam of the stocking. Turn the stocking right side out.
5. Topstitch the trim to the stocking over the cuff seam, lapping the trim's raw ends at the center back seam. Add a fabric hanger loop at the top of the back seam.
6. If you wish, add a tassel at the toe. Wrap the yarn 30 times around the cardboard. Slip a second length of yarn under the wrapped yarn, and tie it tightly to form a tassel (leaving long tie ends). Cut the yarn at the opposite end. Tie a second piece of yarn around the tassel about 1 inch below the top knot. Shake the tassel to loosen and fluff the yarn. Thread the long tie ends through a tapestry needle, and pull them into the toe of the stocking. Knot the tie ends inside the stocking.

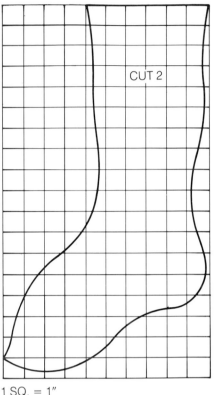

FIG. III, 6   VICTORIAN STOCKINGS

CUT 2

1 SQ. = 1"

T will honor Christmas in my heart, and try to keep it all the year.

— CHARLES DICKENS

Victorian Stockings

Green Gift Box Pillow; Red Present Pillow

GREEN GIFT BOX PILLOW

(17½ x 13½ inches)

Average: For those with some experience in sewing.

Materials: 7⅓ yards of ⅞-inch-wide red tartan plaid taffeta ribbon; 4 yards of ⅞-inch-wide red moire ribbon; 18½ x 14½ inches of red corduroy; 18½ x 14½ inches of green corduroy; matching threads; 2 yards of ¼-inch-wide red covered welting; synthetic stuffing.

**Directions
(½-inch seams allowed):**

1. Cut two 3⅔-yard lengths of plaid taffeta ribbon and one of moire ribbon. Lap one long edge of the taffeta ribbon ⅛ inch over the long edge of the moire ribbon, and topstitch. Repeat at the other long side to make a double-layered ribbon that is 2⅜ inches wide. Set aside the remaining ribbons.

2. Cut a strip of the layered ribbon the length of the green corduroy pillow front. Center the strip lengthwise on the pillow front, and edgestitch the strip in place. Cut and pin a crosswise strip of the layered ribbon over the first, 3 inches from one short end of the pillow front, and edgestitch. Repeat on the red corduroy pillow back.

3. Pin the red welting to the right side of the pillow front, raw edges even. Using a zipper foot, sew as close as possible to the welting cord, lapping the ends.

4. Sew the pillow front to the pillow back, right sides together, around three sides and four corners. Turn the pillow right side out, stuff it firmly, turn in the open edges, and slipstitch the opening closed *(see Stitch Guide, page 240).*

5. Make a nosegay with the remaining ribbons and tie it securely. Stitch the nosegay to the pillow front where the layered ribbons cross *(see photo).*

RED PRESENT PILLOW

(11¾ inches square)

Average: For those with some experience in sewing.

Materials: ⅜ yard of red velveteen; 2 yards of ¼-inch-wide striped or printed grosgrain ribbon; matching threads; 12-inch square knife-edge pillow form.

**Directions
(½-inch seams allowed):**

1. Cut two 12¾-inch squares of the velveteen for the pillow front and back. Cut two 12¾-inch lengths, and one 3-inch length of the grosgrain ribbon.

2. Edgestitch the 12¾-inch ribbon lengths perpendicular to each other on the pillow front. Arrange the remaining ribbon into a big bow with streamer ends *(see photo),* and pin the ribbon in place. Edgestitch the bow and streamers except at the center "knot." Slip the 3-inch ribbon length under the unstitched "knot," lap the ends, and whipstitch the ends together *(see Stitch Guide, page 240).* Rotate the seam to the underside of the "knot."

3. Sew the pillow front and back together following the directions in Green Gift Box Pillow, Step 4 *(at left).* Insert the pillow form and slipstitch the opening closed *(see Stitch Guide).*

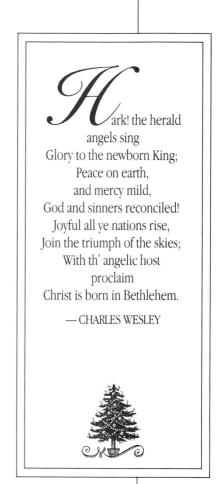

*H*ark! the herald
angels sing
Glory to the newborn King;
Peace on earth,
and mercy mild,
God and sinners reconciled!
Joyful all ye nations rise,
Join the triumph of the skies;
With th' angelic host
proclaim
Christ is born in Bethlehem.

— CHARLES WESLEY

Victorian Touches

Artifacts from the Far East were often a part of lavish Victorian decor, so add a touch of the exotic to your home by filling a Chinese bowl with jasmine potpourri. Import stores offer a wide variety of inexpensive ceramic and lacquer bowls in many sizes. Choose red, the Chinese good luck color, to go with your holiday decor.

❋

If the fireplace is the focal point of your living room, invest in a new hearth rug. Oriental designs are favorites of decorators because they complement all types of furnishings, from Victorian to contemporary. Look for inexpensive wool or acrylic Oriental-style throw rugs at discount chain stores, bed and bath shops, or carpet stores.

❋

Lacy doilies and antimacassars are hallmarks of the Victorian home. Antique lace is a lovely indulgence, but you can find pretty and inexpensive crocheted lace pieces in most department and general merchandise stores. Pick up an oblong table scarf or decorative shelf edging to use on the fireplace mantel.

Check in your sewing basket for unused pearl-type buttons—you can use them to make wonderful Victorian decorations. Draw a miniature stocking front and back on velvet or brocade fabric. Create a design on the stocking with the buttons and sew them on. Cut out the stocking pieces and trim the top edge with a lace scrap. Right sides together, sew the stocking front to the back, turn the stocking right side out and tack on a loop for hanging.

❋

Stitch a holiday bargello throw pillow. An ordinary flame stitch or geometric pattern takes on a different life when you stitch it in holiday colors. Experiment with red, green, white and gold. Try metallic threads and shading, too. Back the pillow with velvet or corduroy.

Wrap your Christmas gifts in floral chintz or opulent brocades, and tie them up with lace, satin and velvet ribbons or gold cord. Trim with doilies or bunches of artificial grapes spray-painted gold or silver.

❋

Your Victorian-style Christmas tree should shine with gold, silver and pearl. Use festoons of glass beads or opalescent plastic beads as garlands. Hang glass balls, mirrored ornaments and medallions from every branch. Fill in with china dolls, small wooden toys, and motifs cut from antique reproduction postcards. If you collect real antique ornaments, display them at adult eye level, out of the reach of little hands or curious pets.

❋

Roses are the favored flowers in Victorian decor. Trim a grapevine wreath with bunches of dried roses from your garden. Cover the mantel with English ivy, using real branches or silk imitations, and more dried roses.

❋

Hang a child's first baby shoes or booties on the tree. If you like, stitch the child's name and birthdate on the shoes.

Make dazzling Victoriana ornaments with a little glue, glass balls and doodads you buy at the five and dime. Create a design on the glass ball with dots of white glue. Gently press sequins, tiny pearl beads, colored beads, ribbons, lace or pretty buttons into the dots of glue; hold each decoration against the ball for a moment to allow the glue to bond.

✳

Fill a cut glass bowl with marzipan strawberries for a delicious accent in red and green.

✳

Make your own Victorian Christmas "crackers." These pretty table favors were, and still are, essential at English holiday celebrations. For each cracker you will need a 5-inch square of oaktag or flexible heavy paper, a 6 x 10-inch rectangle of colored tissue paper, candies, charms or small toys, transparent tape, and ribbons and decals for decoration. Roll the oaktag or heavy paper into a tube, and fill the tube with the candies and charms; traditional English crackers usually contain a tissue paper party hat as well. Roll the tube in the tissue paper, leaving a couple of inches of excess paper at each end. Tie the paper ends with ribbon, and flare out the ends. Decorate the cracker with the decals. To crack the cracker, hold the tissue paper at each end and pull!

✳

Use real or artificial sprigs of English ivy as napkin rings.

✳

Wind evergreen garlands around your bannister rail, then wind strings of imitation pearls (available at card stores) around and through the evergreens. Finish the look with big, white satin or red velvet bows every few feet. If you wish, add strings of little white lights to the arrangement.

Bring your old satin-covered ornaments back to life. Push the threads gently back into place, and mist the ornaments lightly with hairspray.

✳

Don't forget to deck the powder room for your Victorian-style holiday. Put out fancy red and green hand soaps in small, cut glass candy dishes, a lace scarf for the commode, sprigs of holly and evergreen in vases or decorative bottles, and lace-trimmed hand towels. You even can drape a swag of evergreen over the mirror.

No Victorian Christmas celebration was complete without parlor games. A fun game for the whole family to play is Animals in the Manger. The object is for each player to pair off with his or her "mate." On index cards, write the names of the animals that were likely to have been in the manger on Christmas Eve — horse, cow, chicken, pig, cat, dog, and so on — writing two cards for each animal. Write one card for the "lion" and one for the "lamb." Each player is given a card indicating his or her "species." When the game begins, the players act their roles with appropriate noises and gestures — but no words — lumbering around the room until they find their mates. The lion pairs off with the lamb.

✳

Dancing was an important part of Victorian life. This year, why not add some fancy footwork to your celebration. Waltzes and polkas are easy to learn, and fun to do — and dancing is a great way to work up an appetite for the Christmas feast (or to work off the calories after dinner!)

GRAND GIFTS

Gifts of flowers and frills for Mother, Grandma, your best friend, or perhaps a romantic young lady just come of age.

Flowers & Lace Cardigans for Mother and Daughters (directions, pages 121-124)

FLOWERS & LACE CARDIGAN— FOR DAUGHTER

Challenging: Requires more experience in knitting and embroidery.

Directions are given for Child's Size 2. Changes for Sizes 4 and 6 are in parentheses.

Materials: Any sport-weight yarn: 7 (9, 10½) ounces of Off-White or Red; 1 pair each size 5 and size 7 knitting needles, OR ANY SIZE NEEDLES TO OBTAIN GAUGE BELOW; 1 size 7 double-pointed needle (dp); 5 (5, 6) ½-inch-diameter buttons; one ⅜-inch-diameter button; crewel embroidery yarn: small amounts of Red, Yellow and Green; tapestry needle; stitch holder.

Gauge: On size 7 needles in Garter Stitch, 5 sts = 1 inch; 10 rows (5 ridges) = 1 inch.

Measurements:

SIZES:	2	4	6
BODY CHEST:	21″	23″	25″

Finished Measurements:

CHEST:	23″	25″	27″
WIDTH ACROSS BACK AT UNDERARMS:	12″	13″	14″
WIDTH ACROSS EACH FRONT AT UNDERARMS (INCLUDES BORDER):	6″	6½″	7″
WIDTH ACROSS SLEEVE AT UPPER ARMS:	9″	10″	11″

Raised Rib (RR) Pattern, Row 1 (right side): Sl 2 sts as if to p, k 1 leaving yarn on wrong side, sl 2 sts as if to p. **Row 2:** Rep Row 1. **Row 3:** K the 2 sl sts, k 1, k the 2 sl sts. **Row 4:** P 2, k 1, p 2. Rep Rows 1 to 4 for RR pat.

Diamond Pattern, Row 1 (right side): K to within one st of RR pat, sl next st to dp needle, hold in back, k next 2 sts, k 1 from dp needle—**Back Twist (BT) made;** k 1, sl next 2 sts to dp needle, hold in front, k next st, k 2 from dp needle—**Front Twist (FT) made.**

Row 2: K to Diamond, p 2, k 3, p 2. **Row 3:** K to Diamond, sl 2, k 3, sl 2. **Row 4:** Rep Row 3. **Row 5:** K to within one st of Diamond, BT on next 3 sts, k 3, FT on next 3 sts. **Row 6:** K to Diamond, p 2, k 5, p 2. **Row 7:** K to Diamond, sl 2, k 5, sl 2. **Row 8:** Rep Row 7. **Row 9:** K to within one st of Diamond, BT on next 3 sts, k 5, FT on next 3 sts. **Row 10:** K to Diamond, p 2, k 7, p 2. **Row 11:** K to Diamond, sl 2, k 7, sl 2. **Row 12:** Rep Row 11. **Row 13:** K to Diamond, k 2, p 7, k 2. **Row 14:** K to Diamond, p 2, k 7, p 2. **Row 15:** K to Diamond, sl 2, k 7, sl 2. **Row 16:** Rep Row 15. **Row 17:** K to Diamond, sl next 2 sts to dp needle, hold in front, k next st, k 2 from dp needle—**Front Cable (FC) made;** k 5, sl next st to dp needle, hold in back, k next 2 sts, k 1 from dp needle—**Back Cable (BC) made. Row 18:** K to Diamond, p 2, k 5, p 2. **Row 19:** K to Diamond, sl 2, k 5, sl 2. **Row 20:** Rep Row 19. **Row 21:** K to Diamond, FC on next 3 sts, k 3, BC on next 3 sts. **Row 22:** K to Diamond, p 2, k 3, p 2. **Row 23:** K to Diamond, sl 2, k 3, sl 2. **Row 24:** Rep Row 23. **Row 25:** K to Diamond, FC on next 3 sts, k 1, BC on next 3 sts. **Row 26:** K to Diamond, p 2, k 1, p 2. Rep Rows 1 to 26 for Diamond pat.

Directions:

1. Back: Starting at the lower edge with size 5 needles, cast on 60 (64, 70) sts. Work in k 1, p 1 ribbing for 1½ (1¾, 2) inches. Change to size 7 needles and work in garter stitch (k every row) until the total length is 6 (7¼, 8½) inches from beg, ending with a wrong side row. **Note:** *The first row of garter stitch is a right side row.*

2. Back Armhole Shaping: Bind off 3 sts at beg of next 2 rows. Dec one st each end every other row 2 (2, 2) times— 50 (54, 60) sts. Work even until the Armhole is 4¾ (5¼, 5½) inches, end with a wrong side row.

3. Back Shoulder Shaping: Bind off 15 (16, 18) sts at beg of next 2 rows. Place rem 20 (22, 24) sts on the st holder for the back Neck.

4. Left Front: Starting at the lower edge with size 5 needles, cast on 32 (34, 36) sts. Work in k 1, p 1 ribbing for 1½ (1¾, 2) inches.

5. For Sizes 2 and 4: Change to size 7 needles and beg RR pat as follows: **Row 1 (right side):** K 14 (16); follow Row 1 of RR pat over next 5 sts; k 13. **Rows 2 to 4:** Work Rows 2 to 4 of RR pat over established sts and k beg and end sts. Rep Rows 1 to 4 for RR pat until completion of Row 34. **Now** beg Diamond pat as follows: **Row 35 (right side):** K 13 (15); follow Row 1 of Diamond pat over next 7 sts; k 12. **Row 36:** K 12; follow Row 2 of Diamond pat over next 7 sts; k 13 (15). Work in Diamond pat as established until completion of Row 60. **At the same time,** work Armhole shaping *(see Step 6, page 122)* when the total length is the same as the Back to the underarm, ending with a wrong side row. Work RR pat for 6 rows. **Row 67:** Work in Diamond pat over RR pat as before.

For Size 6: Change to size 7 needles and beg RR pat as follows: **Row 1 (right side):** K 11, follow Row 1 of RR pat over next 5 sts; k 7, Row 1 of RR pat over next 5 sts; k 8. **Rows 2 to 4:** Work Rows 2 to 4 of RR pat over established sts, and k all other sts. Rep Rows 1 to 4 for RR pat until completion of Row 38. **Now** beg First Diamond pat as follows: **Row 39 (right side):** K 11, work RR pat over next 5 sts; k 6, follow Row 1 of Diamond pat over next 7 sts for First Diamond; k 7. **Row 40:** K 7; follow Row 2 of Diamond pat over next 7 sts, k 6, work RR pat over next 5 sts, k 11. Work in Diamond pat as established until completion of Row 54. **Row 55 (right side):** K 10; follow Row 1 of Diamond pat over next 7 sts for Second Diamond; k 5; continue working First Diamond over next 7 sts; k 7. Continue working Diamond pat as established. **At the same time,** work Armhole shaping *(see Step 6)* when the total length is the same as the Back to the underarm, ending with a wrong side row. When each Diamond pat is completed, work 4 rows in RR pat over these sts. Work in Diamond pat until completion of Row 70. **Row 71:** Beg next Diamond pat over RR pat nearest Neck edge. **Row 87:** Beg next Diamond pat over RR pat nearest the Armhole edge.

6. Front Armhole Shaping: Bind off 3 sts at beg of next row for the Armhole edge. Dec one st at the Armhole edge every other row 2 times—27 (29, 31) sts. Work even in pat until the Armhole measures 3¼ (3¾, 4¼) inches, ending with a right side row.

7. Neck Shaping: Bind off 4 sts at beg of next row for the Neck edge. Bind off 3 (4, 4) sts at the Neck edge once, then 2 sts once. Dec one st at the Neck edge every other row 3 times—15 (16, 18) sts. Work even in pat until the Armhole measures the same as the Back to the Shoulder, ending with a wrong side row.

8. Front Shoulder Shaping: Bind off 15 (16, 18) sts at beg of the next row for the Shoulder.

9. Right Front: Work the same as the Left Front, reversing the patterns and all the shaping.

10. Sleeves: Starting at the lower edge with size 5 needles, cast on 36 (38, 38) sts. Work in k 1, p 1 ribbing for 1½ (1¾, 2) inches, increasing 3 (3, 5) sts evenly spaced across the last row—39 (41, 43) sts. Change to size 7 needles and beg RR pat as follows: **Row 1 (right side):** K 17 (18, 19); follow Row 1 of RR pat over next 5 sts; k 17 (18, 19). **Rows 2 to 4:** Work Rows 2 to 4 of RR pat over established sts, and k all other sts. Rep Rows 1 to 4 for RR pat, increasing one st each end every 10th row 6 (7, 8) times—51 (55, 59) sts. Work in RR pat until completion of Row 62 (80, 88). **Now** beg Diamond pat as follows: **Row 63 (81, 89) (right side):** K 16 (17, 18); follow Row 1 of Diamond pat over next 7 sts; k 16 (17, 18). Work in Diamond pat as established until the total length from beg measures 8¼ (9¾, 11) inches, ending with a wrong side row.

11. Cap Shaping: Continuing in Diamond pat, bind off 3 sts at beg of next 2 rows. When Diamond is completed,

work in RR pat over these sts. Dec one st each end every other row 18 (20, 22) times. Bind off rem 9 sts.

12. Finishing: Sew the Shoulder seams.

13. Neckband: With the right side up and size 5 needles, pick up and k 18 (21, 22) sts along the Right Front Neck edge, 20 (22, 24) sts from the st holder, 18 (21, 22) sts from the Left Front Neck edge— 56 (64, 68) sts. Work in k 2, p 2 ribbing for 4 rows. Bind off loosely in ribbing.

14. Left Front Band: With the right side up and size 5 needles, pick up and k 52 (60, 64) sts evenly spaced along the Left Front edge (including the Neckband ribbing). Work in k 2, p 2 ribbing for 4 rows. Bind off loosely in ribbing. Mark the positions of 5 (5, 6) buttons evenly spaced, with the first button ¾ inch from the lower edge, and the last button ½ inch from the upper edge.

15. Right Front Band: With the right side up and size 5 needles, pick up and k 52 (60, 64) sts along the Right Front edge. Work in k 2, p 2 ribbing as for the Left Front Band, making buttonholes opposite the markers on Row 2 as follows: K 2 tog, yo for each buttonhole. Sew the side and Sleeve seams. Sew in the Sleeves. Sew on the ½-inch-diameter buttons.

16. Embroidery: With the tapestry needle and crewel embroidery yarn, work a Red rosebud with a Yellow center in bullion stitch at the center of each Diamond if you have made an Off White sweater; work Yellow rosebuds if you have made a Red sweater. Work Green leaves in lazy daisy stitch (see Stitch Guide, page 240).

17. Collar: With size 5 needles and the yarn remaining from the cardigan, cast on 9 sts. **Row 1 (right side):** Sl 1, k 1, yo, k 2 tog, (yo twice, k 2 tog) twice, k 1— 11 sts. **Row 2:** K 3, p 1, k 2, p 1, k 4. **Row 3:** Sl 1, k 1, yo, k 2 tog, k 2, (yo twice, k 2 tog) twice, k 1—13 sts. **Row 4:** K 3, p 1, k 2, p 1, k 6. **Row 5:** Sl 1, k 1, yo, k 2 tog, k 4, (yo twice, k 2 tog) twice, k 1—15 sts. **Row 6:** K 3, p 1, k 2, p 1, k 8. **Row 7:** Sl 1, k 1, yo, k 2 tog, k 11—15 sts. **Row 8:** Bind

off 6 sts, k 8—9 sts. **This completes one leaf.** * Rep Rows 1 to 7. **Short Row 8:** Bind off 6 sts, k 6, *turn;* k 2, (yo twice, k 2 tog) twice, k 1—11 sts. Rep Rows 2 to 8. * Rep from * to * until 12 (12, 13) leaves have been completed. Bind off. Sew the straight edge of the Collar to the Neck edge. Make a loop at the upper right corner of the Collar. Sew the ⅜-inch-diameter button to the opposite corner.

FLOWERS & LACE CARDIGAN— FOR MOTHER

Challenging: Requires more experience in knitting and embroidery.

Directions are given for Size Small (8-10). Changes for Sizes Medium (12-14) and Large (16) are in parentheses.
Materials: Any 4-ply worsted weight yarn: 19½ (21, 23) of Off White; 1 pair each size 5 and size 7 knitting needles, OR ANY SIZE NEEDLES TO OBTAIN GAUGE BELOW; 1 size 7 double-pointed needle (dp); six ½-inch-diameter buttons; one ⅜-inch-diameter button; crewel embroidery yarn: small amounts of Red, Yellow and Green; tapestry needle; stitch holder; shoulder pads *(optional).*
Gauge: On size 7 needles in Garter Stitch, 5 sts = 1 inch; 10 rows (5 ridges) = 1 inch.

Measurements:

	SMALL	MEDIUM	LARGE
SIZES:	(8-10)	(12-14)	(16)
BODY BUST:	32½"	36"	38"

Finished Measurements:

BUST:	36"	38"	40"

WIDTH ACROSS BACK AT UNDERARMS:

	18"	19"	20"

WIDTH ACROSS EACH FRONT AT UNDERARMS (INCLUDES BORDER):

	9½"	10"	10½"

WIDTH ACROSS SLEEVE AT UPPER ARMS:

	14½"	15"	15½"

Directions:

1. Back: Starting at the lower edge with size 5 needles, cast on 92 (96, 102) sts. Work in k 1, p 1 ribbing for 2½ inches. Change to size 7 needles, and work in garter stitch (k every row) until the total length is 10½ (11, 11½) inches from beg, ending with a wrong side row. **Note:** *The first row of garter stitch is a right side row.*

2. Back Armhole Shaping: Bind off 3 (3, 4) sts at beg of next 2 rows, then 2 sts at beg of next 2 rows. Dec one st at each end of every other row 3 (3, 3) times — 76 (80, 84) sts. Work even until the Armhole measures 7½ (8, 8½) inches, ending with a wrong side row.

3. Back Shoulder Shaping: Bind off 26 (27, 28) sts at beg of next 2 rows. Place rem 24 (26, 28) sts on st holder for back Neck.

4. Left Front: Starting at the lower edge with size 5 needles, cast on 52 (55, 58) sts. Work in k 1, p 1 ribbing for 2½ inches. Change to size 7 needles and beg Raised Rib (RR) pat as follows: **Row 1 (right side):** K 9 (12, 15); follow Row 1 of RR pat *(see Daughter's Cardigan, page 121)* over next 5 sts; k 9; Row 1 of RR pat over next 5 sts; k 9; Row 1 of RR pat over next 5 sts; k 10. **Rows 2 to 4:** Work Rows 2 to 4 of RR pat over established sts, and k all other sts. Repeat Rows 1 to 4 for RR pat until completion of Row 14. **Row 15:** Inc one st at beg of row for Armhole edge, and work in RR pat to end. Continue in RR pat, increasing one st at Armhole edge **only** every 14th row, 3 times more — 56 (59, 62) sts. Work even in RR pat until completion of Row 62. **Now** beg First Diamond pat as follows: **Row 63 (right side):** K 13 (16, 19); work RR pat over next 5 sts; k 9; RR pat over next 5 sts; k 8; follow Row 1 of Diamond pat *(see Daughter's Cardigan, page 121)* over next 7 sts; k 9. **Row 64:** K 9; follow Row 2 of Diamond pat over next 7 sts; k 8; work RR pat over next 5 sts; k 9; RR pat over next 5 sts; k 13 (16, 19). Work in Diamond pat as established until completion of Row 82. **Row 83 (right side):** K 13 (16, 19);

work RR pat over next 5 sts; k 8; follow Row 1 of Diamond pat over next 7 sts for Second Diamond; k 7; continue working First Diamond over next 7 sts; k 9. Continue working in Diamond pat as established. **At the same time,** work the Armhole shaping *(see Step 5)* until the total length is the same as the Back to the underarm, ending with a wrong side row. When each Diamond is completed, work 6 rows in RR pat over these sts. Work in Diamond pat until completion of Row 102. **Row 103:** Beg next Diamond pat over first and third RR pats. **Row 123:** Beg next Diamond pat over second RR pat. **Row 143:** Beg next Diamond pat over third RR pat.

5. Front Armhole Shaping: Bind off 3 (3, 4) sts at beg of next row for Armhole edge, then 2 sts at Armhole edge. Dec one st at the Armhole edge every other row 3 times — 48 (51, 53) sts. Work even in pat until the Armhole measures 5¼ (5¾, 6¼) inches, ending with a right side row.

6. Neck Shaping: Bind off 7 (8, 9) sts at beg of next row for the Neck edge. Bind off 5 (6, 6) sts at the Neck edge once, then 3 (3, 3) sts twice. Dec one st at the Neck edge every other row 4 times — 26 (27, 28) sts. Work even in pat until the Armhole measures the same as Back to Shoulder, ending with a wrong side row.

7. Front Shoulder Shaping: Bind off 26 (27, 28) sts at beg of the next row for the Shoulder.

8. Right Front: Work the same as the Left Front, reversing the patterns and all the shaping.

9. Sleeves: Starting at the lower edge with size 5 needles, cast on 48 (50, 52) sts. Work in k 1, p 1 ribbing for 2½ inches, increasing 5 sts evenly spaced across the last row — 53 (55, 57) sts. Change to size 7 needles and beg RR pat as follows: **Row 1 (right side):** K 24 (25, 26); follow Row 1 of RR pat over next 5 sts; k 24 (25, 26). **Rows 2 to 4:** Work Rows 2 to 4 of RR pat over established sts, and k all other sts. Repeat Rows 1 to 4 for RR pat, increasing one st at each end every 10th row 12 (13,

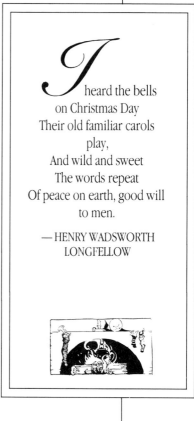

I heard the bells on Christmas Day Their old familiar carols play, And wild and sweet The words repeat Of peace on earth, good will to men.

— HENRY WADSWORTH LONGFELLOW

14) times — 77 (81, 85) sts. Work in RR pat until completion of Row 124 (130, 134). *Now* beg Diamond pat as follows: **Row 125 (131, 135) (right side):** K 35 (37, 39); follow Row 1 of Diamond pat over next 7 sts; k 35 (37, 39). Work in Diamond Pat as established until total length from beg is 14½ (15, 15½) inches from beg, ending with a wrong side row.

10. Cap Shaping: Continuing in Diamond pat, bind off 3 (3, 4) sts at beg of next 2 rows, then 2 sts at beg of next 2 rows. When Diamond is completed, work in RR pat over these sts. Dec one st each end every other row 28 (31, 32) times. Bind off 2 (0, 0) sts at beg of next 2 rows. Bind off rem 7 (9, 9) sts.

11. Finishing: Sew the Shoulder seams.
12. Neckband: With the right side facing and size 5 needles, pick up and k 24 (25, 26) sts along Right Front Neck edge, 24 (26, 28) sts from Back st holder, 24 (25, 26) sts along Left Front Neck edge — 72 (76, 80) sts. Work in k 2, p 2 ribbing for 4 rows. Bind off loosely in ribbing.
13. Left Front Band: With the right side facing and size 5 needles, pick up and k 88 (92, 96) sts evenly spaced along Left Front edge (including Neckband ribbing). Work in k 2, p 2 ribbing for 4 rows. Bind off loosely in ribbing. Mark the positions of 6 buttons evenly spaced, with the first button ¾ inch from the lower edge and the last ½ inch from the upper edge.

14. Right Front Band: With the right side facing and size 5 needles, pick up and k 88 (96, 96) sts along the Right Front edge. Work in k 2, p 2, ribbing as for the Left Front Band, making buttonholes opposite the markers on Row 2 as follows: K 2 tog, yo for each buttonhole. Sew the side and Sleeve seams. Sew in the Sleeves. Sew on the ½-inch-diameter buttons.
15. Embroidery: Follow the directions in Daughter's Embroidered Cardigan, step 16 *(page 122)*.
16. Collar: Follow the directions for the Daughter's Cardigan, Step 17 *(page 122)*, working 17 leaves.
17. If you wish, attach shoulder pads.

ONE MOMENT IN TIME

Holiday time is photo time. Here are a few tips to ensure great pictures of this year's festivities.

Use natural light whenever possible. The glow of the fire is wonderfully romantic, but it makes for very dark pictures. A sunny (but not glaring) window provides much better lighting for picture-taking.

✳

Don't use backgrounds that are brighter or lighter than your photo subject. The subject will be unrecognizable in the shadows. If you must shoot in this type of situation, use a flash to illuminate the subject.

✳

Avoid the red eye effect (those red spots where the subject's eyes should be). Point your flash at the ceiling or wall so the light bounces onto the subject, but not into his or her eyes.

✳

Don't shoot from too far away. Distance makes the subjects appear smaller, and details indistinct. You won't see facial expressions, or shining holiday smiles, from far away.

Take photographs of babies and children from their eye level; that's where the action is! Get down on the floor with the kids and have some fun.

✳

Photograph more than one person at the same time. This is especially important when you are photographing babies and small children. The interaction under the tree on Christmas day makes for some fabulous photos.

✳

Be spontaneous. Be ready to snap a picture at any moment, like when Grandpa has a minute alone with the kids. Be sure to get a shot of the gang in the kitchen as well.

✳

Don't let your pursuit of the perfect shot ruin your holiday fun. Give the camera a rest at times during the festivities. Picture-taking should be relaxed; that's when you and your subjects are at your best.

LACY NET PLACE MATS

Easy: Achievable by anyone.

Materials for Four Place Mats:
21 inches of 6-squares-to-the-inch ecru or white darning net; 2 skeins Filet No. 2 in matching color; 4 skeins of Filet No. 5 in matching color; tapestry needle; narrow lace trim *(optional).*

Note: *Net darning is simply darning in and out of the squares in the net. The squares in* FIG. III, 7 *(page 126) represent the squares of the net.*

Directions:

1. Rectangular Place Mats: For each place mat, cut a net rectangle measuring 80 x 116 squares; this includes 3 squares on each side for a hem.

2. Cut one skein of either Filet No. 2 or Filet No. 5 once to give you forty 1-yard-long strands of yarn, which is a good length for working.

3. Mark the center of each side of the net rectangle for the motif placement *(see the X's and dark solid lines in* FIG. III, 7, *page 126).*

4. Count 35 squares from the center of one net rectangle toward a short side to arrive at Flower **A**, which is in the center of the short side. Start Flower **A** in a corner between the petals. Bring the tapestry needle threaded with Filet No. 2 from the back to the front; leave 2 inches of yarn to be knotted in a square knot when you return to that point. All the outlines of Flowers **A**, **B** and **C** are done with Filet No. 2. There are 25 open squares between the center of the net rectangle and center Flower **B** on the long side. Count the distance between the flowers.

5. The hem is done with Filet No. 2. Turn under 3 squares on each side. Darn first **D** then **E** through the thicknesses of net all around each mat.

6. Stitch the motifs **F** in the four corners.

7. The insides of all Flowers **A**, **B** and **C** are done with Filet No. 5. All dotted squares are filled in four times

alternatively *(see* Fig. III, 7*)*. The yarn ends
are finished on the back with a square
knot or by weaving the ends under the
finished embroidery.

8. *Oval Place Mats:* To make oval place
mats, cut the oval form around the
embroidery plus about 5 squares. Attach a
narrow lace edge on top using a small
zigzag machine stitch; do not hem.

9. *Laundering:* Hand wash the mats
with mild soap. Add bleach if the mats are
white. Iron the mats on the reverse side
with a medium-hot steam iron to restore
stiffness to the net.

FIG. III, 7   LACY NET PLACE MATS

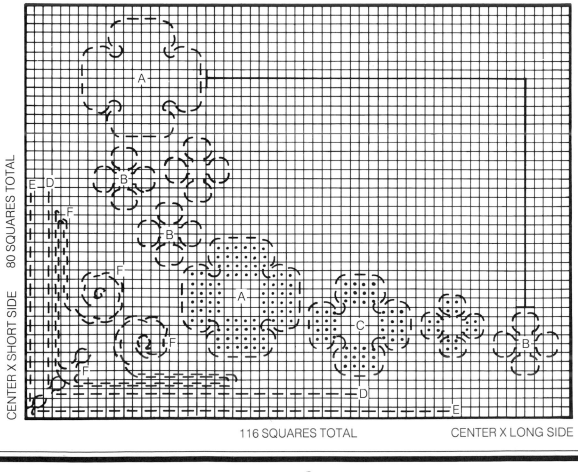

CENTER X SHORT SIDE   80 SQUARES TOTAL

116 SQUARES TOTAL   CENTER X LONG SIDE

BEAUTIFUL DREAMER PILLOWCASE

Easy: Achievable by anyone.

Materials: One pillowcase; matching thread; 4- to 5-inch-wide lace trim whose length is twice the width of the pillowcase plus 2 inches for seam.

Directions:

1. Pin the short ends of the lace right sides together, and sew them together using a 1-inch seam allowance. Press the seam open.

2. Turn the pillowcase and lace wrong side out. Slip the lace just 1 inch over the pillowcase opening, lining up the seams, and press.

3. Using large stitches, sew two rows of stitches by machine or by hand, the first row along the pillowcase edge, and the second row along the lace edge. Turn the pillowcase right side out, and press it.

VICTORIAN HAT BOX

Easy: Achievable by anyone.

Materials: Hat box; several yards of floral patterned wallpaper; scissors or utility knife; white glue or hot glue gun.

Directions:

1. Trace the hat box lid onto the wrong side of the wallpaper, and cut out a circle ⅛ inch inside the traced line. Cut a wallpaper strip 1½ inches wider than the depth, and 1 inch longer than the girth of the lid side. In the same way, trace, measure, and cut two pieces of wallpaper for the box bottom and side.

2. Center the lid strip around the lid side. Turn the strip's bottom edge under to the inside of the lid, and glue it in place. Turn the strip's top edge over the top of the lid and glue it in place, clipping the strip as needed to flatten the paper. Glue the lid circle to the lid top, covering the edges of the side strip. Glue the remaining wallpaper strip and circle to the box side and bottom in the same way.

PRETTY PEACH SHAWL

(22 x 60 inches, plus fringe)

Average: For those with some experience in knitting.

Materials: Paton's Promise yarn (40-gram ball): 7 balls of Pale Peach; one pair size 9 knitting needles, OR ANY SIZE NEEDLES TO OBTAIN GAUGE BELOW; crochet hook.

Gauge: In Garter Stitch, 11 sts = 3 inches; 6 rows (3 ridges) = 1 inch.

Directions:

1. Shawl: Starting at the bottom edge, cast on 80 sts. Sl the first st, and k across the row. Continue in garter stitch (k every row), slipping the first stitch of each row, until the total length is 60 inches from beg. Bind off.

2. Fringe: Cut 16-inch-long strands of yarn. Attach two strands to each st along the bottom and top edges of the shawl; use the crochet hook to feed the strands through the sts. Trim the fringe evenly.

FANCY FOOTSTOOL

(12 inches in diameter; 8½ inches high)

Average: For those with some experience in woodworking and crafting.

Materials: ¾-inch-thick plywood at least 13 inches square; 3-inch-thick 12-inch-diameter foam circle; 1 square yard of synthetic batting; ¾ yard of floral chintz fabric; 3½ yards of upholstery fringe to match fabric; 9 inches of ¾-inch-diameter screw dowel; three 3-inch-diameter ball finials; jigsaw; drill with ¾-inch bit; sabre saw; staple gun; white glue or hot glue gun; compass.

Directions:

1. Cut the plywood into a 12-inch-diameter circle. Using the compass, scribe an inner circle with a 4½-inch radius. Divide the inner circle into 3 equal segments. Drill a ¾-inch hole through the plywood at the intersections of the inner circle and the segments.

2. Place the foam circle on top of the plywood, and cover it with 2 sheets of the batting *(see* FIG. III, 8*)*.

3. Cut a circle from the floral fabric large enough to cover the foam and batting, and to lap under the plywood. Pull the fabric taut, and staple it to the bottom of the plywood about 1 inch from the plywood edge; ease the fabric into pleats as you go. Cut off any excess fabric.

4. Glue the fringe along the lower side edge of the stool, smoothing it as you go.

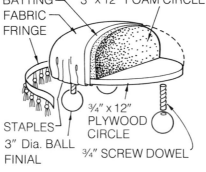

FIG. III, 8   FANCY FOOTSTOOL
BATTING — 3″ x 12″ FOAM CIRCLE
FABRIC —
FRINGE —
STAPLES —
3″ Dia. BALL FINIAL
¾″ x 12″ PLYWOOD CIRCLE
¾″ SCREW DOWEL

5. Cut the ¾-inch-diameter screw dowel into three 3-inch-long pieces. Insert glue in the ball finial holes, and insert a screw dowel into each hole. Insert glue in the holes in the plywood, and insert the dowels with the finials attached to form the stool legs and feet. Before the glue dries, adjust the legs so the stool sits level.

NOSEGAY PILLOW

(18 inches square, plus ruffle)

Average: For those with some experience in sewing.

Materials: 1⅜ yards of 44-inch-wide muslin; flower cut from floral chintz fabric; matching thread; synthetic stuffing.

Directions:

1. Cut two 19-inch muslin squares. Cut and piece together a muslin ruffle strip that is 5½ inches wide and 5½ yards long.

2. Pin the fabric flower to a muslin square; zigzag stitch around the edges.

3. Fold the ruffle strip in half lengthwise, wrong sides together. Stitch a gathering row ½ inch from the long raw edges. Pin the ruffle strip to the pillow front, right sides together and raw edges even. Pull up the gathers to fit the pillow front, and stitch over the gathering row.

4. Stitch the pillow back to the pillow front, right sides together, around three sides and four corners. Turn the pillow right side out, stuff it, turn in the open edges, and slipstitch the opening closed *(see Stitch Guide, page 240).*

Victorian Hat Box; Pretty Peach Shawl; Fancy Footstool; Nosegay Pillow

JUST FOR KIDS

The magic of Christmas morning—gaily wrapped bundles full of wonderful presents peeping out from under a beautiful tree.

T he earth has grown cold with its burden of care, But at Christmas it always is young, The heart of the jewel burns lustrous and fair, And its soul full of music breaks forth on the air, When the song of the Angels is sung.

— PHILLIPS BROOKS

CHRISTENING GOWN, SLIP & BONNET

Challenging: Requires more experience in sewing and embroidery.

Materials: 4¼ yards of 45-inch-wide white batiste; 2½ yards of ⅝-inch-wide scalloped lace edging; 2 yards of ⅞-inch-wide lace panel; 1¾ yards of 1¾-inch-wide crocheted lace; 1 yard of ⅜-inch-wide white ribbon; white sewing thread; embroidery floss: White; embroidery needle; embroidery hoop; 6 snap fasteners; dressmaker's carbon; tracing paper; paper for patterns; yardstick.

General Directions:
Enlarge the patterns in FIG. III, 9A *(page 133)* onto paper, following the directions on page 241. From the batiste, cut one Gown Skirt Front, two Bodice Fronts, one pair each of the Sleeve, Bonnet Midsection, Gown Skirt Side and Gown Skirt Back, and two pairs each of the Bodice Back and Bonnet Side. Also cut two 2 x 9¼-inch Sleeve Bands, a 2½ x 21-inch Bonnet ruffle, two 2 x 14-inch bias strips for the neck bindings, and two 22 x 30-inch pieces for the Slip Skirt Front and Slip Skirt Back.

Gown Directions
(½-inch seams allowed):
1. Front Bodice: Trace the full-size motif in FIG. III, 9B *(page 133)* onto tracing paper. Using the dressmaker's carbon, trace the motif onto one of the

Bodice Fronts, matching centers. Place the Bodice Front in the embroidery hoop. Using the embroidery needle and White floss, work the stems in stem stitch, the blossoms in satin stitch, the baby's breath in French knots, the bow outline in stem stitch, and the enclosing circle in pairs of small lazy daisy petals *(see Stitch Guide, page 240).* Gather a 24-inch length of the ⅝-inch-wide scalloped lace edging, and stitch it to the Bodice Front along the broken line, with the lace's straight edge inside.
2. Bodice: Sew the Bodice Front to a pair of Bodice Backs at the shoulders and side edges. Press the seams open.
3. Sleeves: Sew a gathering row on each Sleeve at the cap edge between the dots, and another gathering row along the bottom edge. At one long edge of each sleeve band, turn ½ inch to the wrong side, and press. Fold each band in half, right side together, and stitch the short ends. Stitch the underarm edges of each Sleeve together. With right sides together, pin the raw edge of each band to the lower edge of a Sleeve, underarm seams matching, pull up the gathers to fit, and stitch. Turn the folded edge of each band to the wrong side, and slipstitch it along the seam line *(see Stitch Guide).*
4. Armholes: With right sides together, pin the Sleeves to the armholes. Match the circles to the Bodice Front, the notches to

Continued on page 132

Christening Gown, Slip & Bonnet

the Bodice Back, and the underarm seams to each other. Pull up the gathers to fit, and stitch.

5. Skirt Front: Measuring from the top edge, draw five horizontal lines across the Gown Skirt Front at the following intervals: 7 inches, 5 inches, 5 inches, 5 inches and 3 inches. Fold the Gown Skirt Front in half lengthwise to make a center front crease. Open the Gown Skirt Front. Plan the embroidery designs and their placement as you wish; they all are based on the full-size motif in FIG. III, 9C. Trace the full-size motif onto tracing paper. The large, broken-line leaf can be substituted for the double leaf, the leaf to the right can be omitted, the middle spray can be shortened by two blossoms. Use the dressmaker's carbon to trace your chosen designs onto the Gown Skirt Front, centering the designs between the horizontal lines. First trace from the center fold toward the left, ending no closer than ¾ inch from the side edge. Then turn the tracing paper patterns wrong side up, and trace the reversed designs to the right of the center fold. Embroider the design following the directions in Step 1, working the leaf outlines in stem stitch, and filling in their lower section with herringbone stitch *(see Stitch Guide, page 240)*.

6. Lace Insets: Pin five bands of the ⅞-inch-wide lace panel across the Gown Skirt Front, centering them over the five horizontal lines. Edgestitch the lace bands. From the wrong side, carefully cut the fabric across the lines. Fold the cut fabric up or down so the lace will be transparent. Stitch along the folds, and trim the excess cut fabric to about ¼ inch.

7. Skirt: Stitch the Gown Skirt Front between the two Gown Skirt Sides, and press the seams toward the sides. Topstitch a length of ⅝-inch-wide scalloped lace along each seam, with the scallops facing away from the Skirt Front. Stitch the slanted edge of a Gown Skirt Back to each Skirt Side, and press the seams open.

8. Waist Seam: Sew two rows of gathering stitches ½ inch from the top edge of the Skirt. With right sides together, pin the Skirt to the Bodice at the waist edges, matching the front seams to the notches on the Bodice, and the side seams to each other, back edges flush. Pull up the gathers to fit, adjust the fullness evenly, and stitch. Press the seam allowance upward.

9. Back Closing: At the back edges, turn ¼ inch to the wrong side and stitch. Then turn under 1¼ inches and press. Bind the neck edge with one of the neck bias strips. Turning under each end, stitch the straight edge of a length of ⅝-inch-wide scalloped lace along the seamline, scalloped edge upward. Sew three snap fasteners on the back edges, one at the waist, one at the neck, and one between. Hem the skirt. Turning under each end, lap the 1¾-inch-wide crocheted lace over the hem edge, and topstitch.

Bonnet Directions (½-inch seams allowed):
1. Stitch one Bonnet Midsection between a pair of Bonnet Sides, notches matching. Press the seams open, clipping them as needed. Repeat with the remaining Bonnet Midsection and Bonnet Sides to make the lining.
2. Topstitch a length of ⅞-inch-wide lace panel ½ inch from the front edge of the Bonnet. Fold the Bonnet ruffle strip in half, right side together. Stitch ½ inch from each end, and turn the strip right side out. Every ¾ inch, make a ¼ inch tuck. Press and pin the tucks. With right sides together and raw edges even, pin the tucked strip to the front edge of the Bonnet, starting and stopping ½ inch from the lower edge of the Bonnet. If necessary, adjust the tucks to fit, and stitch ½ inch from the raw edge.
3. Place the Bonnet lining on the Bonnet, right sides together, and stitch ½ inch from all raw edges, leaving 3 inches open at the back for turning. Turn the Bonnet right side out, turn in the open edges,

and slipstitch the opening closed. Cut the white ribbon in half, and sew one end of each half to opposite inside lower edges of the cap against the front seam.

Slip Directions (½-inch seams allowed):
1. Fold the Slip Skirt Front in half vertically, to 22 x 15 inches. At the top end, mark 11 inches from the fold. Using the yardstick, draw a tapered side edge from this mark to the end of the bottom edge. Cut along the line through both layers. Repeat on the Slip Skirt Back.
2. Slash the Skirt Back down the center fold. Stitch each Skirt Back half to a side of the Skirt Front. Stitch the Slip together following the directions in Gown, Steps 2, 8 and 9, omitting the lace. Bind the armhole edges like the neck edge.

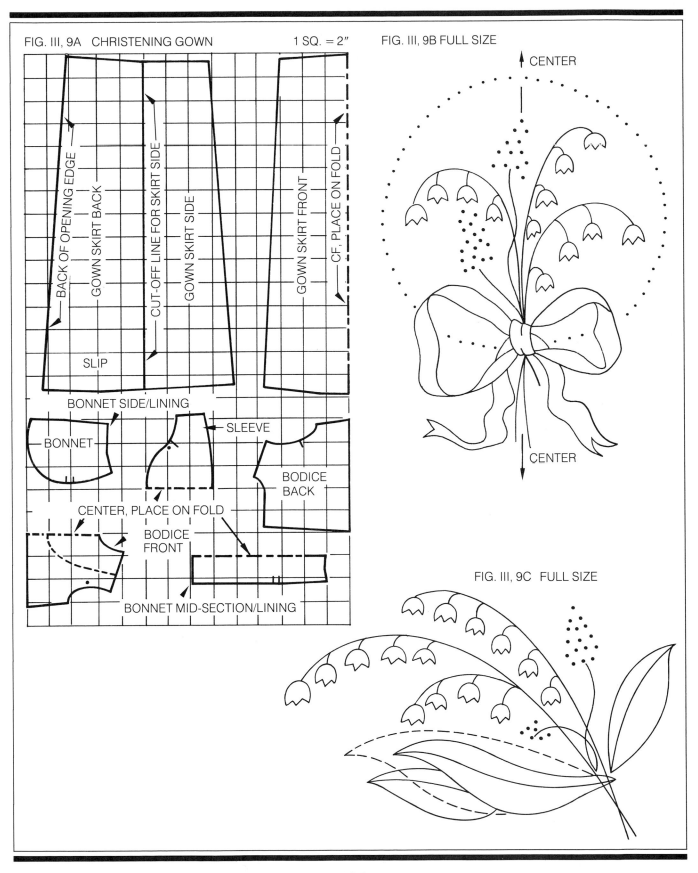

FIG. III, 9A   CHRISTENING GOWN   1 SQ. = 2"   FIG. III, 9B FULL SIZE

CENTER

BACK OF OPENING EDGE

GOWN SKIRT BACK

CUT-OFF LINE FOR SKIRT SIDE

GOWN SKIRT SIDE

GOWN SKIRT FRONT

CF, PLACE ON FOLD

SLIP

BONNET SIDE/LINING

BONNET

SLEEVE

BODICE
BACK

CENTER, PLACE ON FOLD

BODICE
FRONT

BONNET MID-SECTION/LINING

CENTER

FIG. III, 9C FULL SIZE

Sweet & Simple Sock Dolls

SWEET & SIMPLE SOCK DOLLS

(21 inches tall)

Average: For those with some experience in sewing and doll making.

Materials for One Boy Doll and One Girl Doll: 2 pairs of cotton or nylon anklet socks; string; fabric scraps: 9 x 11 inches for legs, 10 x 18 inches for knickers, 8 x 28 inches for boy's jacket, 4 x 44 inches for boy's scarf, 10 x 18 inches for boy's pants, 10 x 44 inches for girl's blouse and 10½ x 44 inches for skirt or ⅝ yard of 44-inch-wide fabric for girl's dress; 5 x 8 inches of felt for shoes; ladies' synthetic stretch wig or acrylic yarn for hair; matching sewing threads, plus blue *(optional)*, black *(optional)*, white and rust for facial features; synthetic stuffing; assorted lace trims for girl; 1 yard of 2½-inch-wide lace for girl's hat *(optional)*; assorted ribbons for girl's bows; ribbon for girl's hat *(optional)*; fabric flowers for girl's hat *(optional)*; child's plastic headband for girl's hat *(optional)*; ladies' lace collar or small doily for girl's collar *(optional)*; two $^7/_{16}$-inch-diameter 2-hole black buttons or white scrap felt for eyes; false eyelashes *(optional)*; blusher; 6 tea bags; 3 small snap fasteners; hard pencil; tracing paper; paper for patterns.

DOLLS

Directions:

1. Cutting: For each doll, enlarge the patterns in Fig. III, 10A *(page 136)* onto paper, following the directions on page 241. From the fabric scraps, cut one pair of Knickers pieces and two pairs of Legs. Trace the Face onto tracing paper.

2. Arms: Steep the tea bags in 2 quarts of hot water. Put in the socks to dye them. If you are using nylon socks, take them out almost immediately; cotton will take longer to dye. When the socks are completely dry, draw two arms on one sock for each doll following the diagram in Fig. III, 10B *(page 136)*. Machine-stitch on the drawn lines, and cut out the arms

about ¼ inch beyond the stitch lines. Turn the arms right side out, and stuff them. Turn in the open edges, and slipstitch the opening closed *(see Stitch Guide, page 240)*.

3. Head and Torso: Stuff the other two whole socks, turn in the open edges, and slipstitch the openings closed. Each head/body should be about 10 inches long. Tie the string around each doll at the neck. Sew the top edge of an arm at each side of a body.

4. Knickers: For each doll, unfold the two Knickers pieces, and stitch them, right sides together at the crotch edges. Fold them so that the seams are matched and centered, and stitch both inseams. Turn the Knickers right side out. Pull them over the doll's torso, slipstitch the top edge in place, and stuff the Knickers.

5. Legs: Stitch each pair of Legs together except at the top edge. Turn the Legs right side out and stuff them. Lap the Knickers ½ inch over the tops of the Legs, turn under the raw edges, and slipstitch the Legs to the Knickers securely.

6. Face: Pin a Face tracing to each doll's head, with center fronts matching. Using the sharp, hard pencil, puncture the tracing paper to mark the eye centers, mouth and nose with pencil dots. Using doubled rust sewing thread, make three straight stitches at the mouth and one at each nostril *(see Stitch Guide)*. Brush on a touch of blusher to the cheeks. Sew eyelashes on the girl, if you wish.

7. Eyes: Using the white thread for highlights, sew the black buttons over the eye centers, starting and ending at a side of the head that will be covered by hair. Or draw two whole eyes on the white felt scrap, and use single sewing thread to embroider the eyes with blue, black and white straight stitches *(see photo)*.

8. Hair: Arrange the ladies' synthetic wig, or part of it, on the girl's head and sew it in place. For the boy, assemble three bundles of the yarn, each with fourteen strands 1 yard long. Starting at the center back of the head, draw a spiral up to the

*C*ome bring, with a noise,
My merrie, merrie boys
The Christmas Log to the firing;
While my good dame, she
Bids ye all be free,
And drinke to your heart's desiring.

— ROBERT HERRICK

hairline with the lines about ⅝ inch apart. Starting at one side of the head, carry one bundle along the line, and sew across the yarn at about ½-inch intervals, leaving a loop of yarn about 1 inch high between the stitches. For a short-haired girl doll, follow the same procedure but sew the yarn at about 1-inch intervals.

CLOTHES
Directions
(¼-inch seams allowed):

1. Cutting: From the shoe felt, cut two pairs of Shoe pieces for each doll. For the girl, from the fabric scraps, cut a 10½ x 44-inch skirt rectangle, two pairs of the Bodice Back, and two each of the Bodice Front, Plain Sleeve and Puffy Sleeve. For the boy, add 2 inches to the length of the Bodice Back and Bodice Front patterns. From the jacket fabric, cut two pairs of the Bodice Back, and two each of the Bodice Front and Plain Sleeve. To make the boy's Pants pattern, add ¼ inch all around to the Knickers pattern. From the pants fabric, cut one pair of Pants pieces. From the shoe felt, cut two felt shoe Tongues.

2. Girl's Double Bodice: Stitch one Bodice Front to a pair of Bodice Backs at the shoulders. Repeat. Pin the two Bodices right sides together, and stitch them together at the back and neck edges. Turn the double Bodice right side out, and baste the two layers together at the raw edges.

3. Girl's Sleeves: Sew lace trim to the bottom edge of each Sleeve. Sew a gathering row between the notches of each Puffy Sleeve. Sew each Puffy Sleeve to a Plain Sleeve, right sides up, at the top edge, pulling up the gathers to fit. Pin the Sleeves to the armholes, right sides together, and stitch. Fold the Bodice at the shoulders, right sides together, and stitch the underarm and side seams.

4. Skirt: Stitch the short edges of the skirt together, leaving 3 inches open at the top. Turn in the opening edges, and stitch. Sew a gathering row along the top edge. Pin the top edge of the skirt to the lower

edge of the double Bodice, back edges even, pulling up the gathers to fit.

5. Finishing: Sew the three snap fasteners along the back opening of the double Bodice. Sew on additional lace trim where you wish. If you wish, make a V-neck lace collar with the ladies' lace collar, brought down to the back waist and folded into a V. If you wish, make a round collar with the small doily folded in half and cut out at the center to fit against the neck.

6. Girl's Hat (optional): Gather a yard of 2½-inch-wide lace, and sew it to a child's plastic headband. Sew on fabric flowers and a bow.

7. Boy's Jacket: Sew the boy's jacket together following the directions for the girl's double Bodice in Clothes, Step 2. Sew the jacket Sleeves to the armholes. Fold the jacket at the shoulders, right sides together, and stitch the underarm and side seams. Turn the jacket right side out, and put it on the doll with the opening in front.

8. Boy's Pants: Sew the boy's Pants together following the directions for the Knickers in Doll, Step 4. Turn under a narrow hem at the top and bottom edges.

9. Boy's Scarf: Fold the scarf fabric in half, right sides together, to 4 x 22 inches. Stitch the two long edges together. Turn the scarf right side out, turn in the open edges, and slipstitch the openings closed.

10. Shoes: Pin each pair of Shoe pieces together, and stitch them from the front to the notch. Turn under ⅛ inch at each top edge, and stitch the hem. Stitch each pair of Shoe pieces together from the notch to the top back. Turn the Shoes right side out. For the girl, tie a narrow satin ribbon bow around each ankle. For the boy, fold each shoe Tongue in half (along the broken line on the pattern), slide the raw edges under the front edges of a Shoe, and hand-stitch the Tongue in place along the hem.

FIG. III, 10A
SWEET & SIMPLE SOCK DOLLS

1 SQ. = 1"

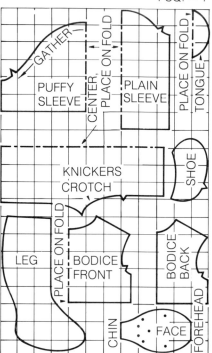

FIG. III, 10B
SWEET & SIMPLE SOCK DOLLS

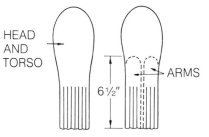

Pierrot and Pierrette Dolls

PIERROT AND PIERRETTE DOLLS

Average: For those with some experience in sewing and doll making.

Materials: 45-inch-wide cotton or polyester/cotton fabric: ¼ yard of pink, and ½ yard of white; ½ yard of 45-inch-wide white polyester crepe-backed satin, or similar fabric; 1 yard of 72-inch wide white nylon tulle (not net); 9 x 12 inches of black felt; 9 x 12 inches of white felt; 3¾ yards of 1-inch-wide old gold cotton fringe; matching sewing threads; 1 pair of girl's size 6-8½ pink stretch socks; 1 pair of girl's size 6-8½ white stretch socks; synthetic stuffing; eleven ¾-inch-diameter black pompons; embroidery floss: Black, Royal Blue and Rose Pink; heavy crochet thread; embroidery needle; upholstery needle; 15 small snap fasteners; 4 small 2-hole buttons; 5-inch square of poster weight cardboard or cereal box; compass; paper for patterns.

DOLLS

Directions

(¼-inch seams allowed):

1. Enlarge the patterns in Fig. III, 11 *(page 139)* onto paper, following the directions on page 241.

2. To make the head, mark a 2¾-inch-diameter circle on the cardboard with the compass, and cut out the circle. Stuff the toe of one sock, white for Pierrot and pink for Pierrette, until you have a round and very firm ball that will just fit through the hole in the cardboard. Tie off the sock directly under the ball with heavy crochet thread to keep the ball firm. Slip the remaining sock over the ball, pull the sock firmly, and tie it off. To make a neck, bind sewing thread around the sock end below the ball for about 1 inch. Cut off the remaining portion of the socks.

3. Cut the fabric doll and clothing pieces from the paper patterns, following the color directions on the patterns. Cut the doll pieces from the cotton or polyester/cotton, the clothing from the satin, the Hat from the white felt, and the Shoes from the black felt.

4. Right sides facing, sew each pair of Leg, Arm and Body pieces together, leaving openings as indicated. Turn the Arms right side out, and stuff them. Sew the top openings closed. Sew each Foot Sole to the bottom of a Leg. Turn the Legs right side out, and stuff them up to the top seam line. Position the front and back seams so that the front seam lies against the back seam. Sew across the top seam line; do not turn in the top seam. Turn in and baste the seam allowance on the neck and bottom edges of the Body. Turn the Body right side out.

5. Wrap the neck end of the head with additional cotton fabric until it fits snugly into the neck opening. Tack the fabric wrap in place. Insert the neck into the neck opening, and sew the top edge of the opening to the head where they meet. Stuff the Body very firmly.

6. Sew the bottom front of the Body to the front of the Legs at the seam allowance. Sew the back of the Body to the back of the Legs, adding stuffing if necessary.

7. To attach the Arms, thread a length of heavy crochet thread on the upholstery needle. Insert the needle through one Arm at the X, through the Body from X to X, and through the second Arm at the X. Thread one of the small buttons on the needle, and return the needle in the opposite direction. Remove the needle, and insert the ends of the thread through a second button. Pull the Arms and Body together very tightly, and knot the thread ends. Cut two quarter-size circles from the Arm fabric, and sew a gathering row along the edges. Gather the circles so the edges turn under. Cover each Arm button with a circle and stitch them in place.

8. Sew the gold fringe around the head for hair. Begin at the hairline and work to the top center, overlapping the fringe so that about ¼ inch of the previous row is visible. For Pierrot, begin the hair rather far back from the face area. For Pierrette, use a lower hairline.

9. For Pierrot, cut one ⅞-inch-diameter circle from the leftover white sock fabric. Gather the circle near the edge, and stuff it. Sew the circle to the face for the nose. For Pierrette's nose, use the pink sock fabric and a ½-inch-diameter circle. Using the photo as a guide, embroider the eyes and mouth with satin and outline stitches *(see Stitch Guide, page 240)*.

PIERROT'S CLOTHES:
Directions:
1. Pants: Sew the front and back crotch seams. Sew the leg seams and hem the legs. Hem the back opening. Pleat the top to fit the doll's waist. Cut a 1½ x 9-inch waistband, and sew it to the pleated edge. Sew a snap fastener to the waistband.

2. Jacket: Treat the lining and Jacket pieces as one. Sew the shoulder and underarm seams. Sew the Sleeves and ease the top of each Sleeve to fit an armhole. Hem the Sleeves, Jacket bottom and front edges. Gather the neck edge to fit the doll. Cut a 1¼-inch-wide satin bias strip, and bind the neck edge with it. Take a tuck on each Sleeve *(see photo)* to raise the front hem to the wrist edge. Sew snap fasteners to the front of the Jacket. Sew three black pompons to the jacket front.

3. Neck Ruffle: Cut two 2-inch-wide tulle strips the full width of the fabric. Place the strips together, all edges even. Gather one long edge to fit the doll's neck. Cut a 1 x 14-inch satin strip. Center the gathered edge of the ruffle on the strip, turn under the strip edges and topstitch. The excess strip ends will become the ties.

4. Hat: Right sides together, sew the back seam. Turn the Hat right side out. Turn up the brim edge ¼ inch, then again 1 inch and press. Sew two black pompons to the center front of the Hat.

5. Shoes: Right sides together, sew the back seams. Sew the shoe tops to the soles. Turn the Shoes right side out.

PIERRETTE'S CLOTHES:
Directions:
1. Underpants: Sew the crotch and leg seams. Make a rolled hem at each leg edge and the back opening. Gather the leg edges to fit the doll's Legs. Pleat the top to fit the doll's waist; sew the pleats.

2. Bodice: Sew the shoulder and underarm seams. Make a rolled hem at the armhole, neck and back edges. Dress the doll in the Underpants and Bodice, and mark the overlap. Remove the clothing. Sew the Bodice and Underpants together, turning in the raw edges. Sew snap fasteners to the back of the suit.

3. Neck Ruffle: Make the neck ruffle following the directions in Pierrot's Clothes, Step 3.

4. Skirt: Cut five 4½-inch-wide tulle strips the full width of the fabric. Place the strips together, and handle them as one strip. Gather the stack along one long edge to fit the doll's waist. Cut a 2-inch-wide satin strip that is 2 inches longer than the doll's waist measurement. Turning under the raw edges, topstitch the waistband to the tulle skirt. Sew two snap fasteners to the waistband. Sew the back seam of the skirt. Sew a black pompon to the center front of the waistband. Using the photo on page 137 as a guide, sew two pompons to the Bodice. Dress the doll.

5. Shoes: Make the Shoes following the directions in Pierrot's Clothing, Step 5, but cut the fronts a little lower. Cut four 24-inch lengths of Black embroidery floss, fold each in half, and attach one to each side of each Shoe. Lace the floss up the legs, knotting the ends at the back.

6. Headband: Cut an 11 x 2½-inch satin strip, and fold it in half lengthwise with right sides together. Sew the long edges, and turn right side out. Fit the headband to the head, allowing a ½-inch overlap plus hems. Hem the short ends. Sew two snap fasteners to the headband. Cut a 2½ x 6-inch satin strip, and fold it lengthwise. Sew the long edge and one short end. Turn the strip right side out, and slipstitch the open short end closed *(see Stitch Guide)*. Fold the strip at the center and sew the strip at the fold to the headband to make ties. Sew three black pompons over the fold as a "knot."

FIG. III, 11   PIERROT AND PIERRETTE DOLLS   1 SQ. = 1"

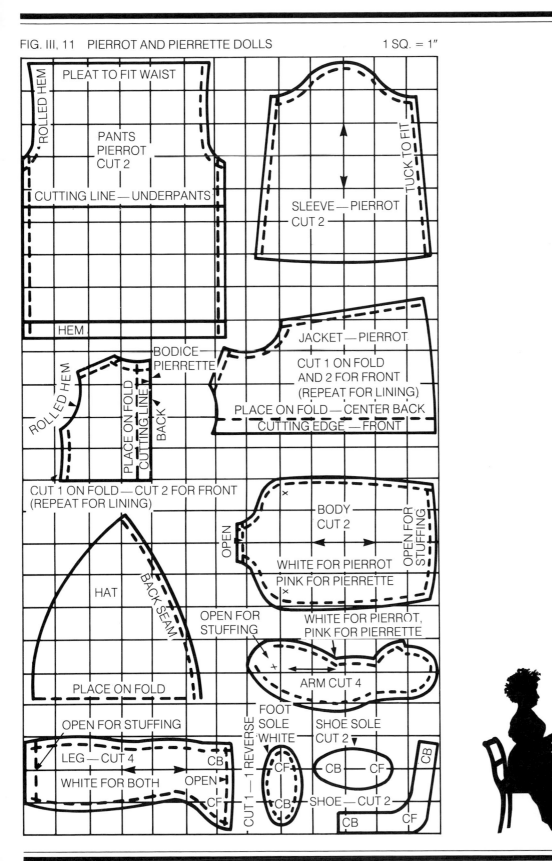

ROLLED HEM

PLEAT TO FIT WAIST

PANTS
PIERROT
CUT 2

CUTTING LINE — UNDERPANTS

HEM

TUCK TO FIT

SLEEVE — PIERROT
CUT 2

ROLLED HEM

BODICE
PIERRETTE

PLACE ON FOLD
CUTTING LINE

BACK

JACKET — PIERROT

CUT 1 ON FOLD
AND 2 FOR FRONT
(REPEAT FOR LINING)
PLACE ON FOLD — CENTER BACK
CUTTING EDGE — FRONT

CUT 1 ON FOLD — CUT 2 FOR FRONT
(REPEAT FOR LINING)

OPEN

BODY
CUT 2

OPEN FOR STUFFING

WHITE FOR PIERROT
PINK FOR PIERRETTE

HAT

BACK SEAM

WHITE FOR PIERROT,
PINK FOR PIERRETTE

OPEN FOR
STUFFING

ARM CUT 4

PLACE ON FOLD

OPEN FOR STUFFING

LEG — CUT 4

WHITE FOR BOTH

CB

OPEN

CF

CUT 1 — 1 REVERSE

FOOT
SOLE
WHITE

CF

CB

SHOE SOLE
CUT 2

CB   CF

SHOE — CUT 2

CB

CF

CB

Stuffed Crown Roast of Pork (recipe, page 147); Butter-Glazed Spinach Dumplings and Sauerkraut Supreme (recipes, page 148); Sweet Red Pepper Soup (recipe, page 146)

A VICTORIAN CHRISTMAS DINNER

Menu for 12

Champagne

*Cream Puffs with Savory Filling**

*Blini with Sour Cream and Caviar**

*Cherry Tomatoes Stuffed with Walnut Pesto**

*Endive with Smoked Salmon Cream Cheese**

*Sweet Red Pepper Soup**

*Stuffed Crown Roast of Pork**

*Sauerkraut Supreme**

*Butter-Glazed Spinach Dumplings**

*Amaretti Oranges**

✳

*Recipe follows

A Victorian Christmas Dinner — Countdown

UP TO 2 WEEKS AHEAD:
— Prepare and freeze the cream puff shells for the Cream Puffs with Savory Filling.
— Prepare the Amaretti Oranges through Step 2; wrap and freeze them.
— Order the Champagne.
— Order the meat for the Stuffed Crown Roast of Pork.
— Prepare and freeze the Walnut Pesto for the Cherry Tomatoes Stuffed with Walnut Pesto.
— Prepare and freeze the Sweet Red Pepper Soup.

1 WEEK AHEAD:
— Prepare and refrigerate the Walnut Pesto for the Cherry Tomatoes Stuffed with Walnut Pesto, if it was not prepared ahead and frozen.
— Prepare and refrigerate the Sweet Red Pepper Soup, if it was not prepared ahead and frozen.

1 OR 2 DAYS AHEAD:
— Prepare and refrigerate the filling for the Cream Puffs with Savory Filling, but do not fill the cream puff shells.
— Prepare and refrigerate the stuffing for the Stuffed Crown Roast of Pork, but do not stuff the pork.
— Prepare the Sauerkraut Supreme through Step 3, and refrigerate it.
— Place the Champagne in the refrigerator to chill.

THE NIGHT BEFORE:
— Thaw the Walnut Pesto, Sweet Red Pepper Soup and the cream puff shells, if they were prepared ahead and frozen.

— Prepare the cream puff shells for Cream Puffs with Savory Filling, if they were not prepared ahead and frozen.
— Prepare and refrigerate the filling for the Endive with Smoked Salmon Cream Cheese.
— Crush the amaretti cookies for the Amaretti Oranges.
— Thaw the spinach, chop the parsley and scallions, and mix dry ingredients for Butter-Glazed Spinach Dumplings.

SEVERAL HOURS BEFORE:
— Prepare the blini batter and the sour cream topping for the Blini with Sour Cream and Caviar.
— Stuff the Crown Roast of Pork, and start roasting it.
— Prepare the Walnut Pesto for the Cherry Tomatoes, if it was not prepared ahead and frozen.

ONE HOUR BEFORE:
— Finish preparing the Endive with Smoked Salmon Cream Cheese and Cherry Tomatoes Stuffed with Walnut Pesto.
— Finish preparing the Sauerkraut Supreme.
— Finish preparing the Cream Puffs with Savory Filling.
— Prepare the Butter-Glazed Spinach Dumplings.

JUST BEFORE DINNER:
— Reheat the Sweet Red Pepper Soup.
— Prepare the Blini with Sour Cream and Caviar.

DURING DINNER:
— Remove the Amaretti Oranges from the freezer ½ hour before serving them. Prepare the amaretto whipped cream, and garnish the Amaretti Oranges with the whipped cream and the crushed amaretti cookies just before serving them.

VICTORIAN SPLENDOR — EVOCATIVE TOUCHES

Place doilies on top of plates, then place first course bowls or salad plates on top of the doilies.

✳

To decorate a plain cake, such as gingerbread, cover it with a doily and sprinkle with 10X (confectioners' powdered) sugar. Carefully remove the doily and the sugar will remain in a lovely, lacy pattern.

Before dessert, serve a "savory" — a palate-livening nibble. Try olives baked in a rich cheese dough, or mushrooms sautéed in Madeira sauce served over toast circles.

✳

After dinner, serve port wine and Victorian-style sweetmeats, such as marzipan, or chocolate rum truffles.

CREAM PUFFS
WITH SAVORY FILLING

Bake at 425° for 10 minutes, then at 375° for
20 minutes and at 325° for 5 minutes.
Reheat at 350° for 5 minutes.
Makes 25 appetizer cream puffs.

Cream Puff Shells:
- 1   cup water
- ½   cup (1 stick) unsalted butter, sliced
- ½   teaspoon sugar
- ¼   teaspoon salt
- 1   cup all-purpose flour
- 4   eggs

Glaze:
- 1   egg beaten with 1 teaspoon water

Savory Filling:
- 10   medium onions, thinly sliced (about 7½ cups)
- ½   cup (1 stick) unsalted butter
- 1   bottle (750 ml.) dry white wine
- ¼   cup dry-cured olives (such as Greek olives),
       finely chopped
- 1   teaspoon fresh thyme, finely chopped
       OR: ½ teaspoon dried thyme, crumbled

1. Preheat the oven to hot (425°). Lightly grease
2 baking sheets, or line the sheets with parchment
paper, and set them aside.
2. Prepare the Cream Puff Shells: Combine the water,
butter, sugar and salt in a small, heavy saucepan over
medium-high heat until the butter melts. Remove the
saucepan from the heat. Add the flour all at once,
stirring with a wooden spoon until the mixture is
smooth. Return the saucepan to high heat and stir
constantly until the dough forms a smooth mass and
leaves a thin film on the sides of the saucepan. Transfer
the dough to a bowl and let it cool slightly. Add the
eggs, one at a time, beating with the spoon after each
addition until the dough is smooth and glossy.
3. Spoon the dough into a pastry bag fitted with a plain
½-inch tip. Pipe the dough onto the prepared baking
sheets, making mounds that are 1 inch in diameter and
¾ inch high. Space the dough mounds 1 inch apart.

Lightly brush the Glaze over the tops of the dough
mounds, smoothing the tops slightly.
4. Bake the puff shells in the preheated hot oven
(425°) for 10 minutes. Lower the oven temperature to
moderate (375°), and bake the puff shells until they are
golden brown, for 20 minutes. Lower the oven
temperature to slow (325°) and bake the puff shells
until they are firm, for 5 minutes more. Cool the puff
shells on a wire rack.
5. Prepare the Savory Filling: Sauté the onions in the
butter in a very large skillet over low heat, covered,
until they are wilted but not browned, for 35 minutes.
Add half of the wine, raise the heat to medium-low and
cook the mixture, uncovered, until the liquid has
evaporated. Add the remaining wine and cook the
mixture until all the liquid has evaporated, for 25 to
30 minutes. Add the olives and thyme, and cook until
all the liquid has evaporated, for 10 minutes more.
6. At serving time, reheat the puff shells in a preheated
moderate oven (350°) for about 5 minutes. Cut off the
top third from each puff shell. Fill each puff shell with
the warm Filling. (Leftover Savory Filling makes an
excellent side dish for roast meats or poultry.)

THE PERFECT PUFF

*Never use whipped butter or margarine or a diet
substitute to make the dough, since they have a
higher water and air content.*

✳

*Add the flour all at once, and stir it into the boiling
liquid until it is thoroughly blended.*

✳

*Don't be alarmed if eggs added to the mixture
cause it to separate. A bit more stirring will
incorporate the eggs and make the dough shiny
and supple.*

✳

*Once made, the dough should be rapidly spooned
out and baked in a preheated oven.*

BLINI WITH SOUR CREAM AND CAVIAR

Makes 70 blini.

1 package (¼ ounce) active dry yeast
½ cup warm water (105° to 115°)*
1 cup milk, scalded and cooled
1 cup all-purpose flour
½ cup buckwheat flour
3 eggs, separated
½ teaspoon salt
⅛ teaspoon sugar
½ cup (1 stick) unsalted butter, melted
1 cup dairy sour cream
1 tablespoon chopped fresh dillweed
1 teaspoon grated onion
½ cup red caviar

1. Combine the yeast and the warm water in a small bowl. Let the mixture stand until it is foamy, for 5 minutes. Place the yeast mixture in the container of an electric blender or food processor along with the milk, the all-purpose and buckwheat flours, egg yolks, salt, sugar and 6 tablespoons of the melted butter. Blend the mixture for 40 seconds. Scrape down the sides of the container and blend until the mixture is smooth, for about 10 seconds more. Pour the mixture into a large bowl. Cover the bowl and let the batter rise in a warm place, away from drafts, just until it is light and bubbly, for no more than 1½ to 2 hours.
2. Meanwhile, combine the sour cream, dillweed and grated onion in a small bowl until the mixture is well blended. Cover the bowl and refrigerate the sour cream mixture.
3. Just before serving time, beat the egg whites in a small bowl until stiff peaks form. Fold the beaten egg whites into the batter.
4. Heat a heavy skillet or griddle over medium heat. Brush the skillet lightly with some of the remaining melted butter. Drop the batter by measuring tablespoonfuls onto the hot skillet. When the bottoms of the blini are lightly browned, turn the blini over and cook them briefly. Repeat the process with the remaining batter, brushing the pan occasionally with the melted butter. Garnish with the sour cream mixture and the red caviar.
***Note:** Warm water should feel tepid when dropped on your wrist.*

CHERRY TOMATOES STUFFED WITH WALNUT PESTO

Makes 40 stuffed cherry tomatoes.

40 cherry tomatoes
¼ cup Walnut Pesto (recipe follows)
4 ounces orzo or egg pastina
¼ cup walnuts, finely chopped
2 tablespoons grated Parmesan cheese

1. Cut off the tops of the cherry tomatoes and spoon out the seeds and the pulp. Invert the cherry tomatoes onto a wire rack or paper toweling to let them drain. Refrigerate the drained cherry tomatoes.
2. Cook the orzo or pastina following the package directions. Drain the pasta.
3. Combine the pasta with the Walnut Pesto. Fill each cherry tomato with the Walnut Pesto mixture. Sprinkle the tops of the stuffed tomatoes with the chopped walnuts and Parmesan cheese.

Walnut Pesto: Combine ¾ cup of firmly packed fresh basil (or fresh parsley and 1 tablespoon of dried basil), 2 tablespoons of walnut or olive oil, ⅓ cup of grated Parmesan cheese, 1 clove of garlic, ¼ cup of chopped walnuts, ⅛ teaspoon of salt and ⅛ teaspoon of freshly ground pepper in the container of an electric blender or food processor. Whirl or process the mixture to combine the ingredients. With the motor running, add 4 tablespoons more of walnut or olive oil, pouring the oil in a thin stream until the pesto is smooth.

Blini with Sour Cream and Caviar (recipe, page 144); Endive with Smoked Salmon Cream Cheese (recipe, page 146); Cream Puffs with Savory Filling (recipe, page 143); Cherry Tomatoes Stuffed with Walnut Pesto (recipe, page 144)

ENDIVE WITH SMOKED SALMON CREAM CHEESE

Makes 40 appetizer servings.

3   packages (3 ounces each) cream cheese with chives, at room temperature
2   ounces smoked salmon
3   tablespoons heavy cream OR: whipping cream
1   teaspoon lemon juice
1/4 teaspoon grated lemon zest (yellow part of rind only)
1/8 teaspoon freshly ground white pepper
4   heads Belgian endive
    Watercress leaves, for garnish (optional)

1. Combine the cream cheese, salmon, heavy or whipping cream, lemon juice, lemon zest and white pepper in the container of a food processor, and whirl to combine all the ingredients. Refrigerate the cream cheese mixture for at least 30 minutes.
2. Wipe the endive with damp paper toweling. Cut a thin slice from the bottom of each. Break off the leaves at the base. Place the leaves in a plastic bag and refrigerate the endive.
3. No more than 1 hour before serving, soften the cream cheese mixture by stirring it with a wooden spoon. Spoon the cream cheese mixture into a pastry bag fitted with a leaf tip. Pipe the cream cheese mixture down the center of each endive leaf. Garnish with the watercress, if you wish.

ENDIVE: LEAVES OF CLASS

While Belgian or French endive (also known as witloof chicory) is more available today than in the past, it still is fairly expensive. Luckily, a little goes a long way. Leaves can be separated, washed and filled to make a tasty appetizer. Endive also can be shredded for salad or braised whole, topped with a cheese sauce and baked.

SWEET RED PEPPER SOUP

Makes 12 servings.

4   large onions, coarsely chopped
8   shallots, chopped
4   cloves garlic, finely chopped
1/2 cup (1 stick) unsalted butter
8   large carrots, peeled and thinly sliced
3   baking potatoes (8 ounces each), peeled and thinly sliced
12 sweet red peppers (3 pounds), cored, seeded and coarsely chopped
11 cups chicken stock OR: canned chicken broth
2   tablespoons chopped fresh parsley
1/4 teaspoon salt
1/4 teaspoon freshly ground pepper
    Crème fraîche OR: dairy sour cream, for garnish (optional)

1. Combine the onions, shallots and garlic with the butter in a large Dutch oven. Cook the mixture, uncovered, over medium heat until the vegetables are wilted, for 10 minutes.
2. Add the carrots and cook for 10 minutes. Add the potatoes and the red peppers, and cook the mixture for 10 minutes more.
3. Add the stock or broth and the parsley. Bring the mixture to boiling over medium heat. Lower the heat and simmer the soup until the vegetables are just tender, for 15 minutes. Season the soup with the salt and black pepper.
4. Working in batches, purée the soup in the container of a food processor. Reheat the soup gently to serving temperature. Garnish with the crème fraîche or sour cream, if you wish.

STUFFED CROWN ROAST OF PORK

Roast at 375° for 2½ to 3 hours.
Makes 12 servings.

Stuffing:
1 cup onion, finely chopped
1 cup celery, finely chopped
1 tablespoon chopped fresh rosemary
½ cup (1 stick) unsalted butter
1 large carrot, shredded
¾ pound small white onions, peeled
8 cups cubed white bread (about 16 slices)
8 ounces dried pitted prunes
4 ounces dried apricots
4 ounces golden raisins
1 cup chicken stock OR: canned chicken broth
½ cup dry red wine
1 teaspoon ground cinnamon
½ teaspoon freshly ground pepper
¼ teaspoon salt

Crown Roast of Pork:
1 tablespoon chopped fresh rosemary
½ teaspoon salt
1 crown roast of pork (about 7 pounds)

1. Preheat the oven to moderate (375°). Line a roasting pan large enough to hold the crown roast of pork with aluminum foil. Set aside the roasting pan.
2. Prepare the Stuffing: Sauté the onion, celery and rosemary in ¼ cup of the butter in a skillet over medium heat, stirring occasionally, until the vegetables are softened, for about 7 minutes. Transfer the mixture to a large bowl and add the carrot.
3. Sauté the small white onions in the remaining ¼ cup of butter in a large skillet over medium heat until they are lightly browned, for 5 minutes. Add the onions to the mixture in the bowl along with the bread cubes, prunes, apricots, raisins, chicken stock or broth, wine, cinnamon, pepper and salt.

4. Prepare the Crown Roast of Pork: Combine the rosemary and the salt. Place the pork in the prepared roasting pan. Rub the rosemary mixture over the pork. Spoon half of the stuffing mixture into the center of the crown of pork. Cover the ends of the bones and the stuffing with aluminum foil to prevent over-browning. Spoon any remaining stuffing mixture into an 8 x 8 x 2-inch baking dish and cover the dish with aluminum foil.
5. Roast the pork in the preheated moderate oven (375°) until a thermometer inserted into the roast without touching a bone registers 160°, for 2½ to 3 hours. Place the extra stuffing in the oven during the last 45 minutes of roasting time. Let the roast stand for 15 minutes before carving it.

SAUERKRAUT SUPREME

Makes 12 servings.

4 slices bacon, cut in 1-inch pieces
¼ cup (½ stick) unsalted butter
1 large onion, chopped
2 large tart apples, peeled, cored and chopped
4 pounds sauerkraut, drained
1½ teaspoons caraway seeds
¾ pound mushrooms, stems trimmed
      and thinly sliced
½ head green cabbage (1 pound), cored and finely
      shredded (6 cups)
¼ cup Calvados OR: apple brandy OR: cider

1. Sauté the bacon in a large Dutch oven until it is crisp, for 7 minutes. Remove the bacon with a slotted spoon to paper toweling to drain.
2. Add 2 tablespoons of the butter to the bacon fat in the Dutch oven. Add the onion and the apple, and sauté them for 10 minutes. Add the sauerkraut and the caraway seeds, and cook the mixture, covered, over medium-low heat for 20 minutes.
3. Sauté the mushrooms in the remaining 2 tablespoons of butter in a large skillet until they are browned, for 5 minutes.
4. Add the shredded cabbage, mushrooms, Calvados or apple brandy or cider, and the reserved bacon to the Dutch oven and stir to combine the ingredients. Simmer the sauerkraut until the cabbage is wilted.

LIGHT-AS-AIR DUMPLINGS

Dumplings should be mixed quickly and gently for feather-light results. To get a head start making Spinach Dumplings, mix all of the dry ingredients in one bowl. In another bowl, blend the sour cream with the eggs, spinach, parsley and scallion. Set both bowls aside. At cooking time, add the melted butter to the egg mixture, then combine the egg and flour mixtures.

BUTTER-GLAZED SPINACH DUMPLINGS

Makes 24 dumplings.

2 packages (10 ounces each) chopped
      frozen spinach
3 cups sifted cake flour (not self-rising)
1 cup sifted all-purpose flour
2 teaspoons salt
1 teaspoon baking powder
1 cup dairy sour cream
4 eggs, slightly beaten
1 cup (2 sticks) butter, melted
⅓ cup chopped parsley
⅓ cup finely chopped scallions

1. Prepare the spinach, following the package directions. Drain the spinach in a colander set over a bowl, pressing the spinach with a spoon to extract as much liquid as possible. Let the spinach cool.
2. Sift together the cake and all-purpose flours, the salt and baking powder in a medium-size bowl.
3. Beat together the sour cream, eggs, ½ cup of the melted butter, spinach, parsley and scallions in a small bowl. Make a well in the center of the dry ingredients. Pour the sour cream mixture into the well, and stir just until all the ingredients are blended.
4. Butter a large heatproof plate. Place the plate on a wire rack in a saucepan. Pour water into the saucepan until it is just under the level of the wire rack. Bring the water to a simmer over medium heat. Dip a tablespoon in a cup of hot tap water and spoon heaping tablespoons of the dumpling batter onto the plate, spacing the dumplings 2 inches apart. Cover the saucepan and steam the dumplings until they are set, for 10 minutes.
5. Transfer the dumplings to a heated platter and drizzle with the remaining ½ cup of melted butter.

AMARETTI ORANGES

Makes 12 servings.

12 large navel oranges
24 double-packaged amaretti cookies
        (48 small cookies total)
13 pints chocolate-chocolate chip ice cream
1½ cups heavy cream
3 tablespoons amaretto

1. Cut off a half-inch slice from the top of each orange. Carefully remove the pulp and reserve it for another use. Invert the orange "cups" onto paper toweling and refrigerate them.

2. Place 24 amaretti cookies (12 packs) in the container of a food processor or electric blender and pulse-chop until they are fine crumbs. Pack the crumbs onto the inside bottom of each orange cup. Scoop generous portions of the ice cream into the cups, packing the ice cream well and mounding it to a firm round shape. Crush one amaretti cookie and press the crumbs firmly over the top of the ice cream in a cup. Repeat with the remaining orange cups, ice cream and 11 cookies. Wrap each orange cup tightly in aluminum foil and freeze them until serving time.

3. Half an hour before serving time, remove the orange cups from the freezer. Whip the cream with the amaretto until the mixture forms stiff peaks. Unwrap the orange cups and pipe the amaretto cream on top of the ice cream in a decorative swirl. Crumble the remaining 12 amaretti cookies and sprinkle the crumbs over the amaretto cream swirls for garnish.

$\mathcal{H}$eap on more
wood! — the wind is chill;
But let it whistle as it will,
We'll keep our Christmas
merry still.

— SIR WALTER SCOTT

CHAPTER 4

OLD-FASHIONED FESTIVITIES

All hearts come home for Christmas.

The hallmark of an old-fashioned Christmas is simplicity of style: no frills, no flounces, just handmade projects with the flavor of home.

In true pioneer tradition, we have crafts to keep you occupied during winter's chilly nights. A cross stitched tree skirt, poinsettia afghan, and a ring of angels carousel are just some of the ways to decorate your home. You can trim your tree with simply styled ornaments like our easy-to-stitch Bargello tree, or add homespun holiday touches by creating a colorful cross stitch stocking or building a winter window box for your feathered friends.

The kids will love our ready-for-action wooden toys. They roll, they float, they stand up to heavy-duty kid power. And for the bigger kids: a gameboard stitched in needlepoint and framed in wood.

For more homespun ideas, take your cue from our photo at left. Place colorful Indian blankets on the sofa, set out some showy red flowers, display orange pomanders, hang giant chocolate chip cookies and strands of cranberries on the tree. Remember, Christmas starts at home—with a smile, a good wish, a heartfelt hug. We wish you all the wonder and magic of an old-fashioned Christmas.

TURNING BACK THE CLOCK

*Simple decorations—many crafted from natural materials—
recall the days when everything was made by hand.*

A Ring of Angels Carousel

A RING OF ANGELS CAROUSEL

Average: For those with some experience in woodworking.

Materials: 8-inch-diameter, ¾-inch-thick pine base; 7½ inches of ½-inch-diameter dowel; balsa wood planks: ¹⁄₃₂-inch, ¹⁄₁₆-inch, ⅛-inch and ¼-inch thick *(see* Fig. IV, 1A *for amounts)*; ¹⁄₁₆-inch-thick basswood plank; 1 inch of ¼-inch-diameter copper tubing; 1 finishing nail; 1 common nail with ¼-inch head; sewing thread; epoxy glue or solder; white glue; dark pine and light oak wood stains; varnish; graphite paper; stylus or old ballpoint pen; sandpaper; paper for patterns; 4 angel chime candles; drill router *(optional)*; drill with ⅜- and ½-inch bits; hammer; metal file; fine saw; sharp knife or razor blade; hacksaw; soldering iron *(optional)*.

Directions:

1. Enlarge the patterns in Fig. IV, 1A onto paper, following the directions on page 241. Using the graphite paper and stylus or old ballpoint pen, trace the rotor blade pattern onto the basswood for a total of eight blades, and the remaining patterns as noted in Fig. IV, 1A onto the balsa wood. Cut out the wood pieces. Also cut four ¼ x ⅜ x 1¼-inch stands for the standing angels from the balsa wood. If you wish, route a decorative groove on the edge of the round pine base *(see photo and* Fig. IV, 1B*)*. Use the white glue when gluing wood pieces. Assemble the flying, top and standing angels with glue following the diagram in Fig. IV, 1B.

2. Drill a ½-inch-deep, ½-inch-diameter hole in the center of the base. Drill four ⅜-inch-deep, ⅜-inch-diameter holes 1⅜ inches from the center hole and 90° apart *(see* Fig. IV, 1B*)*.

3. Glue the dowel post into the center hole in the base. Glue the tree sections to the post and base at right angles between the candle holes.

4. Tap the finishing nail about ¼ inch into

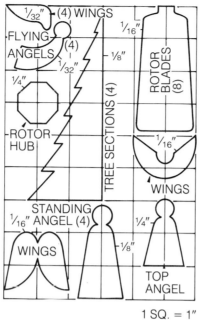

FIG. IV, 1A   A RING OF ANGELS CAROUSEL CUTTING DIAGRAMS

¹⁄₃₂″ (4) WINGS
FLYING ANGELS (4)
¹⁄₃₂″
¼″
ROTOR HUB
STANDING ¹⁄₁₆″ ANGEL (4)
WINGS
¹⁄₁₆″
⅛″
TREE SECTIONS (4)
ROTOR BLADES (8)
¹⁄₁₆″
WINGS
¼″
⅛″
TOP ANGEL

1 SQ. = 1″

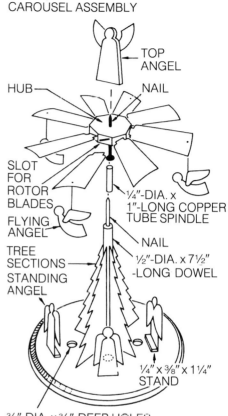

FIG. IV, 1B   A RING OF ANGELS CAROUSEL ASSEMBLY

TOP ANGEL
HUB
NAIL
SLOT FOR ROTOR BLADES
FLYING ANGEL
TREE SECTIONS
STANDING ANGEL
¼″-DIA. x 1″-LONG COPPER TUBE SPINDLE
NAIL
½″-DIA. x 7½″-LONG DOWEL
¼″ x ⅜″ x 1¼″ STAND
⅜″-DIA. x ⅜″-DEEP HOLES FOR CANDLES

the top center of the dowel post. Remove the nail, and file the head to a sharp point. Replace the nail in the post.

5. To make the spindle for the rotor hub, drill or tap an indentation in the center of the common nail head. Glue, with epoxy glue, or solder the nail head to one end of the copper tubing. Shorten the nail to ½ inch and sharpen the cut end.

6. Cut a diagonal groove in each face of the rotor hub, and glue the rotor blades into the hub grooves *(see* Fig. IV, 1B*)*.

7. Stain the base, rotor blades, rotor hub, all the angel bodies and the standing angel stands light oak. Stain the trees, dowel post and angel wings dark pine. Varnish all the pieces.

8. Push the spindle with the nail through the center of the rotor hub. Mount the top angel on the nail point.

9. Make a pinhole in each flying angel wing and in alternate rotor blades *(see* Fig. IV, 1B*)*. Cut four equal lengths of thread. Attach a length of thread to each flying angel wing through the pinhole, and attach the flying angel threads to the alternate rotor blades through the pinholes *(see* Fig. IV, 1B*)*.

10. Place the rotor on top of the sharpened nail in the dowel post. Insert candles into the candle holes. When you light the candles, the heat will cause the carousel to turn.

*O*ne Christmas was so
much like another, in those
years around the seatown
corner now and out of all
sound except the distant
speaking of the voices I
sometimes hear a moment
before sleep, that I can never
remember whether it
snowed for six days and six
nights when I was twelve or
whether it snowed for twelve
days and twelve nights when
I was six.

— DYLAN THOMAS

TINY TREASURES TREE

*These lovely and unique decorations are
made from seeds and beans you probably
have in the pantry. Add pretty bows of
embroidered ribbon and tiny white lights,
if you wish.*

SEED NOSEGAYS

Easy: Achievable by anyone.

Materials: 5-inch-diameter nosegay
holders or white paper doilies; pumpkin
seeds; popping corn; mustard seeds;
poppy seeds; one roll of red streamer
crepe paper; plastic boxwood sprigs; red
stemmed berries *(available in craft and
floral supply stores)*; yellow stamens; tie
wire; floral tape; white glue; floral wire;
1-inch-diameter Styrofoam® balls; stiff
paper; silicone glue.

Directions:

1. Roses: Fold the streamer crepe paper
in half lengthwise, and cut off a 14-inch
length. Gather the paper by hand, rolling
it up along the folded edge, and fluffing
the unfolded edge as needed to
accommodate the flower's fullness. Wrap
tie wire around the gathered edge,
leaving the wire ends long enough to
form a stem. With floral tape, wrap the
stem against a length of floral wire.

2. Corn Flowers: Cut a circle of stiff
paper the size of a dime. Make a small
hole in the center. Cover the paper with
silicone glue, and insert a stemmed red
berry in the hole. Attach corn kernels
onto the glue-covered paper like flower
petals. For the stem, use floral tape to
wrap the berry stem against a length of
floral wire.

3. Pumpkin Seed Flowers: Cut a piece
of stiff paper the size of a nickel. Follow
the corn flower directions in Step 2, using
pumpkin seeds instead of corn kernels,
and adding yellow stamens.

4. Mustard and Poppy Seed Pods:
Dip one end of a length of floral wire in
silicone glue, and push the glued wire
end into a 1-inch-diameter Styrofoam ball.
Cover the ball with white glue, and dip it
into mustard seeds or poppy seeds. Cover
the floral wire stem with floral tape.

5. Assembling the Nosegay: Into each
nosegay holder or doily, insert two each
of the roses, pumpkin seed flowers and
corn flowers, and one each of the poppy
seed pods and mustard seed pods. Also
insert four sprigs of boxwood. Wrap the
stems together with floral tape. Wire the
nosegay to the tree.

ELEGANT EGGS

Easy: Achievable by anyone.

Materials: Eggs; yellow split peas;
green split peas; mung beans; lentils;
barley; darning needle or ice pick; mylar
string; white glue.

Directions:

1. Make a small hole with the darning
needle or ice pick in each end of each
eggshell, making sure to pierce the
membrane, and blow out the eggs. Rinse
and dry the shells.

2. For each shell, run a 6-inch-long
double strand of mylar through the holes.
Knot the mylar at both ends, leaving a
2-inch loop at the large end of the shell
for a hanger.

3. Glue rows of lentils, yellow and green
split peas, mung beans and barley to each
eggshell. Use the photo as a design guide,
or create your own patterns and designs.

Tiny Treasures Tree

BARGELLO TREE ORNAMENT

Easy: Achievable by anyone.

Materials: 8 x 9 inches of 10-mesh interlock needlepoint canvas; masking tape; Persian yarn (10-yard skein): 1 skein each of Olive Green, White and Red; tapestry needle; 21 red glass "E" beads, or any other 4-mm beads; fabric scrap for backing; matching sewing thread; heavy thread; synthetic stuffing.

Directions:

1. Cover the edges of the canvas with the masking tape. Use 3-ply strands of the yarn, separating the three plies and putting them back together again before starting to stitch. Use long, vertical stitches throughout.

2. Stitch the design in FIG. IV, 2, following the color key in the diagram, and taking care to keep the yarn flat as you work.

3. Steam the canvas lightly to block it.

4. Sew one red bead to each point of each Olive Green triangle, including the points on the bottom and side edges *(see photo)*.

5. Trim the canvas to ¼ inch all around, and clip the corners. Fold the excess canvas to the back of the stitchery. Overcast the edges of the tree in Olive Green, and the edges of the base in Red. Cut a 9-inch length of heavy thread, fold it in half, and attach the raw ends to the top of the tree to make a loop for a hanger. Cut the fabric scrap in the shape of the ornament plus ½ inch all around. Fold under the fabric ¼ inch on each edge, and pin it in place. Stitch the fabric backing to the needlepoint ornament, leaving the bottom open. Stuff the ornament lightly, and stitch the bottom edge closed.

FIG. IV, 2 BARGELLO TREE ORNAMENT

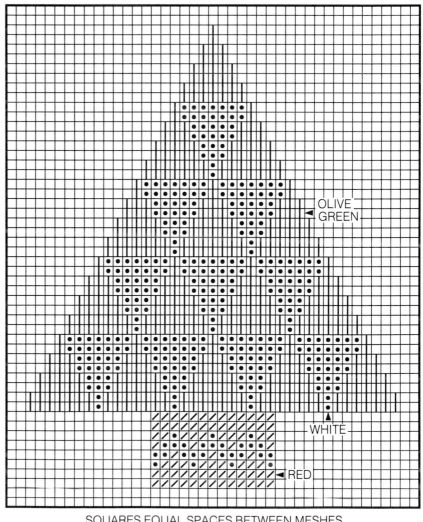

SQUARES EQUAL SPACES BETWEEN MESHES

WINTER WINDOW BOX

A beautiful decoration for your holiday home, this also provides a welcome treat for birds during the hard winter months.

Easy: Achievable by anyone.

Materials: Wood window box; holly branches; pine branches; floral foam or soil; floral wire; wooden picks; pine cones; peanut butter or suet; halved apples; halved oranges; sunflower seeds or bird seed in small dishes *(optional).*

Directions:
1. Line a window box with the floral foam or soil. Arrange the holly and pine branches to fill the box.
2. Spread the pine cones with the peanut butter or suet. Wire the pine cones to wooden picks, and insert the pine cones into the floral foam.
3. Wire the apple and orange halves to wooden picks, and insert the fruit halves into the floral foam.
4. If you wish, place small dishes filled with sunflower seeds or birdseed among the holly and pine branches.

PRANCING REINDEER TREE SKIRT

Average: For those with some experience in sewing and counted cross stitch.

Materials: 1⅜ yards of 52-inch-wide red burlap; 1⅜ yards of 52-inch-wide backing fabric; matching thread; 5¼ yards of white covered cording; worsted knitting yarn: 165 yards of White, 38 yards of Emerald, 10 yards of Dark Green and 4 yards of Yellow; 4 snap fasteners; tapestry needle.
Note: *The diagram below has the trees worked in white; as an alternative, work the trees in Emerald Green as shown in the photo on page 159.*

Directions:
1. Cut a 3-inch strip from one selvage of the burlap, and cut the strip in half widthwise. Cut a slit from the center of the burlap to the center of one side edge. Stitch half the 3-inch strip to one side of the slit. Stay stitch all the edges of the burlap to prevent raveling.
2. Fold the burlap in half to find the center, and baste a line across the center. Repeat, folding the burlap in the other direction. You will begin stitching at the center of one side *(see* FIG. IV, 3*)*, 2 inches in from the edge of the burlap. Using the tapestry needle and worsted yarn, and following the color key below, work all cross stitches over three threads of burlap. Cross stitch around the work, being careful not to miscount threads. Work all the crosses in the same direction, with all the underneath stitches going in one direction, and all the top stitches going in the opposite direction *(see Stitch Guide, page 240).* To begin and end strands, catch the yarn under the

stitches on the back of the work. Make yellow French knots for the poinsettia centers *(see Stitch Guide).*
3. When the embroidery is completed, place the burlap face down and iron it, using a damp pressing cloth. Round the corners of the burlap. Baste or stitch the white cording to the right side of the burlap, along the stitch line on the outer edge, using a ½-inch seam allowance.
4. Prepare the backing fabric the same way you prepared the burlap. Pin the backing to the burlap, right sides together, and stitch, using a ½-inch seam allowance. Leave the underneath side of the slit open.
5. To form an opening for the tree trunk, cut a 3½-inch square in the center of the tree skirt. Clip the corners of the square, and turn the skirt right side out. Turn the edges of the cut square between the layers. Topstitch the burlap and backing together along the slit, and around the trunk opening. Sew the four snap fasteners along the slit. Press the skirt.

FIG. IV, 3 PRANCING REINDEER TREE SKIRT

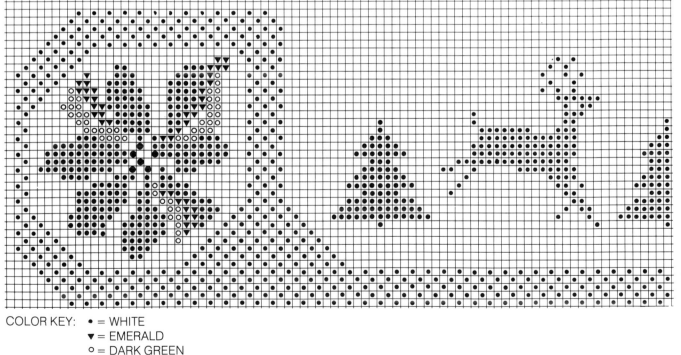

COLOR KEY: • = WHITE
▼ = EMERALD
○ = DARK GREEN
● = YELLOW FRENCH KNOTS

Prancing Reindeer Tree Skirt

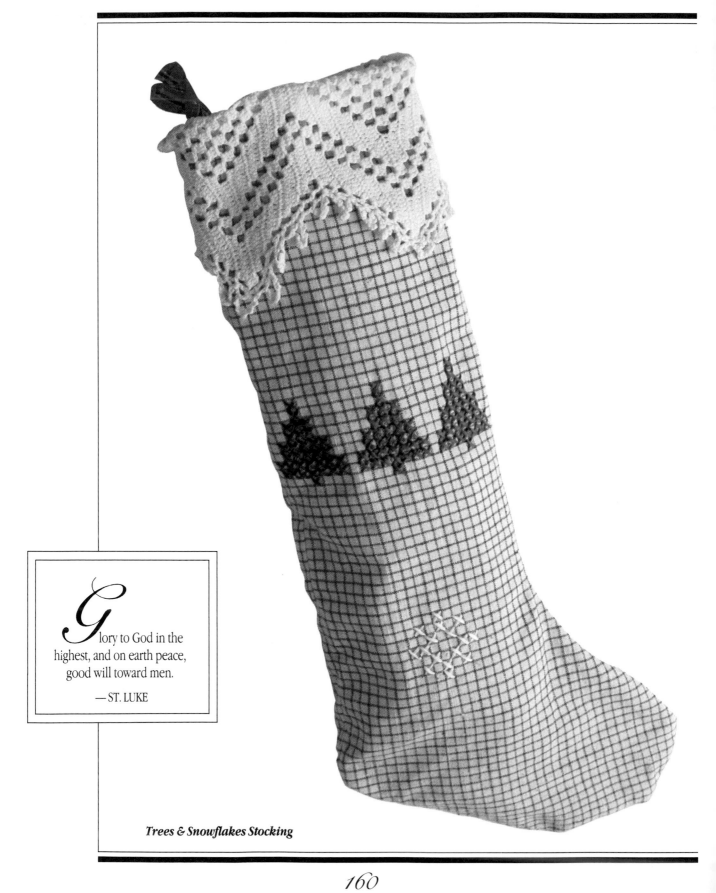

*G*lory to God in the
highest, and on earth peace,
good will toward men.

— ST. LUKE

Trees & Snowflakes Stocking

TREES & SNOWFLAKES STOCKING

Average: For those with some experience in sewing and cross stitch.

Materials: ½ yard of checked fabric; ½ yard of muslin; 15 inches of lace trim; matching threads; embroidery floss: 1 skein each of Green and White; embroidery needle; embroidery hoop; 4 inches of 1-inch-wide red and green plaid ribbon; paper for pattern.

Directions:

1. Enlarge the stocking pattern in Fig. IV, 4 onto paper, following the directions on page 241. Cut out the paper pattern.

2. Using the paper pattern, trace the outline of the stocking shape on the checked fabric two times, turning over the pattern to make the stocking back. Do not cut out the stockings. Place the fabric in the embroidery hoop. Using the embroidery needle and the Green and White floss, cross stitch the trees and snowflakes in Figs. IV, 4A and 4B onto the checked stockings. Use the photo as a placement guide for the snowflakes and trees. There should be one cross stitch per check *(see Stitch Guide, page 240).*

3. When the embroidery is finished, cut out the stockings from the checked fabric. Using the paper pattern, cut out two stockings from the muslin. Leave a ½-inch seam allowance all around on all the stocking pieces.

4. Pin the checked stockings right sides together, and stitch a ½-inch seam all around the stocking except at the straight top edge. Trim the seam, clip the curves, turn the stocking right side out, and press. Repeat with the muslin pieces, leaving a 3-inch opening in the toe. Trim the seam and clip the curves, but do not turn the muslin stocking right side out.

5. Stitch together the short ends of the lace trim. Slide the stocking into the lining, right sides together. Slide the lace trim between the stocking and lining with top edges and back seams matching. Fold

the ribbon in half, and place it between the stocking and trim on the back seam, with the ends matching the top edge of the stocking. Stitch around the top of the stocking. Turn the stocking right side out through the toe opening, and slipstitch the opening closed *(see Stitch Guide).* Tack the lining to the stocking, and press

FIG. IV, 4   TREES & SNOWFLAKE STOCKING   1 SQ. = ½"

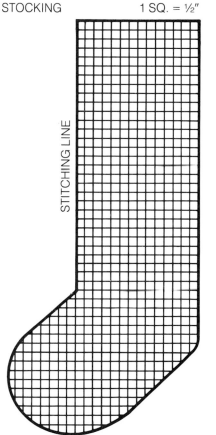

STITCHING LINE

FIG. IV, 4B
CROSS STITCH
SNOWFLAKE

FIG. IV, 4A   CROSS STITCH TREES

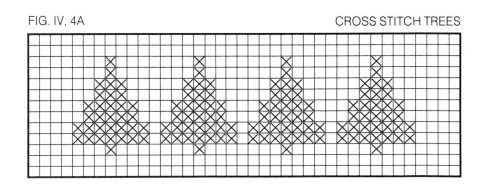

*'T*was the night
before Christmas, when all
through the house
Not a creature was stirring —
not even a mouse;
The stockings were hung by
the chimney with care,
In hopes that St. Nicholas
soon would be there.

— CLEMENT CLARKE MOORE

SUGARPLUM STOCKING

Average: For those with some experience in sewing.

Materials: ⅜ yard of red calico print; ⅜ yard of yellow broadcloth; ⅜ yard of muslin; ⅛ yard of blue calico print; ⅛ yard of yellow calico print; ⅛ yard of green calico print; ⅛ yard of yellow small print fabric; matching threads; ⅜ yard of synthetic batting; ½ yard of ½-inch-diameter yellow ball fringe; ¼ yard of ¼-inch-wide red satin ribbon; paper.

Directions
(½-inch seams allowed):
1. Enlarge the patterns in FIG. IV, 5 onto paper, following directions on page 241.
2. Cutting: From the red calico, cut one stocking front, one 5 x 16½-inch cuff facing, and six 2 x 5-inch strips. *From the yellow broadcloth,* cut a stocking back. *From the blue calico,* cut six 3 x 5-inch strips. *From the yellow calico,* cut five 2 x 5-inch strips. *From the green calico,* cut two 3 x 5-inch strips. *From the yellow print fabric,* cut two 2 x 5-inch strips. *From the muslin and batting,* cut a pair of stockings and a 5 x 16½-inch cuff strip each.
3. Patchwork: Piece together the 5-inch strips, and stitch them along their long edges. Press the seams open. Using the paper patterns, cut one heel and one toe from the patchwork. Also cut one 5 x 16½-inch patchwork cuff strip.
4. Stocking Front: Layer one batting stocking between the red calico stocking and one muslin stocking. Baste them together around the edges. Press under the straight edges of the patchwork heel and toe. Pin the heel and toe to the stocking front, and edgestitch them. Using 8 to 10 stitches per inch, machine-quilt 1-inch-wide diagonal lines across the stocking front. Quilt over all the seams on the patchwork heel and toe.
5. Stocking Back: Place the second batting stocking between the yellow broadcloth and the second muslin

stockings. Baste them together along the edges. Machine-quilt the stocking back following the directions in Step 4.
6. Cuff: Layer the batting cuff strip between the patchwork and muslin cuff strips, and baste them together. Using 8 to 10 stitches per inch, machine-quilt over the patchwork seams. Stitch the ball fringe to the bottom edge of the cuff front, straight edges matching. Stitch together the short ends of the cuff, right sides together. Repeat with the red cuff facing. Press the seams open. Place the cuff front and facing right sides together, and stitch them along the bottom edge. Trim the seam, turn right side out and sew the cuff front and facing together at the top edge.
7. Finishing: Stitch the stocking front to the stocking back, right sides together, leaving the top edge open. Trim the seam, turn the stocking right side out, and lightly press the edges flat. Cut a 7-inch length of the ribbon, fold it in half, and baste the ends together to form a hanger loop. Position the loop, and stitch the right side of the cuff to the wrong side of the stocking at the top edge, catching the loop ends in the seam. Trim the seam and flip the cuff to the outside of the stocking.

FIG. IV, 5 SUGARPLUM STOCKING

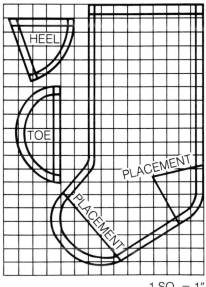

1 SQ. = 1"

Sugarplum Stocking

Old-Fashioned Touches

Create an ambience of yesteryear by decorating with wooden toys. You can make them yourself *(see pages 172-173 and 176-179)*, or start a wonderful collection by searching crafts fairs, antique stores, auctions or even junk shops for timeless treasures. Place toys on the mantel or under the tree. Trim the toys for the holidays: Fill a wooden dump truck with small glass ornaments or red wooden beads; tie a sprig of holly or a tiny plaid scarf around the neck of a wooden animal.

❋

An unfinished wooden bowl takes on the patina of age when you leave it outdoors for a few days. Let the rain and snow give it character, then bring the bowl indoors and fill it with nuts, fruit, pine cones or evergreens.

❋

Toss a woolen blanket over the couch for snuggling on a cold night. Plaids are always winter-warm, or try a red, green, or multi-colored "trader's" blanket.

A tiny potted evergreen is the perfect Christmas touch for a hall table, in the guest room, or on the edge of the bathtub. Leave the evergreen untrimmed to let its natural beauty show, but tie a big red ribbon bow around the pot.

❋

For old-fashioned family fun, toast marshmallows to make s'mores or roast chestnuts in the fireplace — only with Mom or Dad's supervision, of course.

❋

Wrap your Christmas gifts in plain brown paper (available in rolls at office supply stores), or mattress ticking fabric. Tie the boxes with cloth ribbons or twine, and trim them with pine cones, evergreen branches, holly or mistletoe.

Trace the shapes of Christmas cookie cutters onto balsa wood, and cut out the shapes to make simple tree ornaments. These ornaments are pretty as they are, or you can paint or stain them.

❋

Add a peppermint drop or stick to a mug of hot chocolate for a yummy flavor. Adults might prefer a warming splash of peppermint schnappes in their cocoa instead.

❋

If your fireplace is nonfunctional, or if you just want a change of pace, fill the clean, empty fireplace with potted white poinsettias. They're just as pretty as the red variety, but a little more unusual. Or collect all the unmatched candle holders in your home, fill them with white candle and group them together in the fireplace. Use a variety of shapes and sizes — let the color be the unifying feature. Then tuck glass ball ornaments, pretty rocks or figurines among the the candles to complete the look.

❋

Get out the old family photographs — the older the better — and create a visual family history on your mantel or a sideboard. Frame the pictures with ivy or holly, and write a label (pen and ink on parchment paper adds a nice touch) for each photo to identify the relatives. If you have an extended family, this is a particularly nice way to celebrate everyone's heritage.

Choose shades of green as the basis of your holiday decor. Red tends to be used more often because of its warmth and cheerfulness, but green can be beautiful and quite striking for the holidays. Choose a rich evergreen (solid or print) for holiday room accents, such as candles, table coverings, throws and pillows. A brighter green is nice in glass ball ornaments or felt decorations.

❋

Create an ingenious table decoration inspired by Mexican pierced tin lanterns. Place metal cheese graters over votive candles so the candlelight shines through the holes. Tie the graters with red ribbon, and surround the grouping with a carpet of pine boughs and holly.

During the Christmas school holiday, spend a family evening in front of the fire, with no TV, no toys, no distractions. Share some of your favorite Christmas memories with your kids. Drag out the old photo album, if you like, just to prove you really were a kid once! Ask the kids to share their fondest and funniest thoughts about the holidays. Let them stay up extra late as a treat.

❋

Decorate an outdoor tree for the birds. String peanuts in the shell, seeds, dried fruit, popcorn, raisins and pieces of bread to make a garland, and hang the garland on the tree. Make "ornaments" from pine cones spread with peanut butter and rolled in bird seed. Hang them from the tree with string.

For a fragrant fire, throw a handful of one of these natural scent makers into the flames: frankincense, myrrh, pine chips, cedar powder (or tips or shavings), sandalwood chips, red sandalwood powder, balsam fir tips, spearmint leaves, or potpourri.

❋

Never underestimate the power of a sled, a red wagon or a new bike under the tree on Christmas morning. The old types of gifts still are the best, even in the age of video games and skateboards. Need a stocking stuffer? Give jacks, a baseball, a yo-yo, a jump rope, soap bubbles, or a deck of cards; great for young-at-heart adults, too!

❋

With the flurry of holiday merry-making, sometimes the immediate family gets pushed to the back burner. So turn a simple family dinner into a special occasion: serve dinner by candlelight, use the china and silver and cloth napkins, and toast each member of the family for their "invaluable contribution" to the home.

❋

Bring out the old home movies, slides, or videos. Treat the family and close (indulgent) friends to a look at your family's "Christmases Past."

❋

For quick window decorations, tie ribbon loops of varying lengths to Christmas cookie cutters, and hang them from a curtain rod.

❋

Have an old-fashioned skating party (if you live in a warmer climate, going to a indoor skating rink can be just as much fun). Afterwards, bring everyone back to your house for an evening of sandwiches, cider and games like Charades.

TIMELESS TREASURES

A selection of perfect presents that span the ages.

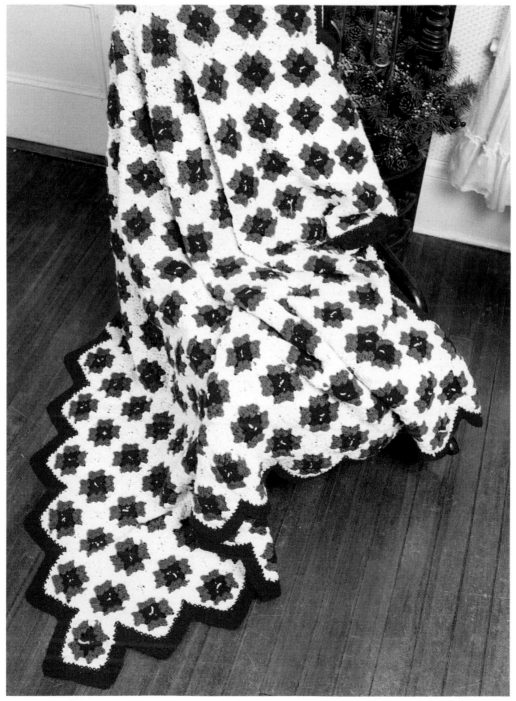

Poinsettia Afghan

POINSETTIA AFGHAN
(about 52 x 62 inches)

Average: For those with some experience in crocheting.

Materials: 4-ply worsted-weight yarn (3½ ounce skeins): 6 skeins of white (A), 3 skeins each of Green (B) and Christmas Red (C), and 1 skein or several yards of Maize (D); size 9 or I aluminum crochet hook, OR ANY SIZE HOOK TO OBTAIN GAUGE BELOW; tapestry needle.

Gauge: Each square = 3¾ x 3¾ inches, and 5 inches across the diagonal.

Directions:

1. Granny Squares (make 219): With C, ch 5, join with sl st to form a ring.
Rnd 1: Ch 3, dc 2 in ring; * ch 1, dc 3 in center of ring; rep from * twice more, ending ch 1, sl st to join in top of ch 3. Fasten off C. **Rnd 2:** Join B in any ch 1 space, (ch 3, dc 2, ch 1, dc 3) in same corner ch 1 space; * (dc 3, ch 1, dc 3) in next corner ch 1 space; rep from * twice more, join with sl st in top of ch 3. Fasten off B. **Rnd 3:** Join A in space between dc 3 on side of square (not corner), ch 3, dc 2 in same space, * (dc 3, ch 1, dc 3) in corner space, dc 3 in side space, rep from * twice more, ending (dc 3, ch 1, dc 3) in corner, sl st to join in top of ch 3. Fasten off.

2. Finishing: Weave in the yarn ends; when weaving in the beginning with the C end, use it to pull the center ring together. Using D and the tapestry needle, make 1 French knot in the center of each square *(see Stitch Guide, page 240)*. Sew the squares right sides together, catching only the back lp of each st on each square. Make 3 strips of 19 squares each, and 2 strips each of 17, 15, 13, 11, 9, 7, 5, 3 and 1 squares. Following the diagram in FIG. IV, 6 for the placement of the strips, sew the strips of squares together using the same method.

3. Crochet Border, Rnd 1: Attach C at the side of any corner square, ch 1, sc to corner of square, * (sc 1, ch 1, sc 1) in corner ch 1, sc in each st to within 1 st of V, dec on next 2 sts (1 st on each side of V), sc to next corner point; rep from * around, working the 2 corner points of each corner square as for the other points, end sl st to join, ch 1. **Rnd 2:** Sc in each sc, working (sc 1, ch 1, sc 1) in each corner point and dec in 2 sc on each side of each V, sl st to join, ch 1. **Rnds 3 and 4:** Repeat Rnd 2.

FIG. IV, 6 POINSETTIA AFGHAN — 219 SQUARES

PLACEMENT OF SQUARES

BLUEGRASS PULLOVER

Challenging: Requires more experience in knitting.

Materials: 4-ply worsted weight yarn, 14 ounces of each color: dark blue (A), medium blue (B) and medium green (C); 1 pair size 8 Knitting needles, OR ANY SIZE NEEDLES TO OBTAIN GAUGE BELOW; 3 cable needles; tapestry needle.

Gauge: With 3 strands of yarn held together in Stockinette Stitch (st st), 12 sts = 4 inches; 16 rows = 4 inches.

Note: *The sweater is loose fitting, and is done in one size only. Work 3 strands of yarn — 1 strand of each color held together throughout.*

Finished Measurements:
One Size

CHEST:	51″
SLEEVE LENGTH:	19¾″
BACK LENGTH:	29″
FRONT LENGTH:	25½″

Stitches Used:

2/2 Ribbing: Row 1: * K 2, p 2; repeat from * to end of row. **Row 2:** Repeat Row 1.

Stockinette Stitch (st st), Row 1 (right side): Knit. **Row 2:** Purl. **Row 3:** Repeat from Row 1.

Reverse Stockinette Stitch (rev st st), Row 1 (right side): Purl. **Row 2:** Knit. **Row 3:** Rep from Row 1.

Cable, Rows 1, 3, 7, 9 and 11: K 6. **All Even Rows:** P 6. **Row 5:** Sl 3 sts onto cable needle and hold at front of work, k 3, k 3 from cable needle. **Row 13:** Rep from Row 5. Always rep Rows 5 to 12.

Directions:

1. Back: With 1 strand each of A, B and C, cast on 78 sts. Work for 2½ inches in 2/2 ribbing. Continue in st st. When the Back measures 29 inches from beg, bind off all sts loosely.

2. Front: With 1 strand each of A, B and C, cast on 78 sts. Work for 2½ inches in 2/2 ribbing. Then work as follows: 15 sts in rev st st with 1 strand of each color, 1 cable of 6 sts with 3 strands of C, 15 sts in rev st st with 1 strand of each color, 1 cable of 6 sts with 3 strands of B, 15 sts in rev st st with 1 strand of each color, 1 cable of 6 sts with 3 strands of A, 15 sts in rev st st with 1 strand of each color. Continue in pat for 6 rows. **Row 7:** With 1 strand of each color, 1 st in st st, 14 sts in rev st st with 1 strand of each color, 1 cable of 6 sts with 3 strands of C, 15 sts in rev st st, 1 cable of 6 sts with 3 strands of B, 15 sts in rev st st with 1 strand of each color, 1 cable of 6 sts with 3 strands of A, 15 sts rev st st. Continue in pat through Row 34, increasing 1 st st at beg of every odd row. **Row 35:** 21 sts in st st with 1 strand of each color, 15 sts in rev st st, 1 cable of 6 sts with 3 strands of B, 15 sts in rev st st with 1 strand of each color, 1 cable of 6 sts with 3 strands of A, 15 sts in rev st st with 1 strand of each color. Continue in pat through to Row 64. **Row 65:** 42 sts in st st with 1 strand of each color, 15 sts in rev st st, 1 cable of 6 sts with 3 strands of A, 15 sts in rev st st with 1 strand of each color. Continue in pat through Row 98. **Row 99:** 63 sts in st st with 1 strand of each color, 15 sts in rev st st. Continue in pat. When the Front measures 25½ inches from beg, shape the neck: Bind off center 24 sts. Join second balls of yarn to the second part, and work it independently. At each neck edge of every 2nd row, bind off 3 sts once. When the Front measures 29 inches from beg, bind off rem 24 sts on each shoulder.

3. Sleeves (make 2): With 1 strand each of A, B and C, cast on 38 sts. Work for 2½ inches in 2/2 ribbing, inc 4 sts evenly spaced across last row — 42 sts. Continue in st st. Inc 1 st at each edge of every 4th row 5 times, then inc 1 st at each edge of every 6th row 8 times, working new sts in st st as you inc — 68 sts. When the Sleeve measures 19¾ inches from beg, bind off all sts.

4. Finishing: Sew 1 shoulder seam. With 1 strand each of A, B and C, pick up and knit 60 sts around the neck. Work 11½ inches in 2/2 ribbing. Bind off. Sew the 2nd shoulder and the neckband seams. Sew the Sleeves to the center 22 inches of the joined side seams, matching the center of the Sleeve with the shoulder seam. Sew the side and Sleeve seams.

Bluegrass Pullover

Winter Nights Sweater

WINTER NIGHTS SWEATER

Average: For those with some experience in knitting.

Materials: White sportweight yarn (16 balls); 1 pair each size 3 and size 8 knitting needles, OR ANY SIZE NEEDLES TO OBTAIN GAUGE BELOW; 9 buttons; 2 stitch holders; tapestry needle.

Gauge: On size 8 needles in Stockinette Stitch (st st), 18 sts = 4 inches, 24 rows = 4 inches.

Finished Measurements:
One Size

FITS BUST SIZES: 32″ to 40″
FINISHED BUST SIZE: 44″

Stitches Used:

Make Bobble (MB): (K 1, p 1, k 1, p 1, k 1) all in next st, slip 2nd, 3rd, 4th, and 5th sts over first st.

Directions:

1. Back: With size 3 needles, cast on 95 sts. Work in ribbing as follows: ***Row 1 (right side):*** K 1; * p 1, k 1; rep from * across. ***Row 2:*** P 1; * k 1, p 1; rep from * across. Rep Rows 1 and 2 for 2¾ inches, inc 4 sts on last row, ending Row 2 — 99 sts. Change to size 8 needles and work ***Rows 1 to 136:*** K odd rows. P even rows, marking each end of Row 81 for underarm. ***Divide for Neck:*** Work across 30 sts, turn, and put rem sts on a holder. Dec 1 st at neck edge on next 3 rows — 27 sts. Complete through Row 144. Bind off. With the right side facing, leave the center 39 sts on the holder, join yarn to rem sts and work to end. Complete as for the first side through Row 141, reversing the shaping. Bind off.

2. Front: Work the same as the back until Row 128 has been completed. ***Divide for Neck:*** Work across 33 sts, turn, and put rem sts on a holder. Dec 1 st at neck edge on next 6 rows — 27 sts. Complete through Row 140. Bind off. With the right side facing, leave the center 33 sts on the holder, join yarn to rem sts and work to end. Complete to correspond to the first side through Row 145.

3. Left Sleeve: With size 3 needles, cast on 43 sts. Work in ribbing as follows: ***Row 1 (right side):*** K 1, p 1; rep across. ***Row 2:*** P 1, k 1; rep across. Work for 2 inches, inc 14 sts on last row, ending Row 2 — 57 sts. Change to size 8 needles and work in st st, beg k row, shaping side by inc 1 st each beg of every 5th row until there are 93 sts. Work 6 rows even. Bind off.

4. Right Sleeve: Work the same as the left Sleeve, shaping the side by inc 1 st each end of every 5th row until there are 96 sts. Work 6 rows even. Bind off.

5. Finishing, Neckband: Sew the right shoulder seam. With the right side facing, and Size 3 needles, pick up 12 sts along the left Front neck edge, k across 33 sts of the Front, inc 8 sts, pick up 16 sts along the right Front neck edge, 8 sts along the right Back neck edge, k across 39 sts of the Back, inc 9 sts, pick up 4 sts along the left Back neck edge — 129 sts. Work in ribbing as follows: ***Row 1 (wrong side):*** K 1; * p 1, k 1; rep from * across. ***Row 2:*** K 2; * p 1, k 1; rep from * to last st, k 1. Rep Rows 1 and 2 three more times, then rep Row 1 once more. Bind off loosely in rib with size 8 needle. Sew the front and back sections of the left Sleeve to the Front and Back, place the center of the right Sleeve top at the shoulder seam, and sew it in place between the markers. ***Button Band:*** With the right side facing and size 3 needles, beg at the neck, pick up 7 sts across the neckband, 33 sts across the left Back shoulder, 105 sts across the Sleeve including the cuff — 145 sts. Work 9 rows of ribbing the same as the neckband. Bind off loosely in rib with Size 8 needle.

Buttonhole Band: With the right side facing and size 3 needles, beg at the lower cuff, pick up 105 sts across the Sleeve, 33 sts across the left Front shoulder, 7 sts across the neckband — 145 sts. Work 4 rows of ribbing same as the neckband.

Buttonhole Row: Rib 4, bind off 2 sts, (rib 15 [including st on needle after bind-off], bind off 2 sts) 8 times, rib 3. ***Next Row:*** (Rib to bind-off, turn, cast on 2 sts, turn) 9 times, rib to end. Work 3 more rows of ribbing. Bind off loosely in rib with Size 8 needle. Sew the side and Sleeve seams. Sew on the buttons.

PINTO ROCKING HORSE

(20 x 8¾ x 12 inches)

Challenging: Requires more experience in woodworking.

Materials: Pine: 4 feet of 1 x 12, and 4 feet of 1 x 4; 12 inches of ¼-inch-diameter dowel; 9 inches of ½-inch-diameter dowel; 4d finishing nails; wood glue; wood putty; white, black and red-brown acrylic paints; graphite paper; stylus or old ballpoint pen; sandpaper; paper for patterns; power saw; jig or sabre saw; drill with ¼- and ½-inch bits; hammer; nail set; vise; clamp.

Cutting Directions:

Code	Pieces	Size	
A (1 x 12)	(2)	¾″ x 10″ x 18″	Horses
B (1 x 4)	(2)	¾″ x 3½″ x 20″	Rockers
C (1 x 12)	(1)	¾″ x 5″ x 7¼″	Seat
C1 (1 x 12)	(1)	¾″ x 6″ x 7¼″	Seat back
C2 (DOW)	(3)	¼″-dia. x 1½″	Seat dowels
D (DOW)	(4)	¼″-dia. x 1¾″	Rocker dowels
E (DOW)	(1)	½″-dia. x 8¾″	Spreader dowel

Directions:

1. Enlarge the pattern in Fig. IV, 7 onto paper following the directions on page 241. Cut out the pattern parts.
2. Using the graphite paper and stylus or old ballpoint pen, trace the A horses and the C and C1 seat parts lightly onto the 1 x 12 pine. Trace the B rockers onto the 1 x 4 pine. Cut out the parts.

3. Clamp the A horses together, flush all around, and then drill a ½-inch diameter hole in the front legs for the E spreader dowel *(see Fig. IV, 7)*. Unclamp the horses. Place the A horses and B rockers in position on a flat surface near a table edge. Drill four ¼-inch-diameter holes through the B rocker into the horses' legs for the D rocker dowels *(see Fig. IV, 7)*.
4. Place the C seat in the vise, angled end up. Position the C1 seat back against the C seat. Drill three ¼-inch-diameter holes, perpendicular to C, through C1 into C. Insert the C2 seat dowels into the holes, and glue C1 to C.
5. Sand the pieces, and paint them following the color key in Fig. IV, 7.
6. Insert the D rocker dowels into their holes, and glue the B rockers to the A horses. Glue and nail the A horses to each side of the C/C1 seat assembly. Set the nails, fill the holes with wood putty, and when the putty is dry, sand it. Touch up the filled nail holes with the appropriate color paint. Glue the E spreader dowel in the holes in the horses' front legs.

ALPHABET BLOCKS

Easy: Achievable by anyone.

Materials: Scrap lumber; green, red, beige, blue, yellow and light fuchsia acrylic paints; paintbrush; stencil brush; white glue; alphabet stencils; gesso *(available at craft and art supply stores)*; masking tape; fine sandpaper.

Directions:

1. To make the blocks in the photo at right, cut the scrap lumber into six 2 x 2 x 4-inch pieces for the smaller 4-inch cube, and six 1¾ x 2⅝ x 5¼-inch pieces for the larger 5¼-inch cube. Glue the pieces together into a block, edges flush. When the glue has dried, sand the edges of the blocks.
2. Fill in the joints with the gesso. Paint the cube edges green to make at least ¼-inch-wide borders, and let them dry. Cover the green borders with the masking tape. Paint each block face beige, yellow, blue or light fuchsia. When the paint is dry, stencil a red letter on each face. Remove the masking tape. Sand each whole block lightly to "distress" it for an antique look.

FIG. IV, 7 PINTO ROCKING HORSE   1 SQ. = 2″

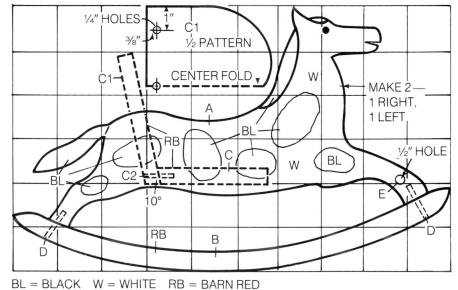

BL = BLACK   W = WHITE   RB = BARN RED

Pinto Rocking Horse; Alphabet Blocks; Sweet Sachets and Dolly's Patchwork Apron & Scarf (directions, page 174)

SWEET SACHETS

Easy: Achievable by anyone.

Materials: Fabric scraps; matching threads; ½ yard of ribbon; potpourri; 4½ x 5-inch piece of paper for pattern.

**Directions
(¼-inch seams allowed):**

1. To make a heart pattern, fold the paper in half along a 5-inch edge. Draw half a heart on the folded side of the paper. Cut out the heart and open the paper for the full pattern. To make a star pattern, draw a star freehand on the paper and cut it out. Using the dressmaker's carbon, trace a pattern onto the fabric twice, and cut out both hearts or stars.

2. Pin the fabric pieces right sides together and edges even. Stitch around the edges, leaving an opening on a straight edge for turning. Clip the seam, turn the shape right side out and stuff it with potpourri. Turn in the raw edges, and slipstitch the opening closed *(see Stitch Guide, page 240).*

3. Cut a 7-inch length of ribbon, fold it in half, and sew it to the top of the sachet for a hanger. Tie the remaining ribbon into a bow, and sew it to the base of the hanger.

DOLLY'S PATCHWORK APRON & SCARF

Easy: Achievable by anyone.

Materials: Fabric scraps in 4 different colors for apron; fabric scrap for lining; 30 inches of ribbon; matching threads; 13-inch square of fabric for head scarf.

**Directions
(¼-inch seams allowed):**

1. Apron Skirt: Cut a 3½-inch square from each of the four fabric scrap colors. Cut each square in half diagonally to make two triangles. Sew together two contrasting color triangles at the long edge to make a 3-inch square. Repeat. Stitch together the remaining two colors of triangles the same way. Using the photo on page 173 as a placement guide, stitch the four squares together to make the apron skirt.

2. Apron Bib: From each color fabric scrap, cut a right triangle with 2¾-inch legs. Using the photo as a placement guide, stitch the triangles together at the short edges to make the bib.

3. Assembling: Stitch the bib to the skirt, centers matching. Pin the apron to the lining fabric scrap, right sides together, and cut out the lining using the apron as a guide. Stitch the apron and lining together, leaving an opening for turning. Turn the apron right side out, press, turn in the open edges, and slipstitch the opening closed *(see Stitch Guide, page 240).* With centers matching, stitch the ribbon over the waist seam. Tie the ribbon ends around a dressed doll. Tack the apron to the doll's dress at the top corners. Fold the scarf in half on the diagonal, and tie it over the doll's head.

DON'T SWEEP THE HOUSE ON CHRISTMAS DAY
And other holiday superstitions.

Don't sweep the house on Christmas day — you'll sweep out all the good spirits.

✳

Becoming engaged on Christmas Day brings good luck to the marriage.

✳

It is unlucky to wear new shoes on Christmas.

✳

If a young woman is kissed under the mistletoe seven times in one day, she will marry within the year.

When you bring evergreen branches into the house at Christmas, you also bring in forest elves and fairies who protect your home from harm. But it's unlucky to bring evergreen into the house before Christmas Eve, or remove it before Twelfth Night (January 5)!

✳

Holly is lucky for men and ivy is lucky for women. This is why the two are used together in Christmas decorations.

✳

Being born on Christmas ensures a carefree life.

TREE TIME TOWELS

Average: For those with some experience in cross stitch.

Materials: Linen towels with large checks; embroidery floss: 1 skein of Green; embroidery hoop; embroidery needle; spray starch; tailor's chalk (optional).

Directions:

1. Starch and press the towels. Following the checked pattern on the towels, plan a border design using the tree diagrams in FIG. IV, 8.

2. If you wish, mark the motif placement lightly on each towel with tailor's chalk. Place a towel in the embroidery hoop. Cross stitch the border design using the embroidery needle and the Green floss *(see Stitch Guide, page 240)*. Decide on the number of floss strands to use according to the weight of the towel linen and the desired weight of the design. Cut the floss into 18- to 20-inch-long strands. To begin, leave a 3-inch tail of floss at the back of the towel, and work cross stitches over the tail. When the strand is about 3 inches long, run the floss end through seven or eight cross stitches at the back of the towel, and cut the excess floss. Begin and end all other strands by running the floss ends through stitches at the back of the towel.

Note: *We included an alternate pattern in* FIG. IV, 8 *to make a cross stitch border of hearts. Use 1 skein of Red embroidery floss and follow the directions as for the tree border.*

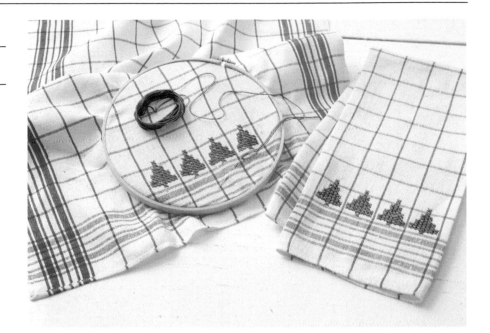

FIG. IV, 8 TREE TIME TOWELS   CROSS STITCH CHRISTMAS TREES

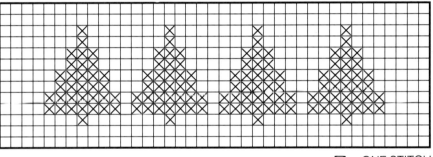

⊠ = ONE STITCH

CROSS STITCH HEARTS (ALTERNATE PATTERN)

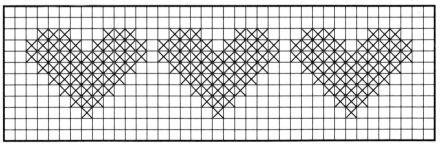

JUST FOR KIDS
Wonderful Wooden Toys
Woodworker's delights, for kids of all ages.

Delivery Truck (directions, page 178); Tanker Truck (directions at right)

TANKER TRUCK
(about 17 x 5 x 6¼ inches)

Average: For those with some experience in woodworking.

Materials: ¾ x 1¼ feet of ¼-inch-thick pine; 5½ feet of ½-inch-thick lattice; 2 feet of ¼-inch-thick lattice; 15 inches of ⅛-inch-diameter dowel; 1 inch of ¼-inch-diameter dowel; six ½-inch-thick, 1½-inch-diameter wooden wheels; four ⅜-inch-diameter wooden plugs; 12 inches of 3-inch-diameter acrylic tubing; two ⅛-inch-thick, 3-inch-diameter acrylic circles; jig or sabre saw; drill with ⅛-, ¼- and ⅜-inch bits; sandpaper; varnish or polyurethane; wood glue; small finishing nails; acrylic paints in your choice of colors *(optional)*.

Directions:

1. Cut out all the pieces for the tractor and trailer, following the cutting directions in FIG. IV, 9. If necessary, sand the edges of the pieces smooth.

2. Drill ⅛-inch-diameter holes in the A, A1 and C4 frame pieces for the A2 axles. Drill a ¼-inch-diameter hole in the C3 frame piece for the C8 hitch. Drill ⅛-inch-deep, ⅜-inch-diameter holes in the B5 and C5 bumpers for the wooden plug headlights.

3. Assemble the tractor and trailer following the diagram in FIG. IV, 9. Glue and nail the parts together. Glue the C8 hitch to the underside of the C3 trailer frame. Fit the A2 axles through the holes in the frame. Glue the wheels to the axles, but do not glue the axles to the frame. Let the glue dry completely.

4. Coat the truck with one or two coats of the clear varnish or polyurethane. If you wish, paint the truck with acrylic paints in the colors of your choice before applying the varnish or polyurethane.

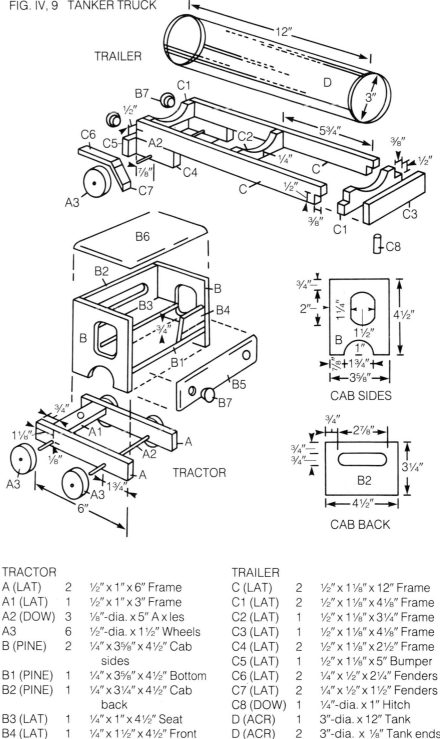

FIG. IV, 9 TANKER TRUCK

TRACTOR		
A (LAT)	2	½" x 1" x 6" Frame
A1 (LAT)	1	½" x 1" x 3" Frame
A2 (DOW)	3	⅛"-dia. x 5" Axles
A3	6	½"-dia. x 1½" Wheels
B (PINE)	2	¼" x 3⅝" x 4½" Cab sides
B1 (PINE)	1	¼" x 3⅝" x 4½" Bottom
B2 (PINE)	1	¼" x 3¼" x 4½" Cab back
B3 (LAT)	1	¼" x 1" x 4½" Seat
B4 (LAT)	1	¼" x 1½" x 4½" Front
B5 (LAT)	1	¼" x 1½" x 5" Bumper
B6 (PINE)	1	¼" x 3⅝" x 5" Roof
B7	4	⅜"-dia. wooden plug headlights

TRAILER		
C (LAT)	2	½" x 1⅛" x 12" Frame
C1 (LAT)	2	½" x 1⅛" x 4⅛" Frame
C2 (LAT)	1	½" x 1⅛" x 3¼" Frame
C3 (LAT)	1	½" x 1⅛" x 4⅛" Frame
C4 (LAT)	2	½" x 1⅛" x 2½" Frame
C5 (LAT)	1	½" x 1⅛" x 5" Bumper
C6 (LAT)	2	¼" x ½" x 2¼" Fenders
C7 (LAT)	2	¼" x ½" x 1½" Fenders
C8 (DOW)	1	¼"-dia. x 1" Hitch
D (ACR)	1	3"-dia. x 12" Tank
D (ACR)	2	3"-dia. x ⅛" Tank ends

DELIVERY TRUCK
(about 16 x 5¼ x 7½ inches)

Average: For those with some experience in woodworking.

Materials: 1 x 3 feet of ¼-inch-thick pine; 3 feet of ½-inch-thick lattice; 1½ feet of ¼-inch-thick lattice; 1 foot of ⅛-inch-diameter dowel; four ¼-inch-thick, 2-inch-diameter wooden wheels; four ⅜-inch-diameter wooden plugs; jig or sabre saw; drill with ⅛- and ⅜-inch bits; sandpaper; varnish or polyurethane; wood glue; small finishing nails; acrylic paints in your choice of colors *(optional)*; alphabet stencils or decals *(optional)*.

Directions:

1. Cut out all the pieces following the cutting directions in FIG. IV, 10. If necessary, sand the edges of the pieces smooth. Sand one vertical edge of each B5 door to round it.

2. Drill ⅛-inch-diameter holes in the A and A3 frame pieces ¼ inch up from the bottom for the A5 axles *(see* FIG. IV, 10*)*. Drill ⅛-inch-diameter holes ¼ inch in from the back and side edges of the B6 roof and B bottom for the B7 door hinges. Drill ¼-inch deep, ⅛-inch-diameter holes on the top and bottom of the B5 doors ¼ inch from the rounded edges *(see* FIG. IV, 10*)*. Drill ⅛-inch-deep, ⅜-inch-diameter holes on the A1 and A4 bumpers for the wooden plug headlights.

3. Assemble the truck, except for the doors, following the diagram in FIG. IV, 10. Glue and nail the parts together. Glue the wheels to the A5 axles, but do not glue the axles to the frame.

4. To assemble the doors, line up one of the holes in the B6 roof with the hole in the top of a B5 door. Fit a B7 door hinge through the roof hole in the door. Repeat with the bottom holes. Do not glue the hinges in place; the door should swing on them. Repeat for the remaining door.

5. When the glue has dried, coat the truck with one or two coats of the clear varnish or polyurethane. If you wish, paint the truck with acrylic paints in the colors of your choice, and add stenciled lettering or decals to the side panels before applying the varnish or polyurethane.

FIG. IV, 10   DELIVERY TRUCK

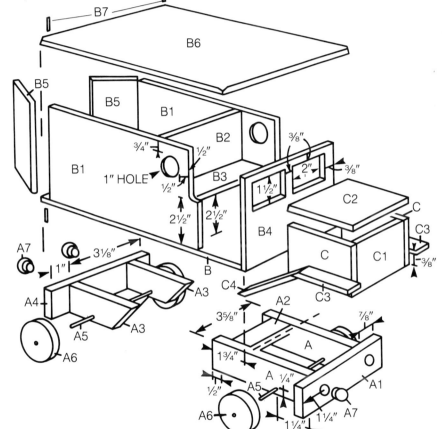

A (LAT)	2	½" x 1¾" x 5½" Frame	
A1 (LAT)	1	½" x 1¾" x 5¼" Bumper	
A2 (LAT)	1	½" x 1" x 2½" Brace	
A3 (LAT)	2	½" x 1¾" x 3½" Frame	
A4 (LAT)	1	½" x 1¾" x 5¼" Bumper	
A5 (DOW)	2	⅛"-dia. x 4¼" Axles	
A6	4	2"-dia. x ¼" Wheels	
A7	4	⅜"-dia. wooden plug headlights	
B (PINE)	1	¼" x 5¼" x 10¼" Bottom	
B1 (PINE)	2	¼" x 5¼" x 8½" Sides	
B2 (PINE)	1	¼" x 4⅝" x 5¼" Divider	

B3 (LAT)	1	¼" x 1⅝" x 4⅝" Seat	
B4 (PINE)	1	¼" x 5" x 5¼" Windshield	
B5 (PINE)	2	¼" x 2⅝" x 5¼" Doors	
B6 (PINE)	1	¼" x 5¼" x 9" Roof	
B7 (DOW)	4	⅛"-dia. x ½" Door hinges	
C (PINE)	2	¼" x 2½" x 3½" Motor sides	
C1 (PINE)	1	¼" x 2½" x 3" Radiator	
C2 (PINE)	1	¼" x 3½" x 3½" Hood	
C3 (LAT)	2	¼" x ¾" x 3" Fenders	
C4 (LAT)	2	¼" x ¾" x 3¼" Fenders	

WOODEN SAILBOAT

Average: For those with some experience in woodworking.

Materials: ½ x 3½ x 10 inches of pine for bottom; ¼ x ¾ x 30 inches of lattice for sides, bow, stern and rudder; ½ x ½ x 3 inches of pine for seat; 1⅛ x 2⅜ x 2⅝ inches of pine for mast support; 35½ inches of ⅜-inch-diameter dowel for mast, booms and sail supports; 3 inches of ⅛-inch-diameter dowel for tiller; fourteen ¼-inch screw hooks; heavy red thread; sewing needle, fabric scraps for mainsail and jib; matching sewing thread; mitering box; varnish; saw; sandpaper; drill with ⅛- and ⅜-inch bits; wood glue.

Directions:

1. Shape the bottom of the boat, and cut the pieces for the sides, stern and bow on the mitering box following FIG. IV, 11. Cut a 2-inch length of the ¾-inch-wide lattice for the rudder. Cut the ⅜-inch-diameter dowel to the following lengths: one 11¼-inch length for the mast, one 9¾-inch length for the mainsail support, one 4-inch length for the mainsail boom, one 8½-inch length for the jib support, and one 2-inch length for the jib boom. Sand all the edges and surfaces smooth. Glue the stern, sides and bow to the bottom. Glue the seat against the stern (*see photo*). Center and glue the mast support 3¾ inches in front of the stern.

2. Varnish the entire boat. When the varnish has dried, drill a ¼-inch-deep, ⅛-inch-diameter hole into one long edge of the rudder near the corner. Glue the tiller into the hole. Drill a ⅛-inch-diameter hole through the stern for the tiller centered just above the seat. Drill a ⅜-inch-diameter hole into the mast support centered ¾ inch from the front support. Glue the mast into the hole.

3. Screw a hook into each end of the remaining booms and supports. Screw a hook into the top mast at the back (*see photo*). Screw a hook into the floor just inside the point of the bow. Screw a hook

into the top edge of the stern just to the side of the tiller.

4. With a fold on the planted edge (*see* FIG. IV, 11*)*, draw the top and bottom of the mainsail and jib directly on the fabric scraps. Cut ½ inch outside the drawn lines. Turn under ¼ inch twice, and stitch hems at the two raw edges.

5. Hook on the booms and sail supports as shown in the photo. Use short pieces of the heavy thread to tie the booms to the hooks in the stern and bow. With the heavy thread and sewing needle, stitch through the top of the mainsail, and tie the thread around the top of the mast. Attach the mainsail in the same way at the remaining two corners, and at the midpoints of the three sides. Repeat for the jib. Slip the tiller through the hole in the stern.

FIG. IV, 11   WOODEN SAILBOAT

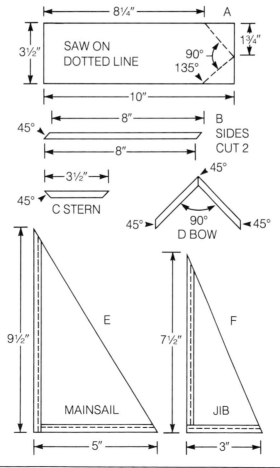

NEEDLEPOINT GAMEBOARD

Average: For those with some experience in needlepoint and framing.

Materials: Tapestry yarn: 5 skeins each of Light Blue and Dark Blue, and 2 skeins of Medium Blue; 22-inch square of 13-mesh-to-the-inch mono needlepoint canvas; tapestry needle; 80 inches of picture molding with $\frac{9}{16}$-inch minimum inside depth; $\frac{1}{8}$-inch-thick Masonite hardboard: one 18-inch square, and one 17¾-inch square; 18 inches square of $\frac{1}{16}$-inch-thick Plexiglas®; piece of heavy cardboard or wood; rust-proof push pins; 1-inch brads; Minwax® special walnut stain and antique oil finish, or paint; 20-inch square of felt; white glue; 1 package of millinery-weight elastic cord; sewing thread; needle; miter box; fine-toothed backsaw; small hammer.

Directions:

1. Gameboard: Starting at the center of the canvas and center of the board, work sixty-four 23-stitch squares, alternating Light and Dark Blue, in continental stitch (*see Stitch Guide, page 240, and photo*). Work one row of continental stitch around each edge of the gameboard in Medium Blue. Work a second row of Medium Blue, extending it by 24 stitches beyond the board to accommodate the arrowheads at each corner of the border (*see* FIG. IV, 12).

2. Border: Following the diagram in FIG. IV, 12, work the borders in bargello stitch (*see Stitch Guide*) over four meshes, except in the corners as shown. Finish the border by working four rows of Medium and Dark Blue bargello around the entire piece.

3. Blocking: Dampen the canvas and pin it, squared, with the push pins to the piece of heavy cardboard or wood. Let the canvas dry completely.

4. Mounting: Stretch the canvas over the smaller piece of hardboard, making sure the work is centered in the front. Fold under the edges of the canvas. Starting in the middle of one side, and using the tapestry needle, pull the elastic cord through one mesh in the folded edge. Extend the elastic to the middle of the opposite side, and pull it through one mesh in the corresponding folded edge. Bring the ends of the cord back to the middle, stretch the cord as far as possible, and tie it in the middle. Using the elastic ends, continue tying the opposite sides of the canvas together in a zigzag fashion, always keeping the front of the canvas even. When you are finished with one direction, do the same with the other two sides. Miter the canvas corners, and stitch them closed with a few stitches using the sewing needle and thread.

5. Frame: Measure four pieces of picture molding which, when put together, will fit around the Plexiglas snugly but not tightly. Cut the ends of the molding in the miter box to 45° angles. Fit each corner together and nail it with two brads on each side of the molding. Stain and finish the frame with the walnut stain and antique oil finish, or paint it. Turn the frame face down. Lay in the Plexiglas, canvas, and larger piece of hardboard. Secure them with brads driven into the frame. Glue the felt square to the back of the frame.

FIG. IV, 12 NEEDLEPOINT GAMEBOARD
EDGE: ALL STITCHES OVER 4 MESHES EXCEPT FOR
COMPENSATING 2, 3, & 5 MESH ONES AT CORNERS

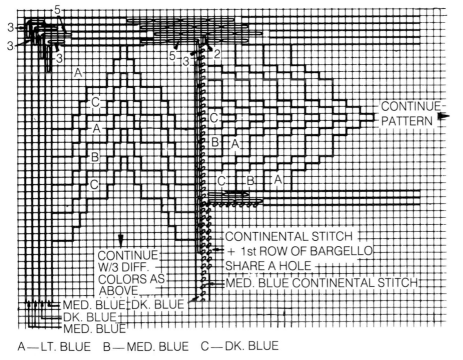

A—LT. BLUE   B—MED. BLUE   C—DK. BLUE

Needlepoint Gameboard

CUDDLY CRITTERS

Stitch up a menagerie of these huggable "best buddies."

Three Little Kittens

THREE LITTLE KITTENS
(about 5 inches tall)

Average: For those with some experience in sewing and crafting.

Materials (for one Kitten): 8-inch square of unbleached muslin; matching thread; black fine-point permanent felt-tip marker; brown, black, orange, pink and green medium-point permanent felt-tip markers; ¼ yard of ¼-inch-wide ribbon; 5 inches of narrow ribbon or cord; synthetic stuffing; paper for pattern.

Directions
(¼-inch seams allowed):

1. Enlarge the patterns in Fig. IV, 13 onto paper, following the directions on page 241. From the muslin, cut one pair each of the body and the tail.

2. Pin the two body pieces right sides together. Fold the 5-inch length of narrow ribbon or cord in half, and insert the folded end between the body pieces at the top of the head for a hanger. Stitch the body pieces together, leaving one leg open between the circles. Clip toward the seam at the inside corners *(see Fig. IV, 13)*. Turn the body right side out. Topstitch across each ear on the dotted lines. Stuff the body, turn in the open edges, and slipstitch the opening closed *(see Stitch Guide, page 240)*.

3. Stitch the two tail pieces right sides together except at the straight end. Clip at the inside corner, turn the tail right side out, and stuff it. Turn in the open edges, and slipstitch the opening closed. Slipstitch the tail to the back of the body.

4. Using the black fine-point marker, outline the toes, paw marks and facial features. When the outlines have dried completely, color the paw pads pink and the eyes green or orange with the medium-point markers. Using the photo as a color and placement guide, color the kitten's spots with the medium-point markers. Make a bow with the ¼-inch-wide ribbon, and tack it to the ornament at the neck.

FIG. IV, 13   THREE LITTLE KITTENS (FOR ONE KITTEN)   1 SQ. = ½″

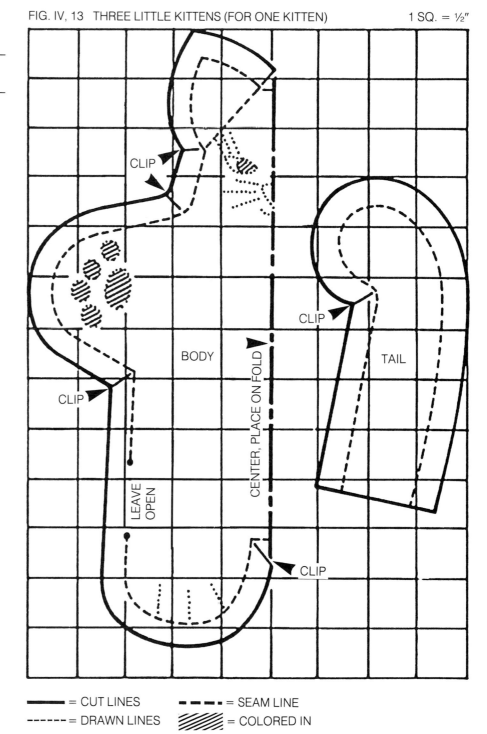

CLIP

CLIP

CLIP

BODY

CENTER, PLACE ON FOLD

TAIL

LEAVE OPEN

CLIP

━━━ = CUT LINES   ▪━▪━▪ = SEAM LINE
------ = DRAWN LINES   ▨▨▨ = COLORED IN

SLEEPYTIME BEARS
(18 inches and 27 inches long)

Average: For those with some experience in sewing.

Materials: 60-inch-wide fleece or furcloth: ½ yard for small bear, and ¾ yard for large bear: scrap of black nonwoven interfacing; matching threads; scrap of Black yarn; embroidery needle; synthetic stuffing; paper for patterns.

Directions
(¼-inch seams allowed):

1. Patterns: Enlarge the patterns in FIG. IV, 14 onto paper, following the directions on page 241. Note the different scales for the large and small bears. Trace a separate pattern for the Underbody. Add ¼-inch seam allowance all around except on the Nose and Eye.

2. Cutting: From the fleece or furcloth, cut one pair each of the Body, Head and Sole. Cut one Underbody, one Gusset, one Tail, and four Ears. From the black nonwoven interfacing, cut one Nose and two Eyes (no seam allowance).

3. Stitching: With right sides together, pin the pieces along the traced seam lines, matching the numbered edges. Stitch the two Body pieces together at the center back (CB 1) from the neck edge to the circle.

4. Tail: Pin the edges of the dart (2) together, right sides facing, and stitch from the point of the dart to the circle. Fold the Tail in half, right sides together, and stitch from the base of the Tail (4) to the circle. Turn the Tail right side out, and stuff it lightly. Pin it to the Body, seams and raw edges matching, along one edge of the Body dart (5). Then stitch the Body dart edges together, enclosing the Tail.

5. Body: Stitch the Underbody to the Body from the Tail to the neckline, except at the neck edges and bottom edges of the back feet. Stitch each Sole to the bottom edge of a back foot, matching the centerline to the seams. Turn the Body right side out, and stuff it.

6. Ears: Stitch each pair of Ears together except at the straight bottom edge (6). Turn the Ears right side out, baste the bottom edges closed, and clip ¼ inch upward on each centerline. With the clip at the top-front corner of the Head dart and right sides together, stitch half of one Ear forward to the top edge of one Head piece. Then swivel the Ear downward, opening the clip, and stitch the other half to the front edge (6) of the Head dart, seam lines matching. Stitch the Head dart closed, over the Ear. Repeat with the remaining Ear and Head piece.

7. Head: Stitch the Head pieces together at the center front (7) from the circle to the neck edge. Stitch the Gusset (8) between the Head pieces, over the Ears, matching the circles. Stuff the Head firmly. Lap the Head over the Body, turning the Head sideways so it will rest on a front foot. Pin, and slipstitch *(see Stitch Guide, page 240)* the neck edge securely, adding more stuffing if necessary.

8. Muzzle: Using small, sharp scissors, trim the nap shorter on the muzzle from the tip of the nose to the broken line on the pattern. Whipstitch *(see Stitch Guide)* the two darts in the Nose piece, and slide the Nose piece over the muzzle over a bit of stuffing. Slipstitch the edges in place.

9. Face: Pin each Eye, longest edge downward, against a seam just above the muzzle, and slipstitch the edges in place. Using the embroidery needle, couch *(see Stitch Guide)* a Black yarn mouth, and stem stitch a line up the center front seam to the Nose.

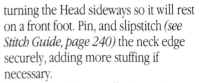

FIG. IV, 14 SLEEPYTIME BEARS

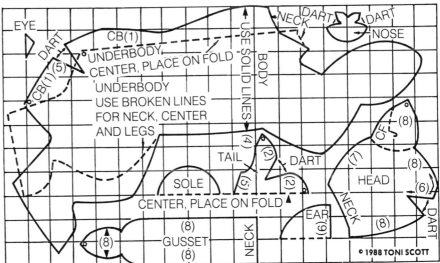

Sleepytime Bears

White Dove (directions at right); Mr. Toucan (directions, page 188); Polly Parrot (directions, page 190)

WHITE DOVE

Average: For those with some experience in sewing.

Materials: ½ yard of 45-inch-wide white or cream cotton fabric; matching thread; synthetic stuffing; Black embroidery floss or two small black beads for eyes; paper for patterns.

Directions
(¼-inch seams allowed):

1. Enlarge all of the patterns in FIG. IV, 15 onto paper, following the directions on page 241. Add a ¼-inch seam allowance all around.

2. Using the paper wing pattern and a double layer of fabric, cut out two pairs of wings. Stitch around the edges of each pair, leaving an opening as indicated on the pattern. Clip the curves and trim the seams. Turn the wings right side out, stuff them firmly, turn in the open edges, and slipstitch the openings closed *(see Stitch Guide, page 240)*.

3. Pin the body pattern to a double layer of the fabric, and cut out two body pieces. Stitch around the edges, leaving an opening between A and B. Clip the curves, and trim the seams.

4. Pin the gusset pattern on the bias of the fabric, and cut out one gusset. Pin and sew the gusset to the lower edges of the body pieces, matching A's and B's and leaving about a 3-inch opening in the middle of one body/gusset seam for turning. Turn the body right side out.

5. Stitch one wing to each side of the body, stitching only along the top edges of the wings where they are slipstitched. Do not sew through the body.

6. Stitch the eyes as indicated on the pattern, using the Black embroidery floss and French knots *(see Stitch Guide)*, or black beads. Stuff the dove body firmly through the remaining opening, turn under the open edges and slipstitch the opening closed.

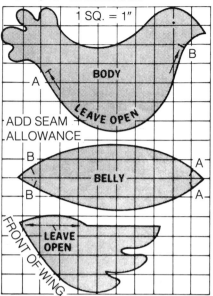

FIG. IV, 15 WHITE DOVE

MR. TOUCAN
(about 5¾ inches tall, and 4 inches wide)

Average: For those with some experience in sewing.

Materials: Short-napped blue imitation fur: ⅓ yard of 60-inch-wide fur, or three 9 x 12-inch pieces; 6-inch square of short-napped yellow imitation fur; wool felt: 1 square each of red, yellow, blue, black and white (if using rayon or other thin felts, use 3 layers); blue, red and white sewing threads; two ½-inch-diameter brown or amber animal eyes with washers, or two buttons; synthetic stuffing; ½ cup of dry beans, peas or rice; white fabric glue; wooden chopstick or ⅜-inch-diameter dowel, for turning and stuffing; paper for patterns.

Note: *Brush off loose fur from the cut edges. Pin or baste the curved pieces together before sewing. Push the nap of the fur aside while sewing.*

Directions:

1. Enlarge the patterns in FIG. IV, 16 onto the paper, following the directions on page 241.

2. Adding a ¼-inch seam allowance all around, cut one Bottom piece, one Back/Side piece and two Wings from the blue fur, and one Chest piece from the yellow fur (if using longer-napped fur, add a ⅜-inch seam allowance). The nap of the fur should run in the same direction for all the fur pieces. Following the color key in FIG. IV, 16, from the felt cut two Eyes, four Foot pieces, and two each of the five Bill pieces (no seam allowance).

3. Wings: In one Wing piece only, cut a 2-inch vertical slash 1 inch below the dot. Pin both Wing pieces right sides together, and stitch completely around them. Turn the wings right side out through the slash. Push the seam out from the inside using the chopstick or dowel. Pull out the nap with a needle where it is caught in the seam.

4. Body: With right sides together, and matching A, B and the center notch, stitch the Chest to the Back/Side piece along the seam from point A to B. Position the blue felt Eyes on the Chest piece, lining up the eye dots. Insert the animal eyes through the felt and fur, or sew on the buttons.

5. Bill: Using a ³⁄₁₆-inch seam allowance, sew together the five pieces for each side of the bill. Sew the red and yellow pieces together for the top, and the two black pieces to the white piece for the bottom. Then sew the top and bottom pieces together. Sew both sides together along the top and bottom.

6. Feet: For each Foot, glue two Foot pieces together along the outside edges, avoiding the stitching line.

7. Assembling Body: Match the center bottom seam of the Bill to the top center notch on the Chest, right sides together. Stitch the Bill to the body from point A to B. Fold the Body/Bill unit right sides together and stitch the entire length of the seam, starting at the tip of the Bill and ending at the bottom of the Body; be sure to match the seams and leave a 2¼-inch opening at the back for turning. Topstitch close to the edge of the Feet for the detail as marked on the pattern. Place the Feet, side by side, on the right side of the Bottom piece, with the toes facing the center of the circle and raw edges flush with the edge of the Bottom piece. Stitch the Feet in place. Insert the Bottom piece into the bottom of the body, right sides together, matching the center of the Feet to the notch. Stitch completely around to close up the body. Turn the body right side out. Using the chopstick or dowel, push out all of the seams, and stuff the body firmly from the Bill down to the Bottom. Fill the Bottom with the ½ cup of dry beans, peas or rice, turn in the open edges and slipstitch the opening closed *(see Stitch Guide, page 240).* With the slashed side of the Wings inside, place the Wings on the body with the front edge of the Wings at the neck. Attach the Wings to the body with the fabric glue or by hand-stitching. Leave the ends of the wings free to hang away from the body to make a tail.

𝒯he Mistletoe hung in the castle hall, The holly branch shone on the old oak wall.

— T.H. BAYLY

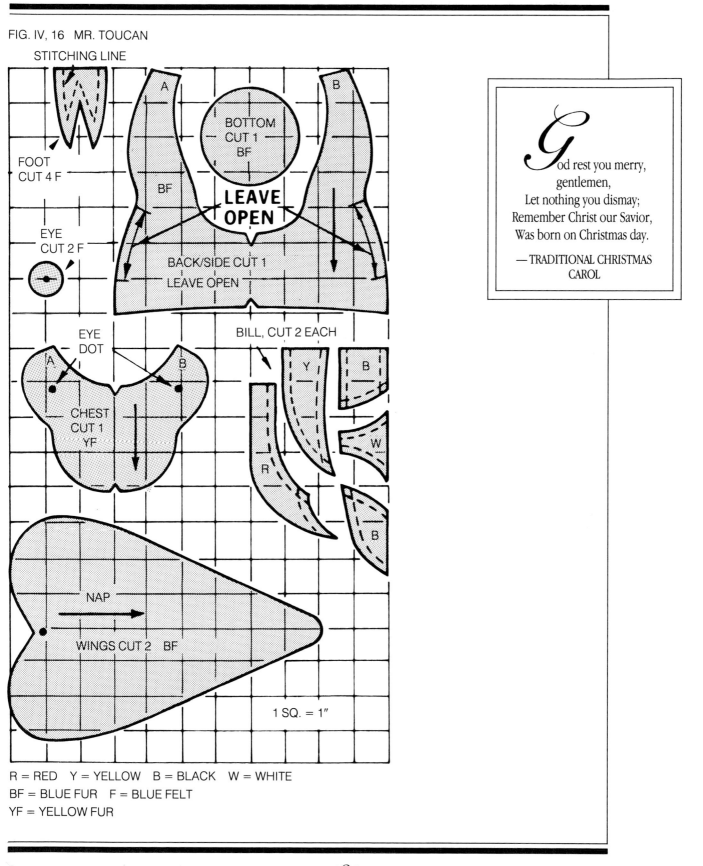

FIG. IV, 16 MR. TOUCAN

STITCHING LINE

FOOT
CUT 4 F

EYE
CUT 2 F

EYE
DOT

A

BF

BOTTOM
CUT 1
BF

LEAVE
OPEN

BACK/SIDE CUT 1
LEAVE OPEN

B

BILL, CUT 2 EACH

Y

B

R

W

B

CHEST
CUT 1
YF

NAP

WINGS CUT 2   BF

1 SQ. = 1″

R = RED   Y = YELLOW   B = BLACK   W = WHITE
BF = BLUE FUR   F = BLUE FELT
YF = YELLOW FUR

God rest you merry,
gentlemen,
Let nothing you dismay;
Remember Christ our Savior,
Was born on Christmas day.

— TRADITIONAL CHRISTMAS
CAROL

POLLY PARROT
(about 9 inches tall)

Average: For those with some experience in crocheting.

Materials: Coats & Clark's Red Heart® Sport Yarn: 2 ounces each of Apple Green, Red and Baby Aqua; size G crochet hook, OR ANY SIZE HOOK TO OBTAIN GAUGE BELOW; marker; tapestry needle; 20 x 25 inches of yellow felt; black and white felt scraps; yellow sewing thread; synthetic stuffing; fabric glue; paper for patterns.

Gauge: With 2 strands of yarn held together, 7 sc = 2 inches; 7 rows = 2 inches

Note: *Work with 2 strands of yarn held together throughout. Always join with a sl st in first sc.*

Directions:

1. Head and Body: Starting at the center top of the Head with 2 strands of Red, ch 10. ***Rnd 1:*** 2 sc in 2nd ch from hook, sc in next 7 ch, 3 sc in last ch. Working along the opposite side of the starting chain, sc in next 7 ch, 2 sc in last ch, join with sl st to first sc. Mark beg of rnd for front. ***Rnds 2 and 3:*** Ch 1, sc in joining and in each sc to center sc of the 3-sc group at center back, 3 sc in center sc, sc in each rem sc, join to first sc — 25 sc on Rnd 3. ***Rnds 4 to 12:*** Ch 1, sc in joining and in each sc around, join. ***Rnd 13:*** Ch 1, sc in joining, inc 2 sc along center back, sc in each sc around, join — 27 sc. ***Rnd 14:*** Ch 1, 2 sc in joining, sc in each sc around, join — 28 sc. ***Rnd 15:*** Ch 1, sc in joining and in next 13 sc, ch 5, sc in 2nd ch from hook and in next 3 ch, sc in rem 14 sc, join — 32 sc. ***Rnd 16:*** Ch 1, sc in joining and in next 13 sc, sc in next 4 ch, 3 sc in next ch at tip at center back, sc in next 18 sc, join — 39 sc. ***Rnd 17:*** Ch 1, sc in joining and in next 19 sc, ch 5, sc in 2nd ch from hook and in next 3 ch, sc in next 19 sc, join — 43 sc. ***Rnd 18:*** Ch 1, sc in joining and in next 19 sc, sc in next 4 ch, 3 sc in next ch at tip, sc in next 23 sc, join — 50 sc. ***Rnd 19:*** Ch 1, sc in joining, inc 2 sc at center back, sc in each sc around, join — 52 sc. ***Rnds 20 to 23:*** Rep Rnd 4. ***Rnd 24:*** Ch 1, sc in joining, dec 1 sc at beg of rnd and 1 sc at end of rnd, sc in each sc around, ***to dec 1 sc***, *draw up a lp in each of 2 sc, yarn over and draw through all lps on hook;* join — 48 sc. ***Rnd 25:*** Rep Rnd 4. ***Rnd 26:*** Ch 1, sc in joining, dec 2 sc along center front and 4 sc along center back, sc in each sc around, join — 42 sc. ***Rnd 27:*** Ch 1, sc in joining, dec 4 sc along center front and 4 sc along center back, sc in each sc around, join — 34 sc. ***Rnd 28:*** Rep Rnd 4. ***Rnd 29:*** Ch 1, sc in joining, sc in next 3 sc; * dec 1 sc over next 2 sc, sc in next 4 sc; rep from * around. Fasten off, leaving an end for sewing. Stuff the parrot, and sew the bottom seam.

2. Wings (make 2): Starting at the top with 2 strands of Apple Green, ch 23. ***Row 1:*** Sc in 2nd ch from hook, sc in next 20 ch, 2 sc in last ch, ch 1, turn. ***Row 2:*** Sl st in first 12 sc, ch 10. ***Row 3:*** Sc in 2nd ch from hook and in next 8 ch to form feather opening, sc in next 11 sc that were used previously for sl sts, 2 sc in last sc, ch 1, turn. ***Row 4:*** Sc in first 11 sc, ch 10. ***Row 5:*** Sc in 2nd ch from hook, sc in next 8 ch, sc in next 11 sc, ch 1, turn. ***Row 6:*** Rep Row 4. ***Row 7:*** Rep Row 5. ***Row 8:*** Sc in first 8 sc. Fasten off. Leaving about ½ inch free at each feather opening, sew the remaining portion of the feathers together. Using the photo as a placement guide, sew the Wings to the Body.

3. Tail (make 2): With 2 strands of Baby Aqua held tog, ch 15. ***Row 1:*** Sc in 2nd ch from hook and in each ch across — 14 sc. Ch 1, turn. ***Hereafter, work in back loop of each st only.*** ***Row 2:*** Sc in each sc across, ch 4, turn. ***Row 3:*** Sc in 3rd ch from hook and in next ch, sc in each sc across, ch 1, turn. ***Row 4:*** Rep Row 2. ***Row 5:*** Rep Row 3. ***Row 6:*** Rep Row 2. ***Row 7:*** Sc in 3rd sc from hook and in next ch, sc in each rem sc across. Fasten off. Sew the two Tail pieces together, matching the corresponding edges to form a tube. Sew the straight opening of the tube to the center back of the parrot *(see photo)*.

4. Finishing: Enlarge the beak and foot patterns in FIG. IV, 17 onto paper, following the directions on page 241. From the yellow felt, cut two beak pieces and four foot pieces. Sew the beak pieces together, leaving the Head edge open. Stuff the beak. Using the photo as a placement guide, sew the beak to the Head. Place four strands of Red yarn around the beak where the beak joins the head. Using one strand of Red, tack the strands in place. For each foot, sew two foot pieces together, leaving the top edge open. Stuff the feet, and close the top edges. Using the photo as a placement guide, sew the feet to the Body. From the white felt scrap, cut two oval shapes, each 1 x ⅝ inch across the centers. From the black felt scrap, cut two circles, each about ½ inch in diameter. Glue each black circle to a white oval. Using the photo as a guide, glue the eyes to the sides of the Head.

FIG. IV, 17   POLLY PARROT   1 SQ. = 1″

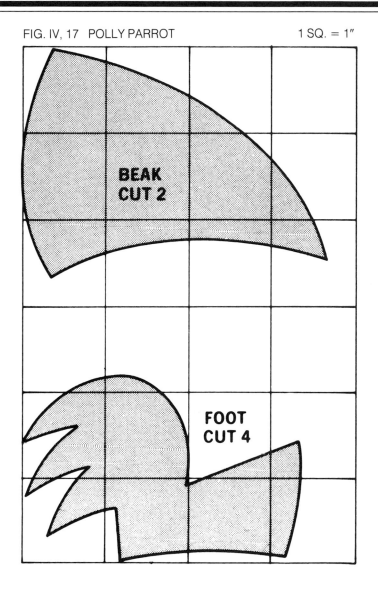

BEAK CUT 2

FOOT CUT 4

Bûche de Noël (recipe, page 199); Honey Whole Wheat Bread; Spicy Gingerbread Squares (recipes, page 197); Pecan Sticky Buns (recipe, page 196); Old-Fashioned Fruitcake (recipe, page 195); Chocolate-Topped Spice Cake (recipe, page 198); Nut Fingers (recipe, page 195)

SWEET SERENDIPITY

Menu for 16

*Nut Fingers**

*Old-Fashioned Fruitcake**

*Pecan Sticky Buns**

*Honey Whole Wheat Bread**
with whipped cream cheese and assorted preserves

*Spicy Gingerbread Squares**

*Golden Raisin Cake**

*Chocolate-Topped Spice Cake**

*Bûche de Noël**

Coffee, Hot Mulled Cider, Cocoa with Crème de
Menthe* and Spiced Wine Punch**

✳

*Recipe follows

Sweet Serendipity — Countdown

UP TO ONE MONTH AHEAD:
— Prepare and freeze the Nut Fingers, Old-Fashioned Fruitcake, Honey Whole Wheat Bread, Pecan Sticky Buns and Golden Raisin Cake.
— Prepare, but do not frost, the Spicy Gingerbread Squares, and freeze them.
— Prepare and freeze the Bûche de Noël. Once the cake is frozen, wrap it tightly in aluminum foil.
— Prepare the Chocolate-Topped Spice Cake up through Step 7, and freeze it.

UP TO TWO WEEKS AHEAD:
— Prepare the Old-Fashioned Fruitcake, if it was not prepared ahead and frozen, and store it in an airtight container.

UP TO A WEEK AHEAD:
— Prepare the Nut Fingers, if they were not prepared ahead and frozen, and store them in an airtight container.

UP TO SEVERAL DAYS AHEAD:
— Thaw the Old-Fashioned Fruitcake, if it was prepared ahead and frozen. Warm the fruitcake in a preheated slow oven (300°), then drizzle the fruitcake with the Sugar Glaze. Let the Glaze set, cover the fruitcake loosely with plastic wrap and store it in a cool place.
— Prepare the Golden Raisin Cake, if it was not prepared ahead and frozen, and cover it loosely.
— Prepare the Chocolate-Topped Spice Cake, if was not prepared ahead and frozen, and cover it loosely.

THE DAY BEFORE:
— Thaw the Nut Fingers, Honey Whole Wheat Bread, Pecan Sticky Buns and Golden Raisin Cake, if they were prepared ahead and frozen.

— Thaw and frost the Spicy Gingerbread Squares, if they were prepared ahead and frozen.
— Thaw the Chocolate-Topped Spice Cake, if it was prepared ahead and frozen, and proceed with Step 8 of the recipe.
— Thaw the Bûche de Noël, if it was prepared ahead and frozen. Place the cake on a serving platter, cover it very loosely with plastic wrap and thaw it in the refrigerator.
— Prepare the Bûche de Noël, if it was not prepared ahead and frozen. Cover the cake loosely with plastic wrap and refrigerate it.
— Prepare the Spicy Gingerbread Squares, if they were not prepared ahead and frozen, and cover them loosely with plastic wrap.
— Prepare the Honey Whole Wheat Bread, if it was not prepared ahead and frozen, and cover it loosely with plastic wrap.

EARLY IN THE DAY:
— Prepare the Pecan Sticky Buns, if they were not prepared ahead and frozen.
— Roll the Nut Fingers in additional 10X (confectioners' powdered) sugar, if necessary.
— Cut the Spicy Gingerbread Squares.
— Decorate the Bûche de Noël with the decorator frostings and candied cherries.
— Prepare the Mulled Cider. Prepare the spiced wine for the Spiced Wine Punch.

JUST BEFORE SERVING TIME:
— Warm the Pecan Sticky Buns and the Honey Whole Wheat Bread.
— Reheat the Mulled Cider. Finish preparing the Spiced Wine Punch.
— Prepare the Cocoa with Crème de Menthe. Prepare a pot of coffee.

NUT FINGERS

Bake at 325° for 25 minutes.
Makes 1½ dozen cookies.

1   cup (2 sticks) unsalted butter
¾   cup 10X (confectioners' powdered) sugar,
      plus extra for garnish
2   cups all-purpose flour
1   teaspoon vanilla
1   cup finely chopped pecans OR: walnuts

1. Preheat the oven to slow (325°).
2. Beat the butter in a large bowl with an electric mixer at high speed until it is light-colored and fluffy. Add the ¾ cup of 10X (confectioners' powdered) sugar, the flour and vanilla and stir to mix all the ingredients well. Add the pecans or walnuts and blend them into the dough.
3. Shape the dough into slender, 3-inch-long "fingers." Place the fingers on an ungreased baking sheet, spacing them 1 inch apart.
4. Bake in the preheated slow oven (325°) until the fingers are golden brown in color, for 25 minutes.
5. Roll the fingers in 10X (confectioners' powdered) sugar while they still are hot. Place the sugar-coated fingers on wire racks to cool. Once the fingers are cool, roll them again in the sugar to coat them evenly. Store the cookies in an airtight container.

OLD-FASHIONED FRUITCAKE

Bake at 325° for 1 hour.
Makes 2 fruitcakes.

1   container (15 ounces) golden raisins
1   container (7 ounces) pitted dates, chopped
1   container (11 ounces) dried currants
1½   cups chopped walnuts
2   tablespoons grated orange zest
        (orange part of rind only)
4   cups all-purpose flour
2   teaspoons apple pie spice
1   teaspoon baking soda

1   teaspoon salt
1   cup (2 sticks) butter, softened
1⅓   cups firmly packed light brown sugar
3   eggs
1   cup port wine
       Sugar Glaze (recipe follows)
       Candied red cherries and walnut halves,
         for garnish

1. Preheat the oven to slow (325°). Grease and lightly flour two 9 x 5 x 3-inch loaf pans. Tap out the excess flour from the pans.
2. Combine the raisins, dates, currants, chopped walnuts and orange zest in a very large bowl.
3. Sift together the flour, apple pie spice, baking soda and salt onto a piece of wax paper. Sprinkle 1 cup of the flour mixture over the fruit and nut mixture, and toss to coat the fruit evenly.
4. Beat the butter, brown sugar and eggs in a large bowl with an electric mixer at high speed until the mixture is fluffy, for 3 minutes.
5. Add the remaining flour mixture to the butter mixture alternately with the port wine, beating after each addition, to form a smooth batter.
6. Pour the batter over the fruit and nut mixture in the very large bowl. Gently fold the batter and fruit and nut mixture just until all the ingredients are well blended. Spoon the batter into the prepared pans.
7. Bake in the preheated slow oven (325°) until a wooden pick inserted in the center of the fruitcakes comes out clean, for 1 hour. Cool the fruitcakes in the pans on wire racks set over wax paper for 15 minutes. Run a thin knife around the edges of the fruitcakes to loosen them. Invert the fruitcakes onto the wire racks.
8. Meanwhile, prepare the Sugar Glaze.
9. Drizzle the Sugar Glaze over the warm fruitcakes. Let the fruitcakes cool completely.
10. To serve, garnish the fruitcakes with the candied red cherries and walnut halves.
Sugar Glaze: Combine ¾ cup of granulated sugar and ⅓ cup of water in a medium-size saucepan. Bring the mixture to boiling over medium heat. Lower the heat and simmer the mixture for 2 minutes. Remove the saucepan from the heat and stir in ¼ cup of 10X (confectioners' powdered) sugar until the glaze is smooth and creamy. *Makes 1 cup.*

PECAN STICKY BUNS

Bake at 375° for 30 minutes.
Makes 12 buns (two 9-inch rounds).

1   package (¼ ounce) active dry yeast
⅓   cup sugar
½   cup warm water (105°-110°) *
1   cup milk
¼   cup (½ stick) butter
1   teaspoon salt
1   teaspoon ground cinnamon
4½ cups all-purpose flour
2   eggs
½   cup (1 stick) butter, melted
2   cups firmly packed light brown sugar
6   tablespoons light corn syrup
6   tablespoons light cream
2   cups pecan halves

1. Sprinkle the yeast and one teaspoon of the sugar over the warm water in a large bowl. Stir the mixture until the yeast dissolves. Let the yeast mixture stand until it is foamy, for 5 minutes.
2. Combine the milk, the remaining sugar, the ¼ cup of butter, the salt and cinnamon in a small saucepan. Place the saucepan over low heat until the milk is warm (the butter does not have to melt).
3. Add the milk mixture to the yeast mixture along with 1½ cups of the flour. Beat the combined mixture with an electric mixer at medium speed for 3 minutes. Add the eggs and 1 cup of the remaining flour. Continue to beat the mixture for 2 minutes. Using a wooden spoon, stir in the remaining 2 cups of flour to form a moderately soft dough.
4. Turn out the dough onto a lightly floured surface. Knead the dough until it is smooth and shiny, for 5 minutes. Cover the dough with the large bowl and let the dough rest in a warm place, away from drafts, until it is doubled in size, for 40 minutes.

5. Divide the dough in half. Roll out one half on a lightly floured surface to a 12 x 9-inch rectangle. Brush part of the ½ cup of melted butter over the surface of the dough, and sprinkle ½ cup of the brown sugar over the buttered surface. Roll up the dough, jelly-roll style, along one short side. Repeat with the second half of the dough, part of the melted butter and ½ cup of the brown sugar.
6. Divide the remaining melted butter between two 9-inch layer cake pans. Combine the remaining 1 cup of brown sugar with the light corn syrup and the light cream, and pour half of the mixture into each pan. Place the pans over low heat, and heat the corn syrup mixture until it bubbles, stirring constantly. Sprinkle 1 cup of the pecan halves into each pan.
7. Using a sharp knife, cut each dough roll into six even slices. Place six of the slices, cut side up, on top of the syrup mixture and the nuts in each pan. Cover the pans with plastic wrap and let the dough rise in a warm place, away from drafts, until it is doubled in size, for 40 minutes.
8. Meanwhile, preheat the oven to moderate (375°).
9. Bake in the preheated moderate oven (375°) until the buns are golden in color, for 30 minutes. Cover the buns with a piece of aluminum foil for the last 5 to 7 minutes of baking time to prevent over-browning. Cool the buns in the pans on wire racks for 5 minutes. Run a thin knife around the edges of the rounds to loosen them, and invert the rounds onto serving platters or pieces of aluminum foil. Serve the buns immediately. Or, cool the buns completely, wrap them in the aluminum foil, label, date and freeze them.
__Note:__ Warm water should feel tepid when dropped on your wrist.

HONEY WHOLE WHEAT BREAD

Bake at 400° for 40 minutes.
Makes 2 loaves.

2   packages (¼ ounce each) active dry yeast
1   cup warm water (105° to 115°) *
⅓   cup honey
2   cups milk
¼   cup (½ stick) butter
1   tablespoon salt
5   cups whole wheat flour
¼   cup wheat germ
3   cups all-purpose flour

1. Sprinkle the yeast over the water. Add 1 teaspoon of the honey and stir until the yeast is dissolved. Let the mixture stand until it is foamy, for about 5 minutes.
2. Combine the remaining honey with the milk, butter and salt in a saucepan over low heat, and stir until the butter has melted. Pour the mixture into a large bowl and let it cool to lukewarm. Stir the yeast mixture into the honey mixture until they are combined.
3. Add the whole wheat flour, wheat germ and enough of the all-purpose flour to form a soft dough.
4. Turn out the dough onto a floured surface and knead the dough until it is smooth and elastic, for 10 minutes. Add more all-purpose flour as needed.
5. Place the dough in a large greased bowl and turn the greased side up. Cover the bowl with a towel. Let the dough rise in a warm place, away from drafts, until it is doubled in size, for 1 hour.
6. Punch down the dough, turn it out onto a floured surface and knead it a few times. Invert the bowl over the dough and let it rest for about 10 minutes.
7. Meanwhile, grease two 9 x 5 x 3 inch loaf pans.
8. Divide the dough in half and knead each half a few times. Shape each dough half into a loaf. Place the loaves into the prepared pans, seam side down.
9. Let the loaves rise in a warm place, away from drafts, until they are doubled in size, for 40 minutes.
10. Meanwhile, preheat the oven to hot (400°).
11. Bake in the preheated hot oven (400°) until the loaves are brown and sound hollow, for 40 minutes. Remove the loaves from the pans to wire racks to cool.
__Note:__ Warm water should feel tepid on your wrist.

SPICY GINGERBREAD SQUARES

Bake at 350° for 30 minutes.
Makes one 13 x 9 x 2-inch cake.

2½   cups all-purpose flour
1½   teaspoons baking soda
2   teaspoons ground ginger
1   teaspoon ground cinnamon
½   teaspoon salt
½   cup vegetable shortening
½   cup sugar
¾   cup molasses
1   egg
1   cup hot water
    Creamy Orange Frosting (recipe follows)
    Pecan halves, for garnish

1. Preheat the oven to moderate (350°). Grease a 13 x 9 x 2-inch baking pan.
2. Sift together the flour, baking soda, ginger, cinnamon and salt onto a piece of wax paper.
3. Beat the shortening with the sugar in a large bowl with an electric mixer at high speed until fluffy. Beat in the molasses and egg until the mixture is creamy.
4. Reduce the speed to low. Add the flour mixture to the molasses mixture, half at a time, just until they are combined. Add the hot water and blend until smooth. Pour the batter into the prepared pan.
5. Bake in the preheated moderate oven (350°) until the top of the gingerbread springs back when lightly touched with your fingertip, for 30 minutes.
6. Cool the gingerbread in the pan on a wire rack for 10 minutes. Run a knife around the edges to loosen the gingerbread. Invert the gingerbread onto the rack, turn it right side up and let it cool completely.
7. Spread the Creamy Orange Frosting over the top of the gingerbread and gently press the pecan halves into the frosting. Serve the gingerbread in squares.

Creamy Orange Frosting: Beat 8 ounces of cream cheese in a bowl with an electric mixer until it is smooth. Add 2 cups of 10X (confectioners' powdered) sugar, 1 tablespoon of grated orange zest (orange part of rind only) and 2 tablespoons of orange juice. Beat until the frosting is smooth. *Makes 2¼ cups.*

GOLDEN RAISIN CAKE

Bake at 325° for 1 hour, 15 minutes.
Makes 1 medium-size loaf cake.

- ⅔ cup (1⅓ sticks) unsalted butter, softened
- 2⅔ cups sifted 10X (confectioners' powdered) sugar
- 2 eggs
- 1 teaspoon vanilla
- 1 cup all-purpose flour
- 1 teaspoon baking powder
- ¼ teaspoon salt
- ⅓ cup yellow cornmeal
- ⅔ cup golden raisins

1. Preheat the oven to slow (325°). Grease and flour an 8½ x 4½ x 2½-inch loaf pan.
2. Beat together the butter and the 10X (confectioners' powdered) sugar in a large bowl with an electric mixer at high speed until the mixture is light and fluffy. Add the eggs and the vanilla to the butter mixture and beat until they are incorporated.
3. Sift together the flour, baking powder and salt in a second bowl. Stir in the cornmeal and raisins. Add the flour mixture to the butter mixture and stir until they are blended. Spread the batter into the prepared pan, smoothing the top with a spatula.
4. Bake in the preheated slow oven (325°) until a wooden pick inserted into the center of the cake comes out clean, for 1 hour and 15 minutes. Cool the cake in the pan on a wire rack for 10 minutes. Run a thin knife around the edges of the cake to loosen it from the pan. Invert the cake onto the rack, turn the cake right side up and let it cool completely.

CHOCOLATE-TOPPED SPICE CAKE

Bake at 350° for 1 hour and 5 minutes.
Makes one 9 x 5 x 3-inch loaf cake.

- 2¾ cups all-purpose flour
- 2 teaspoons baking powder
- ½ teaspoon salt
- 1 teaspoon ground cloves
- 1 teaspoon ground cinnamon
- 1 teaspoon ground nutmeg
- 1 teaspoon ground allspice
- 1 cup (2 sticks) unsalted butter
- 1¾ cups sugar
- 4 eggs
- ⅔ cup milk
- 2 teaspoons vanilla
- 1 cup walnuts, very finely chopped
- 1 package (6 ounces) semisweet chocolate pieces

1. Preheat the oven to moderate (350°). Grease and flour a 9 x 5 x 3-inch loaf pan.
2. Sift together the flour, baking powder, salt, cloves, cinnamon, nutmeg and allspice onto wax paper.
3. Beat the butter and sugar in a large bowl with an electric mixer at high speed until the mixture is light and fluffy, for 3 minutes. Beat in the eggs, one at a time.
4. Reduce the mixer speed to low. Add the flour mixture to the butter mixture, alternately with the milk and vanilla, beating well after each addition.
5. Fold the nuts into the batter just until they are incorporated. Pour the batter into the prepared pan.
6. Bake in the preheated moderate oven (350°) until the top of the cake springs back when lightly touched with your fingertip, for 1 hour and 5 minutes.
7. Cool the cake in the pan on a wire rack for 10 minutes. Run a knife around the edges of the cake to loosen it from the pan. Invert the cake onto the wire rack, turn it right side up and let it cool completely.
8. Melt the chocolate in a saucepan over low heat. Drizzle the melted chocolate over the cooled cake.

BÛCHE DE NOËL

Bake at 375° for 12 minutes.
Makes 12 servings.

1   *cup plain (not self-rising) cake flour*
¼   *cup unsweetened cocoa powder (not a mix)*
1   *teaspoon baking powder*
¼   *teaspoon salt*
3   *eggs*
1   *cup granulated sugar*
⅓   *cup water*
1   *teaspoon vanilla*
     10X (confectioners' powdered) sugar
     Coffee Cream Filling (recipe follows)
     Chocolate Butter Cream Frosting (recipe follows)
     Red and green decorator frosting
     Candied red cherries, for decorating (optional)

1. Preheat the oven to moderate (375°). Grease an 11 x 15 x 1-inch jelly-roll pan. Line the bottom of the pan with wax paper, and grease the wax paper.
2. Sift together the cake flour, cocoa, baking powder and salt onto a piece of wax paper.
3. Beat the eggs in a small bowl with an electric mixer at high speed until they are thick and lemon-colored. Add the granulated sugar, 1 tablespoon at a time, beating constantly, until the mixture is very thick. Using a wooden spoon, stir in the water and the vanilla. Fold the flour mixture into the egg mixture just until they are combined. Pour the batter into the prepared jelly-roll pan, spreading the batter to distribute it evenly.
4. Bake in the preheated moderate oven (375°) until the center of the cake springs back when lightly pressed with your fingertip, for 12 minutes.
5. Meanwhile, heavily dust a clean tea towel with 10X (confectioners' powdered) sugar. When the cake has finished baking, remove it from the oven and set it on a heatproof surface. Run a thin knife around the edges of the cake to loosen it from the pan. Carefully invert the cake onto the sugar-dusted towel, shaking the pan gently to free the cake. Peel off the wax paper. Carefully roll up the cake, jelly-roll style, along one long side using the towel as a guide. Wrap the free ends of the towel around the rolled cake, and let the cake cool completely.

6. Meanwhile, prepare the Coffee Cream Filling and the Chocolate Butter Cream Frosting.
7. Carefully unroll the cake using the towel as a guide. Set aside ¼ cup of the Coffee Cream Filling and spread the remainder on the inside of the roll. Gently reroll the cake.
8. Cut a ½-inch-thick slice from one end of the cake. Reroll the slice tightly to form a "knot" for the log. Place the cake on a serving platter. Frost the sides of the cake with the Chocolate Butter Cream Frosting, leaving the ends unfrosted *(see photo, page 192)*. To create a "bark" effect with the frosting, run the blade of the frosting knife up and down the length of the cake, or draw the tines of a fork up and down the cake instead. Frost the bottom of the "knot," and press it onto the side of the cake. Frost the sides of the "knot," blending the base into the frosting on the sides of the cake. Use the reserved ¼ cup of Coffee Cream Filling to frost the top of the "knot" and the ends of the cake. Use the red and green decorator frosting to make "flowers" *(see photo, page 192)*. If you wish, press a candied cherry half into the center of each frosting flower. Refrigerate the cake until serving time.

Coffee Cream Filling: Combine 1 cup of heavy or whipping cream, 1 tablespoon of instant coffee granules and ½ cup of 10X (confectioners' powdered) sugar in a medium-size bowl. Beat the cream mixture with an electric mixer on high speed until it forms stiff peaks. *Makes 2 cups.*

Chocolate Butter Cream Frosting: Melt ¼ cup (½ stick) of butter and 2 squares (1 ounce each) of unsweetened chocolate in a small saucepan over low heat. Cool the chocolate mixture slightly, and add 2 cups of 10X (confectioners' powdered) sugar, ¼ cup of milk and ½ teaspoon of vanilla. Beat the combined mixture with a wooden spoon until it is smooth and a good spreading consistency. *Makes enough to frost the Bûche de Noël.*

HOT MULLED CIDER

Makes 16 servings.

1	gallon apple cider
1	cup firmly packed light brown sugar
9	whole cloves
9	whole allspice
12	1-inch cinnamon sticks
2	lemons, thinly sliced

1. Combine the apple cider and the brown sugar in a large saucepan or Dutch oven.
2. Place the cloves, allspice and cinnamon sticks on a piece of cheesecloth, gather the ends of the cloth and tie them to make a bag. Place the spice bag in the cider and simmer the mixture for 5 minutes. Remove the spice bag from the cider.
3. Serve the cider in mugs, with a lemon slice floating on top of each serving.

COCOA WITH CRÈME DE MENTHE

Makes 10 servings.

8	envelopes (1 ounce each) instant hot cocoa mix
6	cups boiling water
1/2	cup white crème de menthe

1. Pour the contents of all the hot cocoa mix envelopes into a large, heatproof pitcher.
2. Add the boiling water and the crème de menthe to the pitcher. Beat the cocoa mixture with a wire whisk until all the ingredients are well combined and the mixture is foamy on top. Serve the cocoa in mugs.

SPICED WINE PUNCH

Makes 24 Servings.

4	bottles (1 liter each) Burgundy wine
2	cups sugar
20	whole cardamom seeds, peeled
20	whole cloves
8	two-inch cinnamon sticks
1/4	cup finely grated orange zest (orange part of rind only)
1	bottle (750 ml.) Danish aquavit
2	cups raisins
1	cup sliced blanched almonds

1. Pour the Burgundy wine into a very large saucepan or Dutch oven. Add the sugar, cardamom, cloves, cinnamon sticks and orange zest. Simmer the wine mixture slowly, without letting it boil, until the sugar has dissolved completely.
2. Warm the aquavit in a small saucepan over medium-low heat. Add the warm aquavit to the wine mixture and carefully light the combined mixture using a long fireplace match. Let the flames burn down.
3. Strain part of the punch into a fondue pot or chafing dish set over a lit warmer, and add part of the raisins. Keep the punch hot and serve it in mugs. Add the almonds to each individual serving. Add more punch and raisins to the fondue pot as needed.
Note: To make Spiced Wine Punch ahead, simmer 2 cups of the wine with the sugar, cardamom seeds, cloves, cinnamon sticks and orange zest until the sugar has dissolved completely. Set the mixture aside. At serving time, heat the mixture with the remaining wine. Continue with Step 2 above.

DANISH DELIGHT

Danish aquavit is an unsweetened liquor with a caraway flavor. Add it to Bloody Marys, meat stews and carrot and cabbage dishes.

OLD-FASHIONED FESTIVITIES — EVOCATIVE TOUCHES

When setting your table for the holidays, try an old Scandinavian tradition. Instead of a conventional tablecloth, place a rectangular table runner down the center of your dining table. A lace dresser scarf works beautifully, or create a runner from patchwork.

✳

Serve a Colonial-style Christmas dinner on "pewter" plates. You can find metal ware with the look, but not the cost, of pewter in most department stores.

✳

Grill food for the holiday meal in your fireplace if possible. Fire-smoked sausage imparts a woodsy flavor to stuffing. Grilled vegetables can be brushed with garlic-infused oil, and sprinkled with coarse salt and rosemary. Stuffed apples baked by the side of the fire are a fruity accompaniment to roasted ham.

✳

Clean, flat rocks can be wrapped in aluminum foil and placed by the side of the fire to heat. At dinner time, carefully wrap the rocks in a clean, cotton towel and place them in the bottom of the bread basket to keep rolls fresh-from-the-oven warm during the meal.

Try Café Brûlot, a delicious heart-warmer on a winter evening. To make Café Brûlot: In a deep chafing dish, pan or saucepan, mash together 2 sticks cinnamon, 6 whole cloves, the zest of 2 oranges and 2 lemons (orange and yellow part of rinds only, each cut in one continuous spiral), and 24 sugar cubes, using a sturdy wooden spoon or the back of a ladle. Pour in 1 cup of brandy, $1/3$ cup of coffee-flavored liqueur and $1/3$ cup of Grand Marnier or other orange-flavored liqueur. Cook the mixture over medium-high heat for about 1 minute, stirring occasionally. Very carefully light the mixture using a long fireplace match, then pour in 6 cups of freshly brewed, strong coffee. Continue stirring the mixture until the flames die down. Serve immediately in mugs.

✳

Use a cast-iron skillet to create a special addition for the Christmas feast: Pour a bag of fresh cranberries into a cast-iron skillet. Sprinkle the cranberries with $1^1/2$ cups of sugar and the zest of 1 orange (orange part of rind only). Cover the skillet and bake the mixture in a very slow oven (225°) for about 1 hour. Uncover the skillet and douse the cranberries with $1/4$ cup of cranberry liqueur.

*I*n seed time learn, in harvest teach, in winter enjoy.

— *WILLIAM BLAKE*

CHAPTER 5

WINTER FEST

Make it a New Year to remember.

Don't view the coming months as a series of dreary winter days. This is the time to introduce a new attitude!

Start off the year by inviting your friends to a fabulous party. How about by celebrating New Year's Day with an Open House Cocktail Party—we give you the menu and recipes. But don't stop there! Sometime in January or February, invite the gang over again. Keep it casual. Wear something wild. Have a great time lighting up a winter's night. Serve our hot and hearty meatball hero, with all the fixings. Or make it a theme party—you'll find pages of ideas that chase away the winter blues.

Hold fast to your New Year's resolutions to lose weight, get organized and take better care of yourself and your family. Our timely tips will tell you how.

And when the kids start complaining that there's nothing to do, you'll be ready with our ten great ideas for dismal days. They're guaranteed fun for the kids, and a good time for you, too.

Start the new year off right, and you'll enjoy every minute of it!

THROW A THEME PARTY!

Entertaining shouldn't stop just because the holidays are over. Brighten long winter nights by inviting friends to your place for a casual party with a theme. We've made the entertaining easy on you with serve-yourself main dishes that work at a buffet or a sit-down dinner. Use our suggestions as a starting point, and tailor the party to your personal taste.

Goin' Hollywood Party
Darling, simply everyone will want to be invited!

Invitations: Have your agent call, or design an invitation to look like the front page of *Variety,* the "bible" of the movie industry. Try writing your own *Variety* headline, such as: FLIXS AND KIXS, SATURDAY AT SIX. Sprinkle a little tinsel (left over from Christmas) in each envelope.

Favors: Keychains, magnets and other token items in Hollywood motifs (available at local card and gift shops): miniature director's clappers, film reels, movie cameras, stars and palm trees.

Menu: California cuisine: A light pasta dish made with sun-dried tomatoes and sliced avocado on a bed of lettuce drizzled with oil and vinegar, a citrus fruit salad, and sparkling mineral water or wine spritzers.

Decorations: Cover the table with gold lamé. Buy movie stills of favorite stars (available at card and gift shops, and some record and video stores), and put one at each place setting, prop them behind the dishes at a buffet table, or lay them side-by-side to cover the top of the table. Make your own cardboard cut-out "Walk of the Stars" to lead your guests from the front door to the party.

Tips: Rent a few videos, and keep them running on low volume throughout the party. Stick with upbeat classics and musicals such as *Top Hat* with Fred Astaire and Ginger Rogers, *Gentlemen Prefer Blondes* with Marilyn Monroe and Jane Russell, or any of the Marx Brothers films. Look for *That's Entertainment,* a montage of some of Hollywood's greatest moments. Invite everyone to come incognito—wearing sunglasses—so they won't be mobbed by their fans!

Star Signs Party
Aries to Pisces—everyone's compatible at this astrological theme party!

Invitations: Look to the stars. Decorate plain note cards with gold and silver stick-on stars, or cut out star-shaped invitations from sturdy paper. If you're ambitious, place the stars in the formation of the appropriate constellation for each guests' sign. Write the invitations with gold or silver ink.

Favors: Inexpensive, pocket-size annual horoscope guides (available at book stores, or even the supermarket check-out).

Menu: (Cancer the) Crab Cakes sautéed in (Virgo the) Virgin olive oil with (Pisces the) Fish Chowder. For dessert, (Leo the) Lion-shaped ginger cookies. Set out grapes balanced on a (Libran) scale. Or make up your own innovative references to the astrological charts.

Decorations: Attach aluminum foil stars to chenille pipe cleaners, and insert them in a floral arrangement. Use an astronomer's map of the stars as a covering for the dining table. Turn the lights down, and play ethereal "New Age" music.

Tips: Determine the zodiac sign of each guest beforehand. Get an astrology book, such as Linda Goodman's *Sun Signs*, from the library and use it during the party to read interesting information about each guest. All will enjoy hearing what the stars foretell for them in the coming year.

Red and White Party
With all your guests in red and white, no one could possibly be blue!

Invitations: Red notes written in white ink. Tell everyone to dress in red and white from head to toe.

Favors: Anything in the color scheme: Peppermint candies, roses, inexpensive sunglasses, T-shirts.

Menu: Go Italian: Linguine with white or red clam sauce, cold mozzarella and tomato salad, cherry cheesecake, and red and white wines.

Decorations: Use solid color paper party goods. Buy tablecloths in red and white. Cut one slightly smaller than the other, and place the smaller tablecloth on top of the larger on the table. Arrange red and white carnations or mini-carnations as a centerpiece.

Tips: Wear something a little outrageous such as: one white shoe and one red shoe, or bright red nail polish, or white lipstick, or a red union suit with a white necktie (do you dare?!).

Bring-A-Dish Ethnic Foods Party
The guests supply the meal—what could be easier?

Invitations: Decorate note cards with flags of all nations. Draw them yourself, or use stickers. You'll find charts of world flags in encyclopedias and most dictionaries and almanacs. Be sure your guests understand that they have been asked to bring a dish.

Favors: Token gift items decorated with globes or maps: banks, pencils, pencil sharpeners, even earrings.

Menu: The selection of dishes is up to your guests, but make sure there's a dish for every course: hors d'oeuvres, soup, salad, main course, side dishes, bread, dessert. Ask your guests to prepare enough of their particular dish so everyone can have a taste, but let them know they don't have to feed the whole gang. Try to balance the menu between light and heavy dishes, meat and meatless dishes, spicy and mild dishes.

Decorations: Use a pretty lace tablecloth for the table or, if you prefer a more colorful table covering, an inexpensive map of the world. Make a centerpiece of international flags purchased at a five-and-dime or party supply store.

Tips: Be ready with suggestions for your guests' dishes. Ask an inexperienced cook to bring a salad, simple dessert, or a bottle of wine. Save the challenging dishes for friends who "live" in the kitchen. You might ask each guest to bring a dish that represents his or her family heritage—anything from borscht to lo mein. Set up a bar with specialties of all nations: Sangria, German beer, jasmine tea, citron pressé, and so on.

Midwinter Masquerade Party
Who says "fancy dress" is reserved for Halloween?

Invitations: Get into the Mardi Gras mood by trimming note cards with lace and gold braid. Or try this mischievous approach: Cut photographs of celebrities from magazines (everyone from George Bush to Oprah Winfrey), affix each one to the front of a note card and, with a black marker, draw a Lone Ranger mask on the celebrity.

Favors: Buy inexpensive eye masks, and decorate them with lace, sequins, bows, buttons . . . anything! Personalize one for each guest.

Menu: New Orleans style: Jambalaya or shrimp creole, black-eyed peas, collard greens and pralines. Everything should be festive, spicy and colorful. Don't forget the champagne!

Decorations: Use bright colors such as pink, purple, orange, yellow and green (or all of them, if you can stand it). Decorate with streamers, confetti and masks. Take a cue from old New Orleans, and drape the dining table with strings and strings of faceted, plastic Mardi Gras beads.

Tips: Guests needn't come in costume, but they should wear masks.

"Chili Con Cards" Party

An evening of poker, bridge, or what's-your-pleasure at your ranch.

Invitations: Affix a playing card to the front of each note card, or use the Old West as your inspiration and trim each note card with a tiny twine lasso.

Favors: Decks of cards. You'll find them decorated with everything from flowers to old autos to food product logos. Select an appropriate card deck for each guest.

Menu: Tex-Mex: A steaming pot of chili served with bowls of sour cream, cubes of Cheddar cheese and diced onion on the side. Serve the chili with corn bread (spiked with jalapeño peppers, if you like), a crisp green salad, and apple pie to finish. If you're planning to eat as you play, don't serve finger foods or anything too greasy.

Decorations: Cover the dining table with a plaid wool blanket, or use place mats. The card tables should be covered with felt. Turn an old cowboy hat upside down to hold a bowl of flowers. Or fill a shallow tray with sand and place small potted cacti on top.

Tips: Decide beforehand if you'll be playing a serious game of cards, or just a few informal hands. Set house rules and cash limits, particularly if you are playing poker or bridge for money. It's best to have a reputable rule book on hand to help settle disputes.

A NEW LEAF FOR THE NEW YEAR

The start of a new year is always a good time for changes. This year, make a vow to take better care of yourself and your family by changing bad eating habits, taking off extra pounds, getting organized—even learning to manage stress more effectively.

Smart Dieting

—Keep a diet diary. Before you begin a weight-loss program, keep a diary for two weeks of everything you eat listed under the following headings: Breakfast, Lunch, Dinner, Snacks, Cravings and Triggers (the last category includes stressful situations you encounter, and the foods you crave during those times). The diary will help you understand your eating habits. Be sure to note any meals you skipped; they could be a clue to why you overeat later in the day. Continue keeping the diary once you begin your weight-loss program; it will show a healthy change in your eating habits.

—Instill healthy habits into your cooking techniques. Avoid extra fats by not adding saturated oils, butter, mayonnaise and creamy salad dressings to your dishes. Avoid using salt in cooking and don't add salt at the table. Bake, broil, barbecue, poach or microwave meats and fish, or simmer them in a low-sodium broth. Use herbs, spices, lemon, or flavored vinegars for added zest.

—Drink up. You should drink at least two quarts of fluid a day. We suggest water (fill a pitcher with ice cold water in the morning, and drink a glassful every hour, finishing the pitcher by the end of the work day), seltzer (no sugar, no sodium), tea and iced tea (preferably caffeine-free and without added sugar).

—Exercise regularly. On a serious health and weight-loss program, diet and exercise go hand in hand. Start with a few easy stretching and toning exercises, and move up to a vigorous calisthenics and aerobics workout (low-impact is fine). Walk whenever you can—to the store, the beauty shop, to meet the kids after school. Take the stairs instead of the escalator or elevator.

—Make your kitchen cheat-proof. Keep "danger foods" out of the pantry and refrigerator.

Weigh-In Do's and Don'ts

Don't constantly hop on and off the scale.
Do weigh in once a week. Forget the scale between times.
Do place the scale—and your feet—on the same spot on the floor each time.

Don't be too hard on yourself—don't punish yourself for little lapses in your diet, just try not to repeat them.
Do postpone your weigh-in for a day or so if you're temporarily under extra stress, retaining water, or if you've overeaten.

Relax!

— Reserve time for yourself and mark it on the calendar. Don't let it get bumped!

— Take an occasional "mental health" day off when you're really feeling stressed at work. Use the time to do something nice for yourself; don't use it to do chores.

— Go on a shopping spree. If you can't afford it, go window-shopping and leave your credit cards at home.

— Go alone to a movie, concert or ballet. Learn to enjoy your own company.

— Treat yourself to a facial or manicure.

— Have a free make-up analysis at a department store.

— Have lunch with your best friend at the nicest restaurant you can afford.

— Call an old friend — someone who will make you smile — and have a nice long chat.

— Look through old photographs, letters or journals.

— Get completely involved in a crossword puzzle, jigsaw puzzle or hobby.

Getting Organized

— Prepare for a year of fiscal organization. Buy a file box with dividers, and use it to hold all of your financial papers for the coming year. Save your bank statements, credit card statements, receipts (especially for major purchases), insurance records and claims, lease or mortgage payment records, travel receipts, paycheck stubs, and so on. At tax time, you'll have everything you need at your fingertips.

— Set aside one recipe box for your quickest, easiest meals. Every week, pick out seven and make sure you have all their ingredients; what's missing forms the basis for your shopping list.

— Use self-sticking notes throughout the house with reminders for the kids.

— Never walk upstairs empty-handed. Carry something that has to be put away.

— Keep a "tickler file" in your weekly planner. List all the things you need to purchase for an upcoming event, such as a birthday party.

— Label laundry baskets for lights, whites and darks, so that clothes are sorted instantly.

— Shop for household staples, such as paper towels and soap, once a month.

Lunch Box Savvy

— Give your kids foods that snap, crackle and pop. Kids love the drama of eating even more than they love the food itself. Pack a lunch box with carrots, celery and other raw vegetables, apples, grapes and other interesting-to-eat fruits.

— Use juices that come in boxes to keep things cool. Put a few boxes of juice in the freezer, and a few more in the refrigerator. Pack one frozen and one chilled box in your child's lunch box. The frozen juice will keep sandwiches and fruit cool, the chilled juice is for sipping at lunch. Your child can drink the frozen juice (thawed by the end of the day) on her way home from school.

— Fix fun food together. Mix up a batch of healthy muffins or a chunky tuna salad with your child's help. He'll have more fun eating the food he made himself.

— Pack an extra snack for the trip home. After-school time often signals nutritional collapse; that's when kids are tired and start eating candy. An extra box of raisins, a package of trail mix, or a bag of air-popped popcorn will tide your child over on the bus ride or walk home.

Just For Kids
Fun Stuff to Do Indoors

1. Organize an activity box of arts and crafts supplies. Include white glue and scissors (try to have one of each for each child), thin cardboard, construction paper, white bond paper, crayons or colored pencils, and empty paper towel and toilet paper rolls. Throw in anything that might inspire creativity: bits of fabric, ribbon and lace; beads and buttons; yarn and string; walnut shells; pine cones and acorns; drinking straws. Clear off the kitchen table, cover it with newspaper or a drop cloth, and let the kids create arts and crafts masterpieces. (Best for school age children.)

2. If you're a crafter yourself, teach your child to knit or crochet. Be patient—young hands can't perform sophisticated movements on the first tries. Have your youngster start by making a scarf—it's simple, not too small, and doesn't require much counting. Finish the ends of the scarf with fringe. Take your child to the yarn store, and let her select the yarn herself. (Ages 7 to teens.)

3. Keep a package of balloons on hand for dismal days. Play balloon "volleyball" by tapping the balloon back and forth. Or try balloon "soccer," passing the balloon around using only your feet. Work some balloon magic. Rub a balloon on your sleeve to create friction, then stick the balloon on the wall; the friction holds it in place, like magic! (All ages.)

4. Make walking finger puppets. On thin cardboard, draw a girl or boy from the waist up. The figure should be about 2 inches wide. Extend the sides of the figure below the waist about ¾ inch. Using a penny as a guide, draw two circles side by side on the extension. Cut out the figure, and cut out the circles. Color the puppet. To make the puppet walk, put your index finger and middle finger through the holes, from back to front, for legs. (Ages 6 to 12.)

5. Paint the latest fashions. Purchase fabric paints at your local craft store or five-and-dime. You'll find them in all the colors of the rainbow, including day-glo shades and glitter paints. Let the kids decorate T-shirts, sweatshirts, jeans or fabric sneakers. (Ages 10 to teen.)

6. Make bean bags. Cut an old washcloth into a 4 x 8-inch rectangle, and fold the rectangle in half, right sides together, to 4 x 4 inches. Stitch around three sides and two corners of the square, leaving an opening for turning. Turn the square right side out, fill it with dried peas or beans, turn in the open edges, and slipstitch the opening closed *(see Stitch Guide, page 240)*. Reinforce the edges by stitching all around in blanket stitch *(see Stitch Guide)*. Play catch with the bean bags, or place empty containers on the floor and challenge the kids to a bean bag toss. (All ages.)

7. Use dried peas, beans, lentils and other legumes to create a food mosaic. You'll also need construction or heavy paper, black yarn, and white glue. Outline a design on the paper with the white glue. Place the black yarn along the glue outlines. Let the glue set for a few minutes. Then spread each space inside the outlines, one at a time, with white glue and sprinkle it with one kind of legume. Sprinkle each adjacent space with a different kind of legume. Sprinkle only a thin layer of the legumes to be sure they cover the spaces and adhere to the paper. (Ages 3 and up.)

8. Tie-dye! The fashion statement of the psychedelic sixties is back in style. Here is a refresher course in a nutshell. Lay a T-shirt on a table, and gather the front of the shirt in the center. Twist a rubber band around the base of the gather. Twist a few more rubber bands tightly on the gathered piece. Repeat on the back and sleeves. Mix liquid or powdered dye in a washtub or bucket (not in your washing machine!), following the manufacturer's directions. Put on rubber gloves and immerse the shirt in the dye for the recommended time. Remove the shirt and let it dry. When the shirt is dry, remove the rubber bands and let it dry completely. (All ages. Little ones will need help; older kids may want to try more complicated designs.)

9. Try sponge painting. Cut cellulose sponges into simple shapes: squares, hearts, triangles, stars. Spread acrylic or other non-toxic paint in a flat dish or tray. Dip the sponge shapes in the paint, and dab them on paper to make a design. The kids can make stationery, decorate brown craft paper for gift wrap or brighten up a canvas-covered loose leaf binder. (Ages 7 and up.)

10. Make your own bird feeder; it's a great way to teach the kids about nature and responsibility. Start with a clean, empty container such as a milk carton, plastic bleach bottle, or plastic milk bottle. Cut a feeding hole 2 inches high and 3 inches long in the side of the container, about an inch up from the bottom. Make another hole on the other side of the container. The bottom of the container should still be attached firmly to serve as a tray for bird seed. Using a scissors point, poke two holes in the 1-inch area below each feeding hole. Cut plastic drinking straws into 2-inch lengths for perches, and insert a perch into each prepared hole. Attach wire or cord to the top of the container for a hanger. Hang the feeder from a tree branch or house eave. Spread bird seed, sunflower seeds, pumpkin seeds, or bread crumbs in the feeder tray. Refer to a bird watcher's guide for feeding tips and identification techniques. (All ages.)

Winterfest Touches

Make some cocoa—the old-fashioned way! Buy some cocoa powder, and follow the directions on the back of the can. Flavor your cocoa with cinnamon sticks, marshmallows or a dollop of freshly whipped cream. It's a once-in-a-while indulgence, but a heavenly one!

✳

Affix paper doilies to the underside of a glass top dining table. They'll look like snowflakes.

✳

Send New Year's greetings to the people you forgot on your Christmas card list. Be sure to update the list—names and addresses—for next year. This also is a good time to send greetings of the season to friends of other faiths who don't celebrate Christmas.

✳

As you and your family fill your closets with the new clothes you received as Christmas gifts, clear out some of the clothes you've outgrown or no longer wear. Make up a nice post-holiday package for the charity clothing drop.

Can't get away for a holiday vacation? Rent a travelogue video, and journey to faraway places without leaving your living room. Make an evening of it by preparing a meal to suit your destination: Moroccan lamb and couscous, Chinese stir-fry, Spanish tapas, Mexican enchiladas, even Japanese sushi if you're game.

✳

Try a different kind of soft drink. Heat your favorite flavor of soda (heating will cause the bubbles to dissipate), and drink it warm. Try sodas in lemon-lime, cherry and cola flavors. It's a delicious and warming way to have your favorite drink.

For great party ice, try placing maraschino cherries, lemon and lime slices, mandarin orange sections, strawberries or seedless grapes in each ice cube square. Fill the tray with water and freeze it. To have a supply of ice that doesn't clump together, empty the ice cube trays into brown paper bags, and store the bags in the freezer.

✳

Make up your bed with some snuggly flannel sheets. They're wonderfully warm and feel terrific on nights when the temperature drops. They're an especially good investment if you're lowering your thermostat to conserve on heating bills. Don't forget them for the kids, too!

✳

The winter months can be particularly hard on your skin and lips, so take extra good care of your face. Before you go outside, even on a short walk, apply a light moisturizer that contains sunscreen. Use a lip balm that protects against cracking and chapping. Take special care of the delicate areas under your eyes by moisturizing them daily.

✳

Frosty, rainy or snowy days in January are the perfect time to reorganize your photo albums—and insert the recent holiday snapshots into a new album. This is a great family activity, sure to provide laughs and good memories for all.

Pamper yourself to avoid the January blues. Give yourself a facial to get your skin deep-down clean. Add 1 teaspoon of chamomile leaves to 4 cups of boiling water in a bowl. Hold your face 10 inches from the bowl for about 8 minutes. Finish the treatment with a honey and egg mask. Mix one egg yolk with one teaspoon of honey and one teaspoon of warm milk. Apply the mask to your face and throat. Sit back, close your eyes and relax for 20 minutes, then gently rinse off the mask with warm water.

✳

If you live in an area that gets snow in the winter, get the whole family outside on a sunny, snowy day and have your own snow sculpture contest. Make sure to take lots of pictures of the finished "works of art."

Learn something new. Start an exercise class, take a Chinese cooking course, learn how to use a home computer. Now that the holiday rush is over, it's time to do something special just for you.

✳

Have breakfast for dinner! Cold winter months are the perfect time of year to serve pancakes and sausage links, French toast and bacon, waffles or omelets as your evening meal. Serve coffee (regular or decaffeinated), milk and tea as the beverage. As a special treat, top pancakes or French toast with thawed, fresh-frozen strawberries or sprinkle chocolate chips into the pancake or waffle batter!

✳

Buy a bouquet of fresh flowers once or twice a month. They will brighten your home and remind everyone that spring is just around the corner.

Brighten dark winter days with thoughts of spring. Plan a garden—even though you can't plant it yet, you'll have fun looking at the gardening books and seed catalogs. Force bulbs for early blooms.

✳

Wear bright colors. You'll find that a ruby red sweater or sunny yellow galoshes can make a dreary day more bearable. The cheerful colors will raise the spirits of the people around you as well.

✳

Instead of automatically turning on the television on a snowy or rainy day, try reading aloud to the family. Take turns reading a chapter and discuss the story as you go. Most classic children's books are just as enjoyable to adults as to the youngsters in the crowd. Or, try renting audiocassette tapes of books from your local library. This way, everyone can listen along as they work on their crafts projects.

✳

Bring a bit of the "bubbly" to your wintertime party. Provide each guest with a bottle of soap bubbles. Most adults have a kid inside them, and it's hard to resist the urge to let your hair down and see who can blow the biggest bubble!

Sausage & Meatball Hero (recipe, page 218); Vegetable Dippers (recipe, page 217);
Soda Fountain "Pizza" (recipe, page 218); Super Hero (recipe, page 217)

A HERO'S WELCOME

Menu for 8

Vegetable Dippers, Tangy Tomato Dip*,
Parsley Chive Dip**

*Super Hero**

*Sausage & Meatball Hero**

Potato Chips, Pretzels

*Soda Fountain "Pizza" **

*Star-Spangled Cake**

*Purple Hawaiians**

Cola Floats

✳

*Recipe follows

A Hero's Welcome — Countdown

THE DAY BEFORE:
— Prepare the crust for the Soda Fountain "Pizza."
— Prepare and bake the layers for the Star-Spangled Cake.

EARLY IN THE DAY:
— Prepare and refrigerate the filling for the Sausage & Meatball Hero.
— Prepare and refrigerate the Vegetable Dippers, Tangy Tomato Dip and Parsley Chive Dip.
— Prepare the strawberry sauce and the chocolate "anchovies" for the Soda Fountain "Pizza."

— Finish preparing the Star-Spangled Cake.
— Prepare the Purple Hawaiians.
— Assemble the Super Hero.

1 HOUR AHEAD:
— Finish preparing the Sausage & Meatball Hero.
— Scoop the ice cream onto the Soda Fountain "Pizza," top with the strawberry sauce and freeze the "pizza."
— Prepare the Cola Floats.

RED IS A GOOD LUCK COLOR
And other superstitions for the New Year

If you place an ivy leaf in a bowl of water on New Year's Eve and leave it until Twelfth Night (January 5), it will predict your fortune for the coming year. If the leaf is green and fresh, the year will be good. If the leaf is spotted, the year will bring illness or even death.

✳

Red is a good luck color, especially during the holidays. Eating red foods at the New Year, such as red peppers, tomatoes, and apples, will bring good luck. Pork is a good luck meat for the New Year; because pigs root forward in the dirt, people who eat pork on New Year's will move forward in the coming year. In Sweden, many people decorate their homes for the holidays with red pig ornaments.

Eat something sweet on New Year's Day to ensure a sweet year.

✳

In Greece and Spain, on New Year's Eve people eat twelve grapes at midnight, one for each time the clock strikes. This ensures twelve months of good luck.

✳

The first visitor of the New Year determines your fortune for the year. A tall, dark-haired visitor brings good luck. Blondes and redheads bring ill fortune.

VEGETABLE DIPPERS

Makes 8 servings.

- 1 pound carrots
- 1 bunch green onions
- 1 bunch radishes
- 1 pint cherry tomatoes
- ½ pound green beans
  Tangy Tomato Dip (recipe follows)
  Parsley Chive Dip (recipe follows)

1. Peel the carrots and cut them into long sticks. Pack the carrot sticks in a plastic bag and refrigerate them.
2. Trim and wash the green onions and the radishes well. Drain the green onions and the radishes, pack them separately in plastic bags and refrigerate them.
3. Wash the cherry tomatoes, pack them in a plastic bag and refrigerate them.
4. Wash and trim the green beans, and cut them into 3-inch pieces. Pack the green beans in a plastic bag and refrigerate them.
5. At serving time, arrange all the vegetables on a serving platter. Serve the Vegetable Dippers with the Tangy Tomato Dip and the Parsley Chive Dip.

Tangy Tomato Dip: Soften 1 package (3 ounces) of cream cheese. Place the cream cheese in a medium-size bowl and stir with a fork. Gradually beat in 1 can of condensed cream of tomato soup, 2 teaspoons of Worcestershire sauce and a few drops of liquid hot red pepper seasoning until the mixture is smooth. Cover the bowl with plastic wrap, and chill the dip for at least 2 hours to allow the flavors to blend. At serving time, pour the dip into a serving bowl. *Makes about 2 cups.*

Parsley Chive Dip: Combine 1 container (8 ounces) of dairy sour cream, ¼ cup of chopped parsley, 2 tablespoons of chopped chives, 1 teaspoon of Worcestershire sauce and ¼ teaspoon of seasoned pepper in a medium-size bowl. Cover the bowl with plastic wrap, and refrigerate the dip for at least 2 hours to allow the flavors to blend. At serving time, pour the dip into a serving bowl and garnish it with chopped parsley. *Makes about 1¼ cups.*

SUPER HERO

Makes 8 servings.

- 1 loaf Italian bread OR: French bread
- ½ cup mayonnaise OR: salad dressing
- 2 tablespoons prepared mustard
  Leaf lettuce
- 1 package (8 ounces) Swiss cheese slices, cut in triangles
- 1 package (8 ounces) boiled ham slices, rolled
- 1 package (8 ounces) American cheese slices, cut in triangles
- 1 package (8 ounces) salami slices, rolled

1. Using a sharp knife, cut the Italian or French bread in half lengthwise. Spread the cut sides with the mayonnaise or salad dressing and the mustard.
2. Place the lettuce leaves on the bottom half of the bread, and layer the Swiss cheese, ham, American cheese and salami on top of the lettuce. Place the top half of the bread over all and gently press it down to make the sandwich hold together. Cut the loaf into 8 slices with a sharp serrated knife.

SAUSAGE & MEATBALL HERO

Bake at 350° for 15 minutes.
Makes 8 servings.

1   *pound sweet or hot Italian sausages*
1   *pound ground beef*
1   *large onion, sliced into rings*
1   *large sweet green pepper, halved, seeded and diced*
1   *large sweet red pepper, halved, seeded, and diced*
½   *cup beef stock OR: canned beef broth*
1   *teaspoon mixed Italian herbs, crumbled*
1   *large, round loaf Italian bread OR: 1 large, long loaf Italian bread OR: French bread*
    Vegetable oil

1. Halve the sausages and brown them in a large skillet over medium-high heat. Remove the sausages from the skillet with a slotted spoon and set them aside. Pour off all but 2 tablespoons of the fat.
2. Shape the ground beef into small meatballs and brown the meatballs in the skillet. Remove the meatballs with the slotted spoon and set them aside. Pour off all but 1½ tablespoons of the fat.
3. Sauté the onion rings in the skillet until they are soft. Add the green and red peppers to the skillet, and sauté them for 2 minutes. Stir in the beef stock or broth and the Italian herbs.
4. Bring the mixture to boiling over medium heat. Add the reserved sausages and meatballs. Lower the heat, cover the skillet and simmer the mixture until the sausages no longer are pink, for 15 minutes.
5. Meanwhile, preheat the oven to moderate (350°).
6. Cut off the top third of the bread, set aside the top and hollow out the bottom of the bread to make a shell. Coat the bread shell and the bread top with the vegetable oil and place them on a large baking sheet.
7. Bake in the preheated moderate oven (350°) until the bread is toasted, for 15 minutes. Spoon the sausage and meatball mixture into the bread shell, and replace the top of the bread.
8. To serve, cut the top of the bread into 8 wedges and place one on each dinner plate. Spoon part of the sausage and meatball mixture onto each plate, then cut the shell into 8 wedges.

SODA FOUNTAIN "PIZZA"

Bake at 400° for 12 minutes.
Makes 8 servings.

1   *package pie crust mix*
4   *tablespoons sugar*
1   *egg, beaten*
1   *tablespoon cornstarch*
1   *package (8 ounces) sliced strawberries, thawed*
1   *package (6 ounces) semisweet chocolate pieces*
1   *teaspoon vegetable shortening*
1   *quart vanilla ice cream*

1. Preheat the oven to hot (400°).
2. Combine the pie crust mix and 2 tablespoons of the sugar in a medium-size bowl. Add the egg and toss the ingredients to make a soft dough.
3. Pat the dough onto the sides and bottom of a 14-inch pizza pan to make a smooth crust. Lightly press the tines of a fork around the edge of the crust. Prick the bottom of the crust with the fork.
4. Bake in the preheated hot oven (400°) until the crust is golden, for 12 minutes. Place the crust in the pan on a wire rack, and let the crust cool completely.
5. Meanwhile, combine the remaining 2 tablespoons of sugar and the cornstarch in a small saucepan. Add the strawberries with their syrup to the saucepan and stir until the mixture is smooth.
6. Cook the strawberry mixture over medium heat, stirring constantly, until the sauce thickens and bubbles for 3 minutes. Pour the sauce into a glass or ceramic bowl and let it cool completely.
7. Place the chocolate pieces with the vegetable shortening in a small metal bowl set in a skillet filled with simmering, not boiling, water. Stir the chocolate mixture until it is melted and well blended. Spread the chocolate mixture into an 8 x 4-inch rectangle on a piece of aluminum foil. Cool the chocolate rectangle until it is firm. Cut the chocolate into thin strips to resemble flat anchovies.
8. At serving time, scoop petals of the ice cream onto the cooled pastry. Drizzle the strawberry sauce over the ice cream and top with the chocolate "anchovies." Cut the pizza into wedges with a sharp knife.

STAR-SPANGLED CAKE

Bake at 350° for 30 minutes.
Makes one layer cake.

1   package (18 ounces) yellow cake mix
    Water
2   eggs
¾   cup (1½ sticks) unsalted butter
6   cups 10X (confectioners' powdered) sugar
⅓   cup milk
2   teaspoons vanilla
    Red and blue food coloring
    Silver dragées

1. Preheat the oven to moderate (350°). Grease 2 star-shaped layer cake pans.
2. Prepare the cake mix with the water and eggs, following the package directions. Pour the batter into the prepared layer cake pans.
3. Bake in the preheated moderate oven (350°) until the tops spring back when lightly pressed with a fingertip, for 30 minutes. Cool the layers in the pans on wire racks for 10 minutes. Run a sharp knife between the layers and the edges of the pans to loosen the layers. Invert the layers onto the wire racks and cool them completely.
4. Beat the butter in a large bowl with an electric mixer at high speed until it is smooth. Gradually beat in the 10X (confectioners' powdered) sugar and the milk until the frosting is smooth and creamy. Beat the vanilla into the frosting.
5. Divide the frosting in the large bowl in half; place ⅓ of one half in a small bowl, and the remaining ⅔ of one half in a medium-size bowl. Tint the frosting in the large bowl a bright red using red food coloring. Tint the frosting in the small bowl a deep blue. Keep the frosting in the medium-size bowl white.
6. Place one cake layer, top side down, on a flat tray or serving platter. Spread part of the white frosting over the bottom side, then place the second layer on top of the first one, top side up. Frost the sides of the bottom layer of the cake with the remaining white frosting.
7. Frost the sides of the top layer of the cake with the red frosting (set aside the remaining red frosting). Frost the top of the cake with the blue frosting.

8. Fit a small star tip into a pastry bag and fill the bag with the remaining red frosting. Pipe the frosting around the top, side and bottom of the cake. Garnish with the silver dragées, using tweezers to place them on the cake.

PURPLE HAWAIIANS

Makes 8 servings.

1   can (6 ounces) frozen concentrate for purple grape juice, thawed
1   can (6 ounces) frozen concentrate for pineapple juice, thawed
1   tablespoon lemon juice
1   bottle (28 ounces) ginger ale, chilled
    Ice cubes
    Fresh pineapple spears
    Fresh mint sprigs

1. Combine the grape juice concentrate, pineapple juice concentrate, lemon juice and 3 juice cans full of cold water in a very large pitcher. Stir until all the ingredients are well blended. Refrigerate the juice mixture until serving time.
2. At serving time, add the ginger ale to the pitcher and stir until it is well blended. Place ice cubes in 8 tall glasses, and pour the juice mixture over the ice cubes. Garnish each serving with a pineapple spear and a sprig of mint.

THE ART OF CUBISM

To add a festive touch to drinks, make decorative ice cubes. Place pieces of lemon rind, edible flowers, fresh mint leaves or maraschino cherries in each compartment of an ice cube tray; fill the tray with water and freeze.

Belgian Endive with Herbed Cheese (recipe, page 223); Vegetable Sushi (recipe, page 228); Hot Crab and Mushroom Puffs (recipe, page 226); Tortellini Zucchini (recipe, page 225); Savory Meatball Mini-Kebabs (recipe, page 224); Scallop Kebabs with Creamy Dijon Sauce (recipe, page 225); Creamy Pesto-Stuffed Cherry Tomatoes (recipe, page 223); Tapenade Crisps (recipe, page 224); Almond Cornets with Grenadine Crème (recipe, page 229)

RING IN THE NEW YEAR! AN OPEN HOUSE COCKTAIL PARTY

Menu for 20

Creamy Pesto-Stuffed Cherry Tomatoes*

Belgian Endive with Herbed Cheese*

Tapenade Crisps*

Savory Meatball Mini-Kebabs*

Scallop Kebabs with Creamy Dijon Sauce*

Tortellini Zucchini*

Hot Crab and Mushroom Puffs*

Turkey Terrine with Pistachios*

Vegetable Sushi*

Almond Cornets with Grenadine Crème*

Cassis Punch Royale*

✳

*Recipe follows

Ring in the New Year!
Open House Cocktail Party — Countdown

UP TO SEVERAL WEEKS AHEAD:
—Prepare and freeze the Tapenade Crisps.

UP TO A WEEK AHEAD:
—Prepare, but do not bake, the Hot Crab and Mushroom Puffs, and freeze them.

UP TO SEVERAL DAYS AHEAD:
—Prepare the Tapenade Crisps, if they were not prepared ahead and frozen. Store them in an airtight container.
—Prepare and refrigerate the Creamy Pesto for the Stuffed Cherry Tomatoes and the Tortellini Zucchini.
—Prepare and refrigerate the Turkey Terrine with Pistachios.
—Prepare the ice block for the Cassis Punch Royale.

UP TO TWO DAYS AHEAD:
—Make the cornets for the Almond Cornets with Grenadine Crème and store them in an airtight container.

THE DAY BEFORE:
—Prepare and refrigerate the cream cheese filling for the Belgian Endive with Herbed Cheese.
—Prepare, but do not bake, the Hot Crab and Mushroom Puffs, if they were not prepared ahead and frozen, and refrigerate them.
—Prepare, but do not bake, the prunes, meatballs, sauce and orange segments for the Savory Meatball Mini-Kebabs, and refrigerate them.
—Prepare and refrigerate the zucchini and tortellini for the Tortellini Zucchini.

EARLY IN THE DAY:
—Partially cook the bacon and thread the skewers for Scallop Kebabs with Creamy Dijon Sauce; refrigerate them.

SEVERAL HOURS BEFORE:
—Prepare the tomatoes for Creamy Pesto-Stuffed Cherry Tomatoes, but do not fill them.
—Finish preparing Belgian Endive with Herbed Cheese and refrigerate them.
—Prepare the Creamy Dijon Sauce for the Scallop Kebabs.
—Prepare and dress the rice for the Vegetable Sushi.

UP TO TWO HOURS BEFORE:
—Finish preparing the Vegetable Sushi, and cover them with damp paper toweling.

ONE HOUR BEFORE:
—Finish preparing the Creamy Pesto-Stuffed Cherry Tomatoes.
—Bake the Hot Crab and Mushroom Puffs.

HALF AN HOUR BEFORE:
—Finish preparing the Savory Meatball Mini-Kebabs.
—Reheat the Tapenade Crisps for 5-10 minutes in a 350° oven.
—Finish preparing the Tortellini Zucchini.
—Prepare the Grenadine Crème for the Almond Cornets.

JUST BEFORE THE PARTY:
—Finish preparing the Scallop Kebabs with Creamy Dijon Sauce.
—Prepare the Cassis Punch Royale.
—Finish preparing the Almond Cornets with Grenadine Crème. Or serve the Almond Cornets and Grenadine Crème separately, and have the guests fill the cornets themselves.

CREAMY PESTO-STUFFED CHERRY TOMATOES

Makes 16 servings.

1   pint ripe cherry tomatoes
1/3 cup Creamy Pesto (recipe follows)
     Toasted pine nuts OR: silvered almonds,
        for garnish (optional)

1. Cut a small slice from the top of each cherry tomato. Scoop out the insides of each tomato with a small spoon. Invert the tomatoes on paper toweling to drain.
2. About 1 hour before serving, fill each tomato with a scant teaspoon of the Creamy Pesto. Garnish with the toasted pine nuts or slivered almonds, if you wish.

Creamy Pesto: Combine ½ cup of mayonnaise, ½ cup of loosely packed fresh basil leaves (or ½ cup loosely packed parsley leaves and 1 teaspoon of dried basil), 2 tablespoons of grated Parmesan cheese and 1 teaspoon of finely chopped garlic in the container of an electric blender. Cover and whirl until the mixture is smooth. Blend in 2 tablespoons of finely chopped pine nuts or slivered almonds. Refrigerate the Creamy Pesto until you are ready to use it.

PESTO PRESTO

Creamy Pesto imparts a fresh green flavor to sandwiches. Try it with roast turkey and tomato, ham and cheese and roast lamb and spinach sandwiches. Mix the pesto with an equal amount of plain yogurt to make a dip for crudités. Or spread the pesto on salmon steaks before broiling them to keep the salmon moist and flavorful.

BELGIAN ENDIVE WITH HERBED CHEESE

Makes 24 servings.

2   heads Belgian endive, preferably with short leaves
2   packages (3 ounces each) cream cheese with
        chives, softened
2   teaspoons chopped parsley
1/8 teaspoon garlic powder
     Alfalfa sprouts, rinsed and well drained

1. Trim the bottom from the endive heads. Separate each head into leaves.
2. Blend together the cream cheese, parsley and garlic powder in a small bowl. Spread about 1 teaspoon of the cream cheese mixture on the bottom third of each leaf. Garnish the top part of the leaves with the alfalfa sprouts. Cover the filled leaves with damp paper toweling and plastic wrap, and refrigerate them until serving time.

AS YOU LIKE IT

If you can't find Belgian endive to use when making the recipe above, try using the herbed cheese filling in celery stalks, or sandwich it between thin slices of cucumber.

TAPENADE CRISPS

Bake at 400° for 15 minutes.
Makes 4½ dozen servings.

- ½ can (2 ounces) flat anchovy fillets, drained
- 1 can (3 ounces) pitted black olives, drained
- 2 tablespoons capers, drained
- 1 teaspoon dry mustard
- 2 teaspoons lemon juice
- 2 tablespoons olive oil
- ½ of a 17½-ounce package frozen puff pastry, thawed according to package directions

1. Coarsely chop the anchovies and the olives, and place them in the container of an electric blender or food processor. Add the capers, mustard and lemon juice. Cover and whirl until the mixture is a smooth purée. With the motor running, gradually add the olive oil to make a smooth tapenade paste. Set aside the tapenade paste.
2. Roll out the unfolded pastry on a floured surface to a 15 x 11-inch rectangle. Spread the tapenade paste over the pastry, leaving a ½-inch border around the edges of the pastry. Roll up the pastry, jelly-roll style, along one long side, but do not roll the pastry too tightly. Cut the roll in half crosswise. Place both halves in the freezer until they are firm enough to slice, for about 1 hour.
3. Preheat the oven to hot (400°).
4. Slice the rolls with a thin knife into ¼-inch-thick slices. Place the slices on baking sheets, spacing them 1½ inches apart.
5. Bake in the preheated hot oven (400°) until the crisps are golden brown in color, for 15 to 18 minutes. Serve the crisps slightly warm.

SAVORY MEATBALL MINI-KEBABS

Bake at 400° for 15 minutes.
Makes 24 servings.

- 24 pitted prunes
- ½ cup port wine
- ¾ pound ground pork
- ¼ cup bread crumbs
- ¼ cup finely chopped walnuts
- ¼ cup chopped green onion
- ¾ teaspoon salt
- ¼ teaspoon freshly ground pepper
- 1 egg
- ½ cup chili sauce
- ½ cup red currant jelly
- 1 tablespoon Worcestershire sauce
- 1 orange, peeled, cut into 24 equal pieces and seeded

1. Place the prunes in a small bowl and pour the port wine over them. Let the prunes soak for several hours, or overnight. Drain the prunes, remove them from the soaking liquid to another small bowl and set both bowls aside.
2. Preheat the oven to hot (400°).
3. Combine the pork, bread crumbs, walnuts, green onion, salt, pepper and egg in a medium-size bowl. Mix all the ingredients well. Shape the mixture into 24 equal-size balls. Arrange the meatballs on an oiled rack set over a broiler pan.
4. Bake in the preheated hot oven (400°) until the meatballs are browned on the outside and no longer pink in their centers, for 15 minutes. Place the meatballs in a pie plate.
5. Combine the chili sauce, currant jelly, Worcestershire sauce and 2 tablespoons of the reserved port wine soaking liquid in a small saucepan. Bring the mixture to boiling, stirring the sauce until the jelly melts. Add just enough sauce to the meatballs to coat them.
6. Thread meatballs on 24 short bamboo skewers, alternating them with the orange pieces and the soaked prunes. Serve the kebabs hot or warm. Pass the extra sauce for dipping.

SCALLOP KEBABS WITH CREAMY DIJON SAUCE

Makes 20 servings.

- 10 slices bacon
- 1 pound sea scallops, halved, or quartered if large
- 1 papaya, peeled, seeded and cut into 1-inch chunks
- 6 green onions, cut into 1½-inch lengths
- ¾ cup heavy cream
- 1 tablespoon Dijon-style mustard
- 1 teaspoon finely chopped parsley

1. Preheat the broiler.
2. Place the bacon on a rack set over a broiler pan. Broil the bacon in the preheated broiler until it is partially cooked, but not crisp. Cut the bacon slices in half.
3. Wrap a piece of bacon around each scallop half or quarter. Thread 20 short bamboo skewers with a piece of papaya, green onion and bacon-wrapped scallop. Arrange the kebabs in a single layer on the rack over the broiler pan.
4. Combine the heavy cream with the mustard in a saucepan. Heat the mixture gently until the sauce is slightly thickened, for 5 minutes. Add the parsley. Brush the sauce over the kebabs.
5. Broil the kebabs, 6 inches from the heat source, until the scallops are firm, for 4 or 5 minutes. Turn the kebabs once during the cooking time and brush them with the sauce. Serve the kebabs hot.

TORTELLINI ZUCCHINI

Makes 20 servings.

- 1 small zucchini, about 1¼ inches in diameter
- 20 cheese-filled tortellini
  Milk OR: heavy cream, as needed
- ¼ cup Creamy Pesto (recipe, page 223)
  Toasted pine nuts OR: slivered almonds, for garnish

1. Cut the zucchini into ¼-inch-thick slices. Cook the zucchini in boiling water for 1 minute. Drain the zucchini and immediately plunge them into ice water to stop the cooking. Drain the zucchini again.
2. Cook the tortellini, following the package directions. Drain the tortellini and rinse them under cold running water.
3. Place the Creamy Pesto in a medium-size bowl. Add milk to the pesto until it is the consistency of thick cream. Add the tortellini to the bowl, and toss to coat the tortellini well.
4. To serve, arrange the zucchini slices on a serving platter. Top each zucchini slice with a tortellini. Garnish with the toasted pine nuts or almonds.

HOT CRAB AND MUSHROOM PUFFS

Bake at 375° for 15 to 20 minutes.
Makes about 4 dozen puffs.

3   tablespoons chopped shallots OR: green onions
1   cup (2 sticks) butter
1   cup chopped mushrooms
1   teaspoon lemon juice
¼   cup all-purpose flour
¾   cup milk
*1   package (6 ounces) frozen crab meat, thawed,
        well drained and broken into pieces*
1   tablespoon dry sherry
1   tablespoon chopped parsley
½   teaspoon salt
¼   teaspoon freshly ground pepper
8   phyllo leaves OR: strudel leaves

1. Sauté the shallots or green onions in 4 tablespoons of the butter in a small saucepan for 3 to 4 minutes.
2. Toss the mushrooms with the lemon juice and add them to the saucepan. Cook the mixture over medium-high heat, stirring often, until the mushrooms are lightly browned, for 5 minutes. Remove the saucepan from the heat.
3. Stir in the flour until the mixture is well blended. Gradually stir in the milk until the mixture is smooth. Return the saucepan to the heat and cook the mixture, stirring constantly, until it thickens and bubbles. Cook the mixture for 1 minute. Stir in the crab meat, sherry, parsley, salt and pepper. Remove the saucepan from the heat and let the mixture cool.
4. Melt the remaining ¾ cup of butter in a second small saucepan. Keep the phyllo or strudel leaves between 2 dampened towels. Remove 1 leaf to a flat work surface. Brush the leaf with the melted butter. Cut the leaf lengthwise into six 2-inch-wide strips. Place a rounded teaspoon of the crab-mushroom filling on one end of a strip. Fold one corner of the strip over the filling to the opposite side to form a triangle. Continue folding the strip as if you were folding a flag, maintaining the triangle shape, until the strip is completely folded. Repeat with the remaining strips, leaves and filling. Arrange the triangles on

lightly buttered baking sheets.
5. Preheat the oven to moderate (375°).
6. Bake in the preheated moderate oven (375°) until the triangles are puffed and golden in color, for 15 to 20 minutes. Cool the puffs on wire racks. Serve the puffs hot or warm.

FOR PHYLLO-PHILES

Paper-thin phyllo (or "filo") dough is used extensively in Middle Eastern cooking, to make both sweet and savory pastries. Because the dough is so delicate, it must be treated with care to prevent it from drying out and becoming unworkable. Always keep the dough covered with very lightly dampened paper toweling and a piece of plastic wrap until just before you use it. If you are not using all of the dough, gently reroll the remaining dough, double-wrap it in plastic wrap, and return it to the refrigerator.

TURKEY TERRINE WITH PISTACHIOS

Bake at 300° for 2½ hours.
Makes about 24 servings.

⅓ cup chopped shallots OR: green onions
2 tablespoons butter
½ pound chicken livers, connective tissue removed
2 teaspoons salt
½ teaspoon freshly ground pepper
½ cup dry vermouth
1¼ pounds ground turkey
¾ pound ground pork
¾ pound ground fatback
1 egg
½ teaspoon dried thyme, crumbled
½ teaspoon dried marjoram, crumbled
½ teaspoon ground allspice
⅓ cup whole pistachio nuts, shelled
¾ pound sliced bacon
2 bay leaves
Boiling water
Sprigs of thyme, for garnish (optional)
Toasted French bread and cornichons (French
   gherkin pickles)

1. Sauté the shallots or green onions in the butter in a medium-size skillet for 3 minutes. Add the chicken livers, ½ teaspoon of the salt and ¼ teaspoon of the pepper. Sauté the mixture just until the chicken livers are tender but still pink inside, for about 5 minutes. Stir in the vermouth. Bring the mixture to boiling, scraping up any browned bits from the bottom of the pan with a wooden spoon. Remove the skillet from the heat and let the mixture cool.
2. Combine the turkey, pork, fatback, egg, the remaining 1½ teaspoons of salt and the remaining ¼ teaspoon of pepper, the thyme, marjoram, allspice and pistachio nuts in a large bowl. Stir to mix the ingredients well. Drain the liver mixture into a small bowl. Set aside the liver mixture, and add the cooking liquid to the turkey mixture. Stir gently to mix the ingredients well.
3. Preheat the oven to slow (300°).
4. Set aside 2 or 3 pieces of the bacon. Line a 6- to

8-cup loaf pan or terrine with the remaining bacon, allowing the ends of the bacon to overhang the sides of the pan by 2 inches. Press one third of the turkey mixture onto the bottom of the prepared pan. Arrange half of the liver mixture over the layer of turkey mixture, and gently press the two layers together. Top the first layer of liver mixture with a second layer of turkey mixture, gently pressing the layers together. Top with the remaining liver mixture and a final layer of the turkey mixture. Smooth the top layer. Gently rap the pan on the counter to pack the layers firmly. Bring up the ends of the bacon over the top of the terrine. Lay the reserved bacon over the top of the terrine, and the bay leaves over the bacon. Cover the pan tightly with aluminum foil. Place the covered pan in a deep roasting pan. Pour boiling water into the roasting pan until it is half way up the side of the loaf pan or terrine. Place the roasting pan on the middle shelf of the oven.
5. Bake the terrine in the preheated slow oven (300°) for 2 hours. Remove the aluminum foil from the pan and bake the terrine until a meat thermometer inserted in the center of the terrine registers 160°, for 30 minutes more. Remove the loaf pan or terrine from the roasting pan. Cool the terrine in the pan on a wire rack for 1 hour. Place the aluminum foil back over the top of the terrine. Fill a second loaf pan with cans, and set the weighted pan on top of the terrine to press the layers together firmly. Refrigerate both pans overnight.
6. Remove the terrine from the refrigerator and remove the weighted pan. Run a thin knife around the edges of the terrine to loosen it from the pan, and unmold the terrine onto a platter. Carefully scrape off the fat and any jellied liquid from the terrine. Wrap the terrine in plastic wrap and refrigerate it until serving time. At serving time, garnish the terrine with the thyme sprigs, if you wish, and serve it with the toasted French bread and cornichons.

VEGETABLE SUSHI

Makes about 30 sushi.

18   to 24 large spinach leaves
2   carrots, trimmed and cut lengthwise into
        1/4-inch sticks
1   cup long-grain white rice
1 1/4 cups cold water
1/4   cup rice vinegar
2   tablespoons sugar
1   teaspoon salt
3   eggs
3   tablespoons water
1/2   teaspoon salt
2   tablespoons finely chopped green onion
     Vegetable oil
     Pickled ginger (optional)

1. Working in batches, blanch the spinach leaves in a large saucepan of boiling water just until they are wilted, for 30 seconds. Remove the spinach leaves with a slotted spoon to a colander and rinse them under cold running water. Drain the spinach leaves.
2. Steam the carrots until they are crisply tender. Drain the carrots and rinse them under cold running water.
3. Rinse the rice in several changes of cold water until the water is clear. Combine the rice with the 1 1/4 cups of cold water in a 2-quart saucepan with a tight-fitting lid. Let the rice soak for 15 minutes.
4. Bring the rice to boiling over high heat. Lower the heat, cover the saucepan and cook the rice for 10 minutes without stirring it. Remove the saucepan from the heat. Let the rice steam in the tightly covered saucepan for 15 minutes.
5. Combine the rice vinegar, sugar and salt in a small bowl, stirring to dissolve the sugar.
6. Transfer the rice to a deep platter or a shallow bowl. Toss the rice with a fork for a few minutes to release the steam. Sprinkle the vinegar mixture over the rice, 1 tablespoon at a time, tossing the ingredients with a fork. Cool the rice mixture to room temperature.
7. Combine the eggs, the 3 tablespoons of water, the salt and green onion in a small bowl. Beat the mixture with a fork until all the ingredients are blended.

8. Heat a 10-inch omelet pan or other shallow skillet over medium heat. Brush the pan with the vegetable oil to coat it lightly. Pour one third of the egg mixture (approximately 1/4 cup) into the hot pan, swirling the pan to spread the mixture evenly into an 8-inch-diameter circle. Cook the egg mixture until it is firm, for about 1 minute. Flip over the "omelet" and cook the raw side for a few seconds. Slide the omelet onto a baking sheet. Repeat with the remaining egg mixture to make as many omelets as possible. Cut each omelet in half.
9. To assemble the sushi, place an omelet half on a bamboo mat or a heavy cloth napkin with a straight side facing you. Unfold 3 to 4 spinach leaves and arrange them, slightly overlapping, over the omelet half, leaving a 1/2-inch border around the edges of the omelet half. With dampened hands, place 1/3 cup of the rice mixture in the center of the spinach leaves and gently spread it into a 5 x 3-inch rectangle. Pat down the rice rectangle neatly. Arrange 1 or 2 carrot sticks across the length of the rice rectangle. Trim the omelet and the spinach to within 1/2-inch of the edge of the rice rectangle.
10. Starting with the edge closest to you, roll the rectangle 1 or 2 turns using the mat or napkin as a guide, to enclose the carrot in the center of the rice. The omelet and the spinach leaves will form the outside of the roll. Squeeze the roll gently to make it firm. Let the roll rest wrapped in the mat for a few minutes. Repeat to make 5 more rolls.
11. Transfer the rolls to a cutting board. Cut each roll into five 1-inch pieces of sushi. Arrange the sushi in a flower petal design on a serving platter. Garnish with the pickled ginger, if you wish.

ALMOND CORNETS WITH GRENADINE CRÈME

Bake at 375° for 6 to 8 minutes.
Makes about 24 cornets.

- ½ cup coarsely ground almonds
- ½ cup 10X (confectioners' powdered) sugar
- ¼ cup (½ stick) butter, very soft
- 1 tablespoon all-purpose flour
- 2 tablespoons heavy cream OR: whipping cream
- 3 to 4 sugar ice cream cones, tightly wrapped in aluminum foil OR: other cone-shaped form
  Grenadine Crème, (recipe follows)
  Strawberries, for garnish (optional)

1. Preheat the oven to moderate (375°). Grease and flour 2 baking sheets.
2. Combine the almonds, sugar, butter and flour in a small bowl with a wooden spoon until the mixture is smooth. Stir in the heavy or whipping cream.
3. Drop 3 level teaspoons of the almond mixture onto the prepared baking sheets, spacing them 4 inches apart. Spread each mound into a 2-inch round.
4. Bake in the preheated moderate oven (375°) until the cookies are light brown in color and bubbly in the centers, for 6 to 8 minutes. Let the cookies stand on the baking sheet on a wire rack for 1 minute. Loosen the cookies with a spatula, one at a time and quickly shape the warm cookie around the sugar cone or cone shape to form a cornet. Carefully remove the cornet from the form. Place the cornets, seam side down, on the wire rack to cool completely. Bake and roll only 3 cookies at a time so they do not become too cool to handle. If the cookies become too stiff to shape, return them to the oven for a minute or two until they soften. Repeat with the almond mixture to make about 24 cornets.
5. To serve, pipe or spoon the Grenadine Crème into each cornet and serve them at once. Or arrange the cornets on a serving platter with a bowl of the Grenadine Crème, and let each guest fill his or her own cornet. Garnish with the strawberries, if you wish.

Grenadine Crème: Beat 1 cup of heavy or whipping cream with 3 tablespoons of grenadine syrup and 1 teaspoon of lemon juice until the mixture forms stiff peaks. Refrigerate the crème until serving time, for up to 2 hours. *Makes 2 cups.*

CASSIS PUNCH ROYALE

Makes about 24 servings.

- Ice block
  Red and green grapes for ice block
- ½ cup crème de Cassis (black currant liqueur)
- 1 bottle (750 ml.) white wine, chilled
- 2 bottles champagne, chilled
  Whole fresh strawberries OR: frozen strawberries, for garnish (optional)

1. Prepare the ice block: Fill a fancy mold that will fit inside the punch bowl with ice cubes. Add enough cold water to almost fill the mold. Arrange clusters of the red and green grapes so they are half in the ice and water and half protruding out of the top of the mold. Place the mold in the freezer until the ice block is firm enough to unmold. Unmold the ice block by dipping it in warm water to loosen the ice. Be careful not to break the grapes. Return the ice mold to the freezer until you are ready to use it.
2. Just before serving time, pour the Cassis and the wine into the punch bowl. Add the ice block with the grapes on top. Slowly pour the champagne into the punch bowl. Add a strawberry to each glass for garnish, if you wish.

A CURRANT AFFAIR

Cassis is a liqueur made from black currants. It is thick in consistency and deep purple in color. Mixed with white wine, it becomes a Kir cocktail. Add a splash of Cassis over vanilla ice cream for a luscious dessert. Or use it to flavor raspberry sauce, for an intense berry experience.

CRAFTS BASICS & ABBREVIATIONS

HOW TO KNIT

THE BASIC STITCHES

Get out your needles and yarn, and slowly read your way through this special section. Practice the basic stitches illustrated here as you go along. Once you know them, you're ready to start knitting.

CASTING ON: This puts the first row of stitches on the needle. Measure off about two yards of yarn (or about an inch for each stitch you are going to cast on). Make a slip knot at this point by making a medium-size loop of yarn; then pull another small loop through it. Place the slip knot on one needle and pull one end gently to tighten (FIG. 1).

FIG. 1

❊ Hold the needle in your right hand. Hold both strands of yarn in the palm of your left hand securely but not rigidly. Slide your left thumb and forefinger between the two strands and spread these two fingers out so that you have formed a triangle of yarn.

　　Your left thumb should hold the free end of yarn, your forefinger the yarn from the ball. The needle in your right hand holds the first stitch (FIG. 2).

FIG. 2

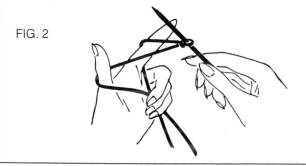

You are now in position to cast on.

❊ Bring the needle in your right hand toward you; slip the tip of the needle under the front strand of the loop on your left thumb (FIG. 3).

FIG. 3

❊ Now, with the needle, catch the strand of yarn that is on your left forefinger (FIG. 4).

FIG. 4

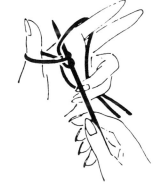

❊ Draw it through the thumb loop to form a stitch on the needle (FIG. 5).

FIG. 5

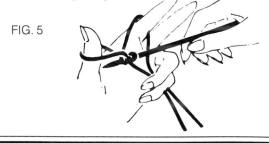

KNITTING ABBREVIATIONS AND SYMBOLS

Knitting directions are always written in standard abbreviations. Although they may look confusing, with practice you'll soon know them:

beg — beginning; **bet** — between; **bl** — block; **ch** — chain; **CC** — contrasting color; **dec(s)** — decrease(s); **dp** — double-pointed; **″** or **in(s)** — inch(es); **incl** — inclusive; **inc(s)** — increase(s); **k** — knit; **lp(s)** — loop(s); **MC** — main color; **oz(s)** — ounces(s); **psso** — pass slipped stitch over last stitch worked; **pat(s)** — pattern(s); **p** — purl; **rem** — remaining; **rpt** — repeat; **rnd(s)** — round(s); **sk** — skip; **sl** — slip; **sl st** — slip stitch; **sp(s),** — space(s); **st(s)** — stitch(es); **st st** — stockinette stitch; **tog** — together, **yo** — yarn over; **pc** — popcorn stitch.

* (asterisk) — directions immediately following * are to be repeated the specified number of times indicated in addition to the first time — i.e. "repeat from * 3 times more" means 4 times in all.

( ) (parentheses) — directions should be worked as often as specified — i.e., "(k 1, k 2 tog, k 3) 5 times" means to work what is in ( ) 5 times in all.

❋ Holding the stitch on the needle with your right index finger, slip the loop off your left thumb (Fig. 6). Tighten up the stitch on the needle by pulling the freed strand back with your left thumb, bringing the yarn back into position for casting on more stitches (Fig. 2).

FIG. 6

❋ **Do not cast on too tightly.** Stitches should slide easily on the needle. Repeat from * until you have cast on the number of stitches specified in your instructions.

KNIT STITCH (k): Hold the needle with the cast-on stitches in your left hand (Fig. 7).

FIG. 7

❋ Pick up the other needle in your right hand. With yarn from the ball in **back** of the work, insert the tip of the right-hand needle from **left to right** through the front loop of the first stitch on the left-hand needle (Fig. 8).

FIG. 8

❋ Holding both needles in this position with your left hand, wrap the yarn over your little finger, under your two middle fingers and over the forefinger of your right hand. Hold the yarn firmly, but loosely enough so that it will slide through your fingers as you knit. Return the right-hand needle to your right hand.

❋ With your right forefinger, pass the yarn under (from right to left) and then over (from left to right) the tip of the right-hand needle, forming a loop on the needle (Fig. 9).

FIG. 9

❋ Now draw this loop through the stitch on the left-hand needle (Fig. 10).

FIG. 10

✳ Slip the original stitch off the left-hand needle, leaving the new stitch on right-hand needle (FIG. 11).

FIG. 11

Note: *Keep the stitches loose enough to slide along the needles, but tight enough to maintain their position on the needles until you want them to slide.* Continue until you have knitted all the stitches from the left-hand needle onto the right-hand needle.

✳ To start the next row, pass the needle with stitches on it to your left hand, reversing it, so that it is now the left-hand needle.

PURL STITCH (p): Purling is the reverse of knitting. Again, keep the stitches loose enough to slide, but firm enough to work with. To purl, hold the needle with the stitches in your left hand, with the yarn in **front** of your work. Insert the tip of the right-hand needle from **right to left** through the front loop of the first stitch on the left-hand needle (FIG. 12).

FIG. 12

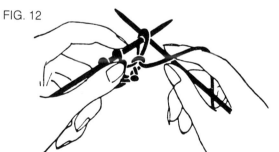

✳ With your right hand holding the yarn as you would to knit, but in **front** of the needles, pass the yarn over the tip of the right-hand needle, then under it, forming a loop on the needle. (FIG. 13).

FIG. 13

✳ Holding the yarn firmly so that it won't slip off, draw this loop through the stitch on the left-hand needle (FIG. 14).

FIG. 14

✳ Slip the original stitch off of the left-hand needle, leaving the new stitch on the right-hand needle (FIG. 15).

FIG. 15

SLIPSTITCH (sl st): Insert the tip of the right-hand needle into the next stitch on the left-hand needle, as if to purl, unless otherwise directed. Slip this stitch off the left-hand needle onto the right, but **do not** work the stitch (FIG. 16).

FIG. 16

BINDING OFF: This makes a finished edge and locks the stitches securely in place. Knit (or purl) two stitches. Then, with the tip of the left-hand needle, lift the first of these two stitches over the second stitch and drop it off the tip of the right-hand needle (Fig. 17).

FIG. 17

One stitch remains on the right-hand needle, and one stitch has been bound off.

✽ Knit (or purl) the next stitch; lift the first stitch over the last stitch and off the tip of the needle. Again, one stitch remains on the right-hand needle, and another stitch has been bound off. Repeat from * until the required number of stitches have been bound off.

✽ Remember that you work two stitches to bind off one stitch. If, for example, the directions read, "k 6, bind off the next 4 sts, k 6 . . ." you must knit six stitches, then knit **two more** stitches before starting to bind off. Bind off four times. After the four stitches have been bound off, count the last stitch remaining on the right-hand needle as the first stitch of the next six stitches. When binding off, always knit the knitted stitches and purl the purled stitches.

✽ Be careful not to bind off too tightly or too loosely. The tension should be the same as the rest of the knitting.

✽ To end off the last stitch on the bound-off edge, if you are ending this piece of work here, cut the yarn leaving a 6-inch end; pass the cut end through the remaining loop on the right-hand needle and pull snugly (Fig. 18).

FIG. 18

SHAPING TECHNIQUES

Once you are familiar with the basic stitches, you can learn the techniques for shaping your knitting projects.

INCREASING (inc): To add stitches in a given area to shape your work. There are three ways to increase.

1. To increase by knitting twice into the same stitch: Knit the stitch in the usual way through the front loop (Fig. 19), but **before** dropping the stitch from the left-hand needle, knit **another** stitch on the same loop by placing the needle into the back of the stitch. (Fig. 20). Slip the original stitch off your left-hand needle. You now have made two stitches from one stitch.

FIG. 19

FIG. 20

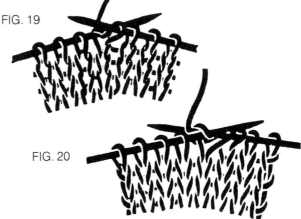

2. To increase by knitting between stitches: Insert the tip of the right-hand needle under the strand of yarn **between** the stitch you've just worked and the following stitch; slip it onto the tip of the left-hand needle (Fig. 21).

FIG. 21

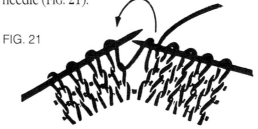

Now knit into the back of the loop (Fig. 22).

3. *To increase by "yarn-over" (yo):* Pass the yarn ***over*** the right-hand needle after finishing one stitch and before starting the next stitch, making an extra stitch (see the arrow in FIG. 23). If you are knitting, bring the yarn ***under*** the needle to the back. If you are purling, wind the yarn ***around*** the needle once. On the next row, work all yarn-overs as stitches.

FIG. 23

DECREASING (dec): To reduce the number of stitches in a given area to shape your work. Two methods for decreasing are:

1. *To decrease by knitting* (FIG. 24) ***or purling*** (FIG. 25) ***two stitches together:***

FIG. 24

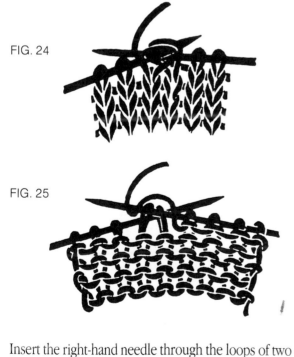

FIG. 25

Insert the right-hand needle through the loops of two stitches on the left-hand needle at the same time. Complete the stitch. This is written as "k 2 tog" or "p 2 tog."

✳ If you work through the ***front*** loops of the stitches, your decreasing stitch will slant to the right. If you work through the ***back*** loops of the stitches, your decreasing stitch will slant to the left.

2. *Slip 1 stitch, knit 1 and psso:* Insert the right-hand needle through the stitch on the left-hand needle, but instead of working it, just slip it off onto the right-hand needle (see FIG. 16). Work the next stitch in the usual way. With the tip of the left-hand needle, lift the slipped stitch over the last stitch worked and off the tip of the right-hand needle (FIG. 26). Your decreasing stitch will slant to the left. This is written as "sl 1, k 1, psso."

FIG. 26

Pass Slipped Stitch Over (psso): Slip one stitch from the left-hand needle to the right-hand needle and, being careful to keep it in position, work the next stitch. Then, with the tip of the left-hand needle, lift the slipped stitch over the last stitch and off the tip of the right-hand needle (FIG. 26).

ATTACHING YARN

When you finish one ball of yarn, or if you wish to change colors, attach the new ball of yarn at the start of a row. Tie the new yarn to an end of the previous yarn, making a secure knot to join the two yarns. Continue to work (FIG. 27).

FIG. 27

HOW TO CROCHET
THE BASIC STITCHES

Most crochet stitches are started from a base of chain stitches. However, our stitches are started from a row of single crochet stitches which gives body to the sample swatches and makes practice work easier to handle. When making a specific item, follow the stitch directions as given.

Holding the crochet hook properly (FIG. 1), start by practicing the slip knot (FIG. 2 through FIG. 2C) and base chain (FIG. 3 through FIG. 3B).

CHAIN STITCH (ch): Follow the steps in FIG. 3 through FIG. 3B. As you make the chain stitch loops, the yarn should slide easily between your index and middle fingers. Make about 15 loops. If they are all the same size, you have maintained even tension. If the stitches are uneven, rip them out by pulling on the long end of the yarn. Practice the chain stitch until you can crochet a perfect chain.

From here on, we won't be showing hands—just the hook and the stitches. ***Note:*** *Left-handed crocheters can use the illustrations for right-handed crocheting by turning the book upside down in front of a free-standing mirror. The reflected illustrations will provide left-handed instructions.*

FIG. 1   HOLDING THE HOOK

FIG. 2   THE SLIP KNOT
(BASIS FOR CHAIN STITCH)

FIG. 2a

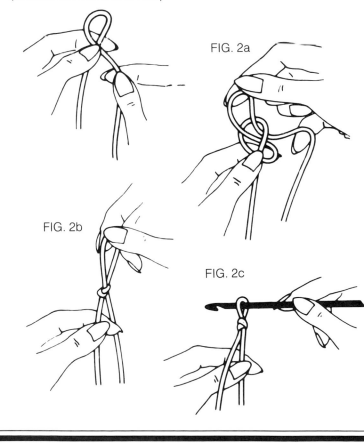

FIG. 2b

FIG. 2c

FIG. 3   CHAIN STITCH (CH)

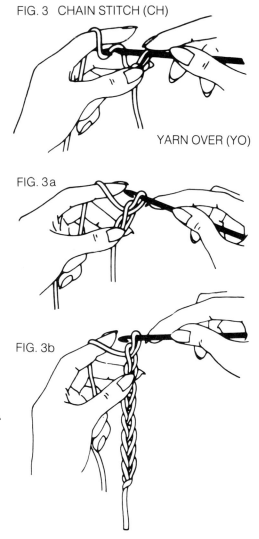

YARN OVER (YO)

FIG. 3a

FIG. 3b

CROCHET ABBREVIATIONS AND SYMBOLS

The following is a list of standard crochet abbreviations with definitions of the terms given. To help you become accustomed to the abbreviations used, we have repeated them throughout our instructions.

beg—begin, beginning; **ch**—chain;
dc—double crochet; **dec**—decrease;
dtr—double treble crochet;
hdc—half double crochet; **in(s)** or ″—inch(es);
inc—increase; **oz(s)**—ounce(s); **pat**—pattern;
pc—picot; **rem**—remaining; **rnd**—round;
rpt—repeat; **sc**—single crochet;
skn(s)—skein(s); **sk**—skip;
sl st—slip stitch; **sp**—space; **st(s)**—stitch(es);
tog—together; **tr**—triple crochet; **work even**—continue without further increase or decrease;
yo—yarn over.
* (asterisk)—directions immediately following * are to be repeated the specified number of times indicated in addition to the first time.
( ) (parentheses)—directions should be worked as often as specified.

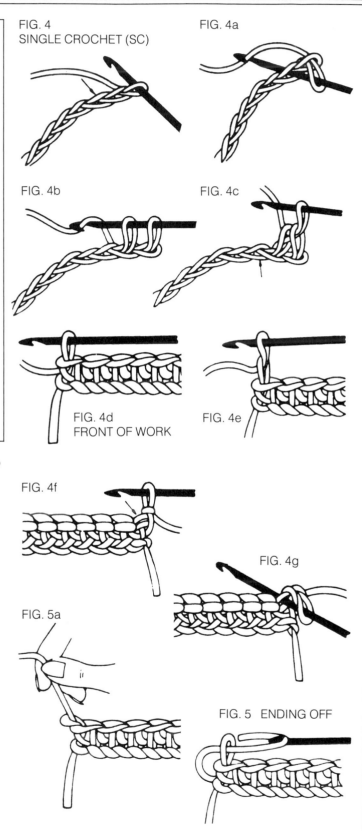

FIG. 4
SINGLE CROCHET (SC)

FIG. 4a

FIG. 4b

FIG. 4c

FIG. 4d
FRONT OF WORK

FIG. 4e

FIG. 4f

FIG. 4g

FIG. 5a

FIG. 5 ENDING OFF

SINGLE CROCHET (sc): Follow the steps in Fig. 4. To practice, make a 20-loop chain (this means 20 loops in addition to the slip knot). Turn the chain, as shown, and insert the hook in the second chain from the hook (see arrow) to make the first sc stitch. Yarn over (yo); for the second stitch, see the next arrow. Repeat to the end of the chain. Because you started in the second chain from the hook, you end up with only 19 sc. To add the 20th stitch, ch 1 (called a turning chain) and pull the yarn through. Now turn your work around (the "back" is now facing you) and start the second row of sc in the first stitch of the previous row (at the arrow). Make sure your hook goes under both of the strands at the top of the stitch. Don't forget to make a ch 1 turning chain at the end before turning your work. Keep practicing until your rows are perfect.

ENDING OFF: Follow the steps in Fig. 5. To finish off your crochet, cut off all but 6-inches of yarn and end off as shown. (To "break off and fasten," follow the same procedure.)

DOUBLE CROCHET (dc): Follow the steps in FIG. 6. To practice, ch 20, then make a row of 20 sc. Now, instead of a ch 1, you will make a ch 3. Turn your work, yo and insert the hook in the second stitch of the previous row (at the arrow), going under both strands at the top of the stitch. Pull the yarn through. You now have three loops on the hook. Yo and pull through the first two, then yo and pull through the remaining two—one double crochet (dc) made. Continue across the row, making a dc in each stitch (st) across. Dc in the top of the turning chain (see arrow in FIG. 7). Ch 3. Turn work. Dc in second stitch on the previous row and continue as before.

FIG. 7

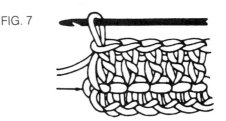

Note: *You also may start a row of dc on a base chain (omitting the sc row). In this case, insert the hook in the fourth chain from the hook, instead of the second (FIG. 8).*

FIG. 6
DOUBLE CROCHET (DC)   FIG. 6a

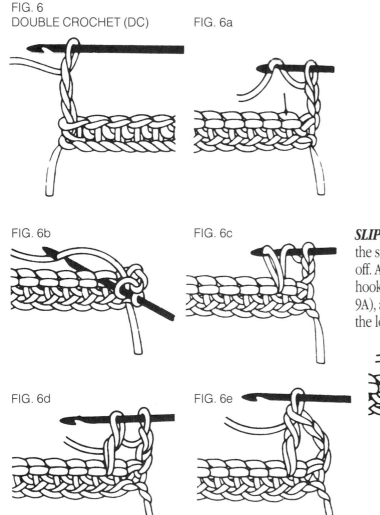

FIG. 6b   FIG. 6c

FIG. 6d   FIG. 6e

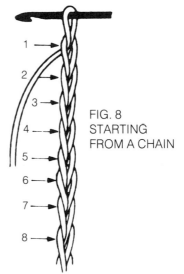

FIG. 8
STARTING
FROM A CHAIN

SLIP STITCH (sl st): Follow the steps in FIG. 9. This is the stitch you will use for joining, shaping and ending off. After you chain and turn, **do not** yo. Just insert the hook into the **first** stitch of the previous row (see FIG. 9A), and pull the yarn through the stitch, then through the loop on the hook—the sl st is made.

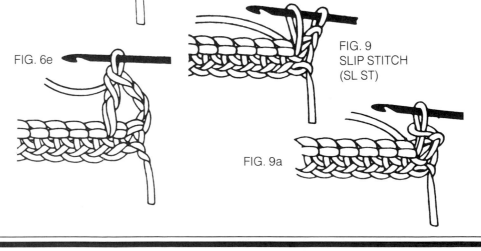

FIG. 9
SLIP STITCH
(SL ST)

FIG. 9a

HALF DOUBLE CROCHET (hdc): Follow the steps in Fig. 10 and 10A.

To practice, make a chain and a row of sc. Ch 2 and turn; yo. Insert the hook in the second stitch, as shown; yo and pull through to make three loops on the hook. Yo and pull the yarn through *all* three loops at the same time—hdc made. This stitch primarily is used as a transitional stitch from an sc to a dc. Try it and see—starting with sc's, then an hdc and then dc's.

FIG. 10
HALF DOUBLE CROCHET

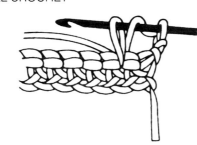

FIG. 10a

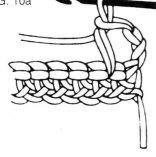

SHAPING TECHNIQUES FOR CROCHETING

Now that you have practiced and made sample squares of all the basic stitches, you are ready to learn the adding and subtracting stitches that will shape your project by changing the length of a row as per the instructions. This is done by increasing (inc) and decreasing (dec).

To increase (inc): Just make two stitches in the same stitch in the previous row (see arrow in Fig. 11). The technique is the same for any kind of stitch.

FIG. 11   INCREASING (INC)
FOR SINGLE CROCHET

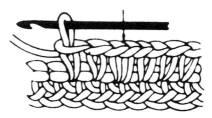

To decrease (dec) for single-crochet (sc): Yo and pull the yarn through two stitches to make three loops on the hook (see steps in Fig. 12). Pull the yarn through all the loops at once—dec made. Continue in the stitches called for in the instructions.

FIG. 12   DECREASING (DEC)

FOR SINGLE CROCHET   FIG. 12a

To decrease for double crochet (dc): In a dc row, make the next stitch and stop when you have two loops on the hook. Now yo and make a dc in the next stitch. At the point where you have three loops on the hook, pull yarn through all loops at the same time. Finish the row with regular dc.

HOW TO BLOCK LIKE A PRO

MATERIALS:

✳ *A Blocking Board* An absolute *must* for professional-looking blocking. You can usually buy a blocking board at craft and sewing centers.

✳ *Rustproof T-pins and Staples* Used to hold the needlework pieces in place.

✳ *Undyed Cotton Cloth* A dampened cloth covers the needlework while it is being pressed.

✳ *Iron* With a dry setting.

✳ *Yellow Soap* Dels Naptha or Kirkman. For blocking needlepoint. Restores natural sizing to canvas and helps prevent infestations of insects.

KNITTED OR CROCHETED WORK:

The purpose of blocking is to align the stitches, loft the yarn and straighten the knitted or crocheted pieces.

✳ Pin the work or the pieces, right side down, to the blocking board with the T-pins. Place the pins close together to avoid ripples in the work.

✳ Dampen a cotton cloth with water and wring it out; the cloth should be moist, not dripping wet. Place the cloth over the work on the board.

✳ Set the iron on "dry" and select a temperature setting suited to the fibers in the work.

✳ Gently iron over the cloth in the direction of the stitches. *Do not* apply pressure to the iron or iron against the grain. You may need to remoisten the cloth and iron the work several times, until it is moist and warm to the touch.

✳ Carefully remove the cloth. If the cloth clings, leaving the work damp and rippled, don't panic. This occurs when a synthetic fiber is pressed with steam that is too hot. No permanent damage can be done unless pressure is used and the stitches are flattened. To restore the work to the desired shape, pat the pieces gently with your hands.

✳ Allow the work to dry on the board in a flat position for at least 24 hours.

✳ When the work is completely dry, remove the pins; the pieces are ready to be assembled.

Note: You can ease or stretch pieces a bit to achieve the desired size, but you can't turn a size 10 sweater into a size 16, or shrink a size 40 vest into a size 34.

NEEDLEPOINT PROJECTS:

Blocking needlepoint realigns the threads of the canvas, lofts the yarn and naturally sets each stitch.

Note: First check the yarn for color fastness. If you've finished a work, and are unsure of the yarn color fastness, do not block. Press the work on the wrong side with a warm iron to avoid color streaking.

✳ Place a bar of yellow soap in a bowl of warm water. Let stand until the water becomes slick to the touch.

✳ Place the work right side down on the board.

✳ Dip a cotton cloth into the soapy water and wring it out. Place the damp cloth over the needlepoint.

✳ Set an iron on "dry" and select a temperature suited to the fibers in the work. Lightly pass the iron over the cloth; *do not* apply pressure.

✳ Repeat dampening the cloth and pressing until the canvas is very soft and flexible; moist, but not wet.

✳ Turn the needlepoint right side up on the board.

✳ Keeping the threads of the canvas parallel to the grid on the blocking board, staple the canvas to the board leaving 1 inch between the staples and the edge of the needlepoint. (Remove tape or selvages before stapling.) The staples should be fairly close together (staples are preferable to pins because they maintain a straight line and even tension across the work).

✳ Staple along the bottom edge of the canvas, again, maintaining an even tension across the work. Gently pull one side of the canvas to align the fabric grain with the grid lines on the board, and staple along this edge. Repeat on the other side of the canvas. (*Do not* stretch the canvas; just pull it gently into its original size.) As you are stretching the third and fourth sides, wrinkles may appear in the center of the work; as the fourth side is eased into alignment, these should disappear. If the canvas is pulled off the grain while being blocked, remove the staples and realign the sides. When the grain of the work is perfectly square, the stitching should be aligned; remember, you are not straightening the stitching, you are squaring the threads of the canvas.

✳ Let the work dry on the board for at least 24 hours.

✳ When the work is completely dry, gently pull it up from the board; the staples will pull out easily.

Note: If the design becomes distorted, start from the beginning again and reblock the piece.

STITCH GUIDE

THE BLANKET STITCH

Work this stitch from left to right, with the point of the needle and the edge of the work toward you. The edge of the fabric can be folded under or left raw. Secure the thread and bring out the needle below the edge of the fabric. For each stitch, insert the needle through the fabric from the right side and bring it out at the edge. Keeping the thread from the previous stitch *under* the point of the needle, draw the needle and thread through, forming a stitch over the edge. The stitch size and spacing can be uniform or varied.

BLANKET STITCH

FRENCH KNOT

SATIN STITCH

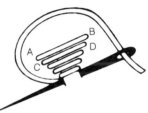

SPLIT STITCH

CONTINENTAL STITCH

STEM STITCH

STRAIGHT STITCH

CROSS STITCH

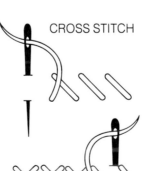

WHIPSTITCH

WHIPPED STEM STITCH

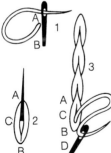

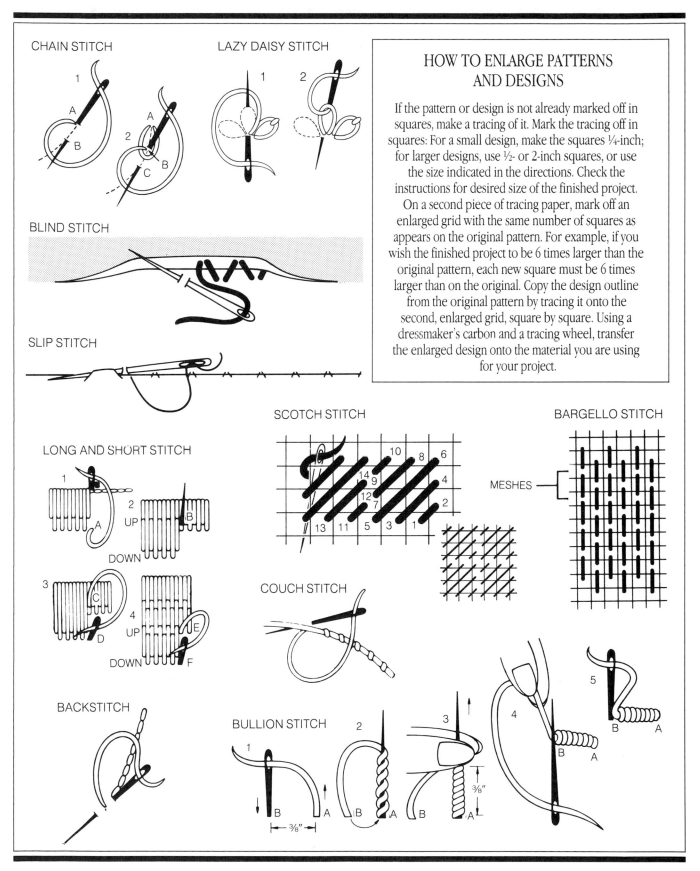

CHAIN STITCH

LAZY DAISY STITCH

HOW TO ENLARGE PATTERNS AND DESIGNS

If the pattern or design is not already marked off in squares, make a tracing of it. Mark the tracing off in squares: For a small design, make the squares ¼-inch; for larger designs, use ½- or 2-inch squares, or use the size indicated in the directions. Check the instructions for desired size of the finished project. On a second piece of tracing paper, mark off an enlarged grid with the same number of squares as appears on the original pattern. For example, if you wish the finished project to be 6 times larger than the original pattern, each new square must be 6 times larger than on the original. Copy the design outline from the original pattern by tracing it onto the second, enlarged grid, square by square. Using a dressmaker's carbon and a tracing wheel, transfer the enlarged design onto the material you are using for your project.

BLIND STITCH

SLIP STITCH

LONG AND SHORT STITCH

UP

DOWN

UP

DOWN

SCOTCH STITCH

BARGELLO STITCH

MESHES

COUCH STITCH

BACKSTITCH

BULLION STITCH

INDEX

Italicized Page Numbers Refer to Photographs

A Ring of Angels Carousel, *152*-153
A Touch of Spice Table Setting, *2*, 5
afghan
　Buffalo Plaid, *13*
　Poinsettia, *166*-167
　Stained Glass, *17*, 16-18
Almond Cornets with Grenadine
　Crème, *220*, 229
angel
　A Ring of, Carousel, *152*-153
　Centerpiece, 100-*101*
appetizer, 142
　Belgian Endive with Herbed Cheese,
　　220, 223
　Blini with Sour Cream and Caviar,
　　144-*145*
　Cherry Tomatoes Stuffed with
　　Walnut Pesto, 144-*145*
　Cream Puffs with Savory Filling,
　　143, *145*
　Creamy Pesto-Stuffed Cherry
　　Tomatoes, *220*, 223
　Endive with Smoked Salmon Cream
　　Cheese, *145*-146
　Hot Crab and Mushroom Puffs,
　　220, 226
　Savory Meatball Mini-Kebabs,
　　220, 224
　Scallop Kebabs with Creamy Dijon
　　Sauce, *220*, 225
　Tapenade Crisps, *220*, 224
　Tortellini Zucchini, *220*, 225
　Turkey Terrine with Pistachios,
　　220, 227
　Vegetable Dippers, *214*, 217
　Vegetable Sushi, *220*, 228

apple
　Wild Rice, Pecan and, Stuffing, *33*, 35
appliqué
　Carolina Lily Quilted Shade, *10*-12
apron
　Child's, *70*-71
　Dad's Denim, *70*-71
　Dolly's Patchwork, & Scarf, *173*-174
Almond Cornets with Grenadine
　Crème, *220*, 229
Alphabet Blocks, 172-*173*
amaretti
　Oranges, *149*
　Ricotta Mousse, 41
Angel Centerpiece, 100-*101*
argyle
　Baby's, Sweater, *80*-81
autumn
　Hues Pillow, *14*-15
　Leaves Table Setting, 6-7

Baby's Argyle Sweater, *80*-81
ball
　Scented Soap, 21
　Silver, with Mauve Flowers, *104*
　Silver, with Pink Flowers, *104*
Bargello Tree Ornament, *156*
baskets, 5, 37, 67, 86
　Beautiful, *65*, *66*, *67*
　Dyed, 67
　Fabric-Lined, *65*
　Slipcovered, 65-66
bean
　Fava, Soup, *38*, 40
　Pinto, Picante, 45
bears
　Sleepytime, 184-*185*

beautiful
　Baskets, *65*, *66*, *67*
　Dreamer Pillowcase, *127*
beef
　Sausage & Meatball Hero, *214*, 218
　Shredded, Filling, 44
Belgian Endive with Herbed Cheese,
　220, 223
beverage, 201
　Cassis Punch Royale, *220*, 229
　Cocoa with Crème de Menthe, 200
　Hot Mulled Cider, 200
　Purple Hawaiians, 219
　Spiced Wine Punch, 200
Bittersweet Candied Orange Peel, 93
Blini with Sour Cream and Caviar,
　144-*145*
block
　Alphabet, 172-*173*
Bluegrass Pullover, 168-*169*
bonnet
　Christening Gown, Slip &, *131*,
　　130-133
box
　Green Gift, Pillow, *116*-117
　Victorian Hat, 128-*129*
　Window, Mirror, *72*-73
　Winter Window, *157*
braid
　Cranberry Orange, 88, 96
bread, 37, 93, 95, 201
　Carrot Hazelnut Twist, 91
　Cranberry Orange Braid, *88*, 96
　German Stollen, 97
　Honey Whole Wheat, *192*, 197
　Pecan Sticky Buns, *192*, 196
　Prosciutto, 41
　Spiced Christmas Brioche, *88*, 92-93
　Streusel-Topped Kugelhopf, 94

Bring-a-Dish Ethnic Foods Party, 206
brioche
    Spiced Christmas, *88*, 92-93
Bûche de Noël, *192*, 199
Buffalo Plaid Afghan, *13*
buns
    Pecan Sticky, *192*, 196
Burnished Beauty Wreath, *111*
Butter-Glazed Spinach Dumplings,
    140-148

——————— *C* ———————

Café Brûlot, 201
cake, 142
    Bûche de Noël, *192*, 199
    Chocolate-Topped Spice, *192*, 198
    Golden Raisin, 198
    Old-Fashioned Fruit, *192*, 195
    Spicy Gingerbread Squares,
        192, 197
    Star-Spangled, 219
calico
    Cat Ornament, 57
    Christmas Stockings, *46*, 53
    Corner Ornaments, *46*, *48*, *49*
    The, Kids, *46*, *50*-52
candied
    Bittersweet, Orange Peel, 93
candles, 86-87
    A Ring of Angels Carousel, *152*-153
cap
    Snow Country, 74-76
cardigan
    Flowers & Lace, — for Daughter,
        120-122
    Flowers & Lace, — for Mother, *120*,
        122-124
Carolina Lily Quilted Shade, *10*-12
carousel
    A Ring of Angels, *152*-153
carrier
    Log, *69*
Carrot Hazelnut Twist, 91
casserole
    Creamy Corn, with Jalapeños, *28*, 35

Enchiladas Olé, 43
cassis, 229
    Punch Royale, *220*, 229
cat
    Calico, Ornament, 57
caviar
    Blini with Sour Cream and, 144-*145*
centerpiece, 8, 37
    Angel, 100-*101*
    Grapes & Pine Cones, Wreath, *4*-5
    How to Dry Flowers for
        Arrangements and Wreaths, 109
Cheddar
    Steamed Vegetables with, Cheese
        Sauce, *28*, 36
cheese, 142
    Amaretti Ricotta Mousse, 41
    Belgian Endive with Herbed,
        220, 223
    Endive with Smoked Salmon Cream,
        145-146
    Steamed Vegetables with Cheddar,
        Sauce, 36
cherry
    Sour, Cranberry Sauce, *28*, 36
    Tomatoes Stuffed with Walnut Pesto,
        144-*145*
chicken
    Shredded, Filling, 44
Child's Apron, 70-71
"Chili con Cards" Party, 207
chive
    Parsley, Dip, *214*, 217
chocolate
    Butter Cream Frosting, 199
    Topped Spice Cake, *192*, 198
Christening Gown, Slip & Bonnet,
    131, 130-133
Christmas, 61, 174
    Calico, Stocking, *46*, *53*
    Cards, 9
    Crackers, 119
    Silent Night, Stocking, *54*-55
    Spiced, Brioche, *88*, 92-93
cider
    Hot Mulled, 200
cleaning ideas, 9, 87, 118

coat rack
    Street Scene, *68*
cocoa, 164, 212
    with Crème de Menthe, 200
coffee, 8
    Café Brûlot, 201
    Cream Filling, 199
coffee cake
    Carrot Hazelnut Twist, 91
    Cranberry Orange Braid, *88*, 96
    Streusel-Topped Kugelhopf, 94
cookies, 85
    Almond Cornets with Grenadine
        Crème, *220*, 229
    Nut Fingers, *192*, 195
    Spicy Gingerbread Squares,
        192, 197
cooking tips, 201
corn
    Creamy, Casserole with Jalapeños,
        28, 35
cornet
    Almond, with Grenadine Crème,
        220, 229
country
    Snow, Caps, 74-76
crab
    Hot, and Mushroom Puffs, *220*, 226
crafting, 210
    Beautiful Baskets, *65*, *66*, *67*
    "Stained Glass" Triptych, 58-60
    Victorian Hat Box, 128-*129*
cranberry
    and Oranges, 6
    Orange Braid, *88*, 96
    Oven-Baked, 201
    Sour Cherry, Sauce, *28*, 36
cream
    Coffee, Filling, 199
    Endive with Smoked Salmon,
        Cheese, *145*-146
    Puffs with Savory Filling, 143, *145*
creamy
    Corn Casserole with Jalapeños,
        28, 35
    Orange Frosting, *192*, 197
    Pesto-Stuffed Cherry Tomatoes,
        20, 223

crisp
　Tapenade, *220*, 224
crochet
　Log Carrier, *69*
　Poinsettia Afghan, *166*-167
　Snow Country Caps, *74*-76
　Stained Glass Afghan, *17*, 16-18
　Sunburst Pillow, *14*-15
cross stitch
　Holiday Home Sampler, *62*-64
　Prancing Reindeer Tree Skirt,
　　158-*159*
　Tree Time Towels, *175*
　Trees & Snowflakes Stocking,
　　160-161
curtain
　Carolina Lily Quilted Shade, *10*-12
custard
　Flan, 45

dumpling, 148
　Butter-Glazed Spinach, *140*, 148
Dyed Basket, 67

Elegant Eggs, 154-*155*
embroidery
　Calico Cat Ornament, 57
　Christening Gown, Slip & Bonnet,
　　131, 130-133
　Flowers & Lace Cardigan
　　—for Daughter, *120*-122
　Flowers & Lace Cardigan
　　—for Mother, *120*, 122-124
　Holiday Home Sampler, *62*-64
　Red Velveteen Stocking, *112*-113
　Rocking Horse, 56
enchilada
　Sauce, 44
　Olé, 43
endive, 146
　Belgian, with Herbed Cheese,
　　220, 223
　with Smoked Salmon Cream
　　Cheese, *145*-146
entertaining ideas, 165, 204-207, 210,
　212-213, 219

fireplace, 118, 165, 201
flannel, 212
　Red Hot, Quilt, *19*-21
flowers, 87, 118, 213
　How to Dry, for Arrangements and
　　Wreaths, 109
　Silver Ball with Mauve, *104*
　Silver Ball with Pink, *104*
　& Lace Cardigan — For Daughter,
　　120-122
　& Lace Cardigan — For Mother, *120*,
　　122-124
footstool
　Fancy, 128-*129*
frosting
　Chocolate Butter Cream, 199
　Creamy Orange, *192*, 197
fruitcake
　Old-Fashioned, *192*, 195

game, 119
gameboard
　Needlepoint, 180-*181*
garland, 87, 119
　Cranberries and Oranges, 6
German Stollen, 97
gift ideas, 27, 67, 118
gingerbread
　Spicy, Squares, *192*, 197
glaze
　Sugar, 195
Goin' Hollywood Party, 204
Golden Raisin Cake, 198
gown
　Christening, Slip & Bonnet, *131*,
　　130-133
Grapes & Pine Cones Centerpiece
　Wreath, *4*-5
Green Gift Box Pillow, *116*-117
grenadine
　Almond Cornets with, Crème,
　　220, 229
grilling, 201

Dad's Denim Apron, *70*-71
decorating ideas, 5-6, 8-9, 27, 37, 56,
　61, 85-87, 90, 118-119, 142, 164-
　165, 201, 204-207, 212-213
Delivery Truck, *176*, 178
dieting tips, 208
Dijon
　Scallop Kebabs with Creamy, Sauce,
　　220, 225
dip
　Parsley Chive, *214*, 217
　Tangy Tomato, *214*, 217
doll
　Angel Centerpiece, 100-*101*
　Dolly's Patchwork Apron & Scarf,
　　173-174
　Little Women, *84*, *82*-85
　Pierrot and Pierrette, *137*-139
　Sweet & Simple Sock, *134*-136
　The Calico Kids, *46*, *50*-52
Dolly's Patchwork Apron & Scarf,
　　173-174
dove
　White, *186*-187

Fabric-Lined Basket, *65*
facial, 213
Fancy Footstool, 128-*129*
Fava Bean Soup, *38*, 40
filling
　Coffee Cream, 199
　Cream Puffs with Savory, 143, *145*
　Shredded Beef, 44
　Shredded Chicken, 44
filo, 226
　Hot Crab and Mushroom Puffs,
　　220, 226
fingers
　Nut, *192*, 195

ℋ

hat
Christening Gown, Slip & Bonnet, *131*, 130-133
Snow Bunny Suit and, *24-26*
Snow Country Caps, *74-76*
Victorian, Box, 128-*129*
Hawaiian
Purple, 219
hazelnut
Carrot, Twist, 91
health tips, 208-209, 212-213
hero
Sausage & Meatball, *214*, 218
Super, *214*, 217
Holiday Home Sampler, *62-64*
home
Holiday, Sampler, *62-64*
Honey Whole Wheat Bread, *192*, 197
horse
Pinto Rocking, 172-*173*
Rocking, *56*
hot
Crab and Mushroom Puffs, *220*, 226
Mulled Cider, 200
Red, Flannel Quilt, *19-21*
How to Dry Flowers for Arrangements and Wreaths, 109

𝒥

jalapeños
Creamy Corn Casserole with, *28*, 35

𝒦

kebab
Savory Meatball Mini-, *220*, 224
Scallop, with Creamy Dijon Sauce, *220*, 225
kids, 27, 85, 87, 118, 164-165, 210
The Calico, *46*, *50*-52
kittens
Three Little, *182*-183

knitting
Baby's Argyle Sweater, *80*-81
Bluegrass Pullover, 168-*169*
Buffalo Plaid Afghan, *13*
Flowers & Lace Cardigan
—for Daughter, *120*-122
Flowers & Lace Cardigan
—for Mother, *120*, 122-124
Pretty Peach Shawl, 128-*129*
Snow Bunny Suit and Hat, *24-26*
Snow Country Caps, *74-76*
Snowflake Mittens, *74*, 77
Winter Nights Sweater, *170-171*
Woolly Bully Pullover, 22-*23*
"Washing Day" Sweater, 78-79
kugelhopf
Streusel-Topped, 94

ℒ

lace
Flowers &, Cardigan,
—for Daughter, *120*-122
Flowers &, Cardigan,
—for Mother, *120*, 122-124
Lavender and, Wreath, *108-109*
Lacy Net Place Mats, *125*-126
Lavender and Lace Wreath, *108*-109
leaves
Autumn, Table Setting, 6-7
lily
Carolina, Quilted Shade, *10-12*
liqueur, 200, 201, 229
Café Brûlot, 201
Cassis Punch Royale, *220*, 229
Cocoa with Crème de Menthe, 200
Little Women Dolls, *84*, *82-85*
Log Carrier, *69*

ℳ

Mandolin, *102*-103
microwave
Enchilada Sauce, 44
Enchiladas Olé, 43
Flan, 45
Pinto Beans Picante, 45

Shredded Beef Filling, 44
Shredded Chicken Filling, 44
Spanish Rice, 44-45
meatball
Sausage &, Hero, *214*, 218
Savory, Mini-Kebabs, *220*, 224
Midwinter Masquerade Party, 206
mirror
Window Box, *72*-73
mittens
Snowflake, *74*, 77
mousse
Amaretti Ricotta, 41
Mr. Toucan, *186*, 188-189
mulled
Hot, Cider, 200
mushroom
Hot Crab and, Puffs, *220*, 226
mustard
Scallop Kebabs with Creamy Dijon Sauce, *220*, 225

𝒩

napkin
A Touch of Spice Table Setting, *2*, 5
Autumn Leaves Table Setting, 6-7
needlepoint
Bargello Tree Ornament, *156*
Gameboard, 180-*181*
Rainbow Pillow, *14*-15
Silent Night Christmas Stocking, *54*-55
net
Lacy, Place Mats, *125*-126
night
Winter, Sweater, *170*-171
nosegay
Pillow, 128-*129*
Seed, 154-*155*
nut
Almond Cornets with Grenadine Crème, *220*, 229
Carrot Hazelnut Twist, 91
Cherry Tomatoes Stuffed with Walnut Pesto, 144-*145*
Fingers, *192*, 195

Pecan Sticky Buns, *192*, 196
Perfect Pecan Pie, *30*, 37
Turkey Terrine with Pistachios, *220*, 227
Wild Rice, Pecan and Apple Stuffing, *33*, 35

O

Old-Fashioned Fruitcake, *192*, 195
O' Christmas Tree, 106-107
orange
 Amaretti, *149*
 Bittersweet Candied, Peel, 93
 Cranberries and, 6
 Cranberry, Braid, *88*, 96
 Creamy, Frosting, *192*, 197
organization tips, 209
ornament, 118-119, 164
 Bargello Tree, *156*
 Calico Cat, 57
 Calico Corner, *46*, 48-49
 Elegant Eggs, 154-*155*
 Mandolin, *102*-103
 Plaid Ribbon Pinwheel, 57
 Rocking Horse, *56*
 Seed Nosegays, 154-*155*
 Shining Star, *105*
 Silver Ball with Mauve Flowers, *104*
 Silver Ball with Pink Flowers, *104*

P

parrot
 Polly, *186*, 190-191
Parsley Chive Dip, *214*, 217
party ideas
 Bring-a-Dish Ethnic Foods, 206
 "Chili con Cards", 207
 Goin' Hollywood, 204
 Midwinter Masquerade, 206
 Red and White, 205
 Star Signs, 205
pasta
 Tortellini Zucchini, *220*, 225
patchwork
 Autumn Hues Pillow, *14*-15

Dolly's, Apron & Scarf, *173*-174
Red Hot Flannel Quilt, *19*-21
Sugarplum Stocking, 162-*163*
pecan
 Perfect, Pie, *30*, 37
 Sticky Buns, *192*, 196
 Wild Rice, and Apple Stuffing, *33*, 35
pepper
 Creamy Corn Casserole with Jalapeños, *28*, 35
 Sweet Red, Soup, *140*, 146
Perfect Pecan Pie, *30*, 37
pesto
 Cherry Tomatoes Stuffed with Walnut, 144-*145*
 Creamy Pesto-Stuffed Cherry Tomatoes, *220*, 223
photograph, 124, 164
picante
 Pinto Beans, 45
pie
 Perfect Pecan, *30*, 37
 Pumpkin, *30*, 37
Pierrot and Pierrette Dolls, *137*-139
pillow, 8, 118
 Autumn Hues, *14*-15
 Green Gift Box, *116*-117
 Nosegay, 128-*129*
 Rainbow, *14*-15
 Red Present, *116*-117
 Sunburst, *14*-15
pillowcase
 Beautiful Dreamer, *127*
pine cone
 Grapes &, Centerpiece Wreath, *4*-5
pinto
 Beans Picante, 45
 Rocking Horse, 172-*173*
pinwheel
 Plaid Ribbon, 57
pistachios
 Turkey Terrine with, *220*, 227
"pizza"
 Soda Fountain, *214*, 218
place mat
 Autumn Leaves Table Setting, 6-7
 Lacy Net, *125*-126

plaid
 Buffalo, Afghan, *13*
 Ribbon Pinwheel, 57
Poinsettia Afghan, *166*-167
Polly Parrot, *186*, 190-191
pomander, 56
popcorn ball, 8
pork
 Sausage & Meatball Hero, *214*, 218
 Savory Meatball Mini-Kebabs, *220*, 224
 Stuffed Crown Roast of, *140*, 147
potpourri, 9, 37, 86, 90, 118
 Sweet Sachets, *173*-174
Prancing Reindeer Tree Skirt, 158-*159*
Pretty Peach Shawl, 128-*129*
Proscuitto Bread, 41
puff pastry
 Cream, with Savory Filling, 143, *145*
 Hot Crab and Mushroom, *220*, 226
 Tapenade Crisps, *220*, 224
pullover
 Baby's Argyle Sweater, *80*-81
 Bluegrass, 168-*169*
 "Washing Day" Sweater, 78-79
 Winter Nights Sweater, *170*-171
 Woolly Bully, 22-*23*
Pumpkin Pie, *30*, 37
punch
 Café Brûlot, 201
 Cassis, Royale, *220*, 229
 Spiced Wine, 200
Purple Hawaiians, 219

Q
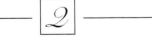

quilt
 Carolina Lily, Shade, *10*-12
 Red Hot Flannel, *19*-21

R

Rainbow Pillow, *14*-15
raisin
 Golden, Cake, 198

red
 and White Party, 205
 Hot Flannel Quilt, *19*-21
 Present Pillow, *116*-117
 Sweet, Pepper Soup, *140*, 146
 Velveteen Stocking, *112*-113
reindeer
 Prancing, Tree Skirt, 158-*159*
ribbon
 Plaid, Pinwheel, *57*
rice
 Spanish, 44-45
 Wild, Pecan and Apple Stuffing, *33*, 35
ricotta
 Amaretti, Mousse, 41
ring
 A, of Angels Carousel, *152*-153
roast
 Stuffed Crown, of Pork, *140*, 147
 Turkey with Wild Rice, Pecan and Apple Stuffing, *28*, 32-*33*
rocking
 Horse, *56*
 Pinto, Horse, 172-*173*

S

sachet
 Sweet, *173*-174
sailboat
 Wooden, *179*
salad
 Sicilian, 41
salmon
 Endive with Smoked, Cream Cheese, *145*-146
sampler
 Holiday Home, 62-64
sandwich
 Sausage & Meatball Hero, *214*, 218
 Super Hero, *214*, 217
Santa Claus, 61
sauce
 Enchilada, 44
 Scallop Kebabs with Creamy Dijon, *220*, 225

Sour Cherry Cranberry, *28*, 36
 Steamed Vegetables with Cheddar Cheese, *28*, 36
Sauerkraut Supreme, *140*, 148
Sausage & Meatball Hero, *214*, 218
savory, 142
 Cream Puffs with, Filling, 143, *145*
 Meatball Mini-Kebabs, *220*, 224
Scallop Kebabs with Creamy Dijon Sauce, *220*, 225
scarf
 Dolly's Patchwork Apron &, *173*-174
Scented Soap Balls, 21
seafood
 Hot Crab and Mushroom Puffs, *220*, 226
 Scallop Kebabs with Creamy Dijon Sauce, *220*, 225
Seed Nosegays, 154-*155*
sewing
 A Touch of Spice Table Setting, *2*, 5
 Angel Centerpiece, 100-*101*
 Autumn Hues Pillow, *14*-15
 Autumn Leaves Table Setting, 6-7
 Beautiful Dreamer Pillowcase, *127*
 Calico Cat Ornament, *57*
 Calico Christmas Stockings, *46*, 53
 Carolina Lily Quilted Shade, *10*-12
 Child's Apron, 70-71
 Christening Gown, Slip & Bonnet, *131*, 130-133
 Dad's Denim Apron, 70-71
 Dolly's Patchwork Apron & Scarf, *173*-174
 Fabric-Lined Basket, *65*
 Green Gift Box Pillow, *116*-117
 Little Women Dolls, *84*, 82-85
 Mr. Toucan, *186*, 188-189
 Nosegay Pillow, 128-*129*
 Pierrot and Pierrette Dolls, *137*-139
 Polly Parrot, *186*, 190-191
 Prancing Reindeer Tree Skirt, 158-*159*
 Rainbow Pillow, *14*-15
 Red Hot Flannel Quilt, *19*-21
 Red Present Pillow, *116*-117
 Red Velveteen Stocking, *112*-113
 Shining Star, *105*

Sleepytime Bears, 184-*185*
Slipcovered Basket, 65-66
Sugarplum Stocking, 162-*163*
Sunburst Pillow, *14*-15
Sweet Sachets, *173*-174
Sweet & Simple Sock Dolls, *134*-136
The Calico Kids, *46*, 50-52
Three Little Kittens, *182*-183
Tree Top Star, *105*
Trees & Snowflakes Stocking, *160*-161
Victorian Stockings, 114-*115*
White Dove, *186*-187
shade
 Carolina Lily Quilted, *10*-12
shawl
 Pretty Peach, 128-*129*
Shining Star, *105*
shredded
 Beef Filling, 44
 Chicken Filling, 44
Sicilian Salad, 41
Silent Night Christmas Stocking, *54*-55
silver
 Ball with Mauve Flowers, *104*
 Ball with Pink Flowers, *104*
Sleepytime Bears, 184-*185*
slip
 Christening Gown, & Bonnet, *131*, 130-133
Slipcovered Basket, 65-66
snow
 Bunny Suit and Hat, *24*-26
 Country Caps, 74-76
snowflake
 mittens, *74*, 77
 Trees &, Stocking, *160*-161
soap
 Scented, Balls, 21
sock
 Sweet & Simple, Dolls, *134*-136
Soda Fountain "Pizza," *214*, 218
soup, 8, 40
 Fava Bean, *38*, 40
 Sweet Red Pepper, *140*, 146
Sour Cherry Cranberry Sauce, *28*, 36

sour cream
    Blini with, and Caviar, 144-*145*
Spanish Rice, 44-45
spice
    A Touch of, Table Setting, *2*, 5
    Chocolate-Topped, Cake, *192*, 198
spiced
    Christmas Brioche, *88*, 92-93
    Wine Punch, 200
Spicy Gingerbread Squares, *192*, 197
spinach
    Butter-Glazed, Dumplings, *140*, 148
squares
    Spicy Gingerbread, *192*, 197
stained glass
    Afghan, *17*, 16-18
    Triptych, *58*-60
star
    Shining, *105*
    Signs Party, 205
    Spangled Cake, 219
    Tree Top, *105*
Steamed Vegetables with Cheddar
    Cheese Sauce, *28*, 36
stocking
    Calico Christmas, *46*, *53*
    Red Velveteen, *112*-113
    Silent Night Christmas, *54*-55
    Sugarplum, *162*-163
    Trees & Snowflakes, *160*-161
    Victorian, 114-*115*
stollen
    German, 97
Street Scene Coat Rack, *68*
Streusel-Topped Kugelhopf, 94
Stuffed Crown Roast of Pork, *140*, 147
stuffing
    Wild Rice, Pecan and Apple, *33*, 35
sugar
    Glaze, 195
sugarplum
    Stocking, *162*-163
    Wreath, *110*
suit
    Snow Bunny, and Hat, *24*-26
Sunburst Pillow, *14*-15

Super Hero, *214*, 217
sushi
    Vegetable, *220*, 228
sweater
    Baby's Argyle, *80*-81
    Bluegrass Pullover, 168-*169*
    Flowers & Lace Cardigan
        —for Daughter, *120*-122
    Flowers & Lace Cardigan
        —for Mother, *120*, 122-124
    Snow Bunny Suit and Hat, *24*-26
    "Washing Day", 78-79
    Winter Nights, *170*-171
    Woolly Bully Pullover, 22-*23*
sweet
    Red Pepper Soup, *140*, 146
    Sachets, *173*-174
    & Simple Sock Dolls, *134*-136

T

tablecloth
    A Touch of Spice Table Setting, *2*, 5
    Autumn Leaves Table Setting, 6-7
table decorations, 5, 8-9, 56, 86-87, 119,
    142, 165, 204-207
    A Touch of Spice Table Setting, *2*, 5
    Angel Centerpiece, 100-*101*
    Autumn Leaves Table Setting, 6-7
    Grapes & Pine Cones Centerpiece
        Wreath, *4*-5
    Lacy Net Place Mats, *125*-126
Tangy Tomato Dip, *214*, 217
Tanker Truck, *176*-177
Tapenade Crisps, *220*, 224
terrine
    Turkey, with Pistachios, *220*, 227
The Calico Kids, *46*, *50*-52
Three Little Kittens, *182*-183
Tiny Treasures Tree, 154-*155*
tomatoes
    Cherry, Stuffed with Walnut Pesto,
        144-*145*
    Creamy Pesto-Stuffed Cherry
        Tomatoes, *220*, 223
    Tangy, Dip, *214*, 217

Tortellini Zucchini, *220*, 225
Toucan
    Mr., *186*, 188-189
towel
    Tree Time, *175*
toy, 164-165
    Alphabet Blocks, 172-*173*
    Delivery Truck, *176*, 178
    Little Women Dolls, *84*, 82-85
    Mr. Toucan, *186*, 188-189
    Needlepoint Gameboard, 180-*181*
    Pierrot and Pierrette Dolls, *137*-139
    Pinto Rocking Horse, 172-*173*
    Polly Parrot, *186*, 190-191
    Sleepytime Bears, 184-*185*
    Sweet & Simple Sock Dolls, *134*-136
    Tanker Truck, *176*-177
    Three Little Kittens, *182*-183
    White Dove, *186*-187
    Wooden Sailboat, *179*
tree, 106-107, 164-165
    Bargello, Ornament, *156*
    Prancing Reindeer, Skirt, 158-*159*
    Time Towels, *175*
    Tiny Treasures, 154-*155*
    Top Star, *105*
    & Snowflakes Stocking, *160*-161
triptych
    "Stained Glass," *58*-60
truck
    Delivery, *176*, 178
    Tanker, *176*-177
turkey, 34-35
    Roast, with Wild Rice, Pecan and
        Apple Stuffing, *28*, 32-*33*
    Terrine with Pistachios, *220*, 227
twist
    Carrot Hazelnut, 91

V

vegetable, 37
    Belgian Endive with Herbed Cheese,
        220, 223
    Butter-Glazed Spinach Dumplings,
        140, 148
    Cherry Tomatoes Stuffed with
        Walnut Pesto, 144-*145*

Creamy Corn Casserole with
    Jalapeños, *28*, 35
Creamy Pesto-Stuffed Cherry
    Tomatoes, *220*, 223
Dippers, *214*, 217
Sauerkraut Supreme, *140*, 148
Steamed, with Cheddar Cheese
    Sauce, *28*, 36
Sushi, *220*, 228
Tortellini Zucchini, *220*, 225
velveteen
    Red, Stocking, *112*-113
victorian
    Hat Box, 128-*129*
    Stockings, 114-*115*

—— 𝒲 ——

walnut
    Cherry Tomatoes Stuffed with, Pesto,
    144-*145*
"Washing Day" Sweater, 78-79

wheat
    Honey Whole, Bread, *192*, 197
White Dove, *186*-187
Wild Rice, Pecan and Apple Stuffing,
    33, 35
window
    Box Mirror, 72-73
    Winter, Box, *157*
wine
    Spiced, Punch, 200
winter
    Nights Sweater, *170*-171
    Window Box, *157*
women
    Little, Dolls, *84*, 82-85
Wooden Sailboat, *179*
woodworking
    A Ring of Angels Carousel, *152*-153
    Alphabet Blocks, 172-*173*
    Delivery Truck, *176*, 178
    Fancy Footstool, 128-*129*

Mandolin, *102*-103
Pinto Rocking Horse, 172-*173*
Street Scene Coat Rack, *68*
Tanker Truck, *176*-177
Window Box Mirror, 72-73
Wooden Sailboat, *179*
Woolly Bully Pullover, 22-*23*
wreath, 8, 118
    Burnished Beauty, *111*
    Grapes & Pine Cones Centerpiece,
    4-5
    How to Dry Flowers for
        Arrangements and, 109
    Lavender and Lace, *108*-109
    Sugarplum, *110*

—— 𝒵 ——

zucchini
    Tortellini, *220*, 225

PHOTOGRAPHERS

Barbara Bersell
David Bishop
Ralph Bogertman
Richard Chestnut
Deborah Feingold
David Glomb
Joshua Green
Richard Jeffery
Jeffrey Jenkins
David Lawrence
Taylor Lewis
Leombruno-Bodi
Virginia Liberatore
Bill McGinn
Teresa Montalvo

Jeff Niki
Leonard Nones
Bradley Olman
Frances Pellegrini
Dean Powell
Carin Riley
Ron Schwerin
Ariel Skelley
Gordon E. Smith
William Steele
Steve Steigman
William Stites
Bob Stoller
Rene Velez

CONTRIBUTING CRAFT EDITORS

Pam Allen
Robert L. Anderson &
Alexandra Eames
Shirley Botsford
Jacqueline Cadovious
Lyn Le Grice
Blake Hampton

Millie Hines
Alla Ladyzhensky
Jeannette Marconi-Martin
Constance Spates
Mary Lou Stribling
Jean Wilkinson

CONTRIBUTING FOOD EDITORS

A.T. Callen
Beth Hensperger

Grace Manney
Angela Phelan